FLOWER COTTON bap. at A 2 Jan. 1642/3

```
A = Arrington, co. Cambridge
B = Boxworth    "      "
L = Lolworth    "      "
St L.P. = St Laurence Pountney,
          London.
C = Clapham, Surrey
```

FLOWER of Longstow m. at St Edward's, Cambridge, 15 Apr. 1703, Robert Rogers of Longstow

JOHN COTTON: b.3 Aug 1699 bap. at Childerley 5 Oct folling: of Knapwell 1730: later of Caxton. — MARY KING m.at Knapwell 8 Oct 1730

Issue

MARY in g-f's will 3 Jan. 1704/5 m.at Knapwell 15 Oct. 1721 Henry Rigwell.

MIRIAM bap. at B. 7 Nov. 1700: d young

MIRIAM b 29 Apr 1703: bap. at Knapwell 18 May folng

MICHAEL COTTON bap. at L. 22 Mar. 1729/30: bur there 6 Sep. 1730

WILLIAM COTTON bap at B. 22 Dec. 1731: of St Laurence Pountney, London: Admitted to Freedom of City as citizen & Glover, 23 Nov. 1756: a freeholder at Hardwicke 1780: d. 10 Dec. 1791 — CHARLOTTE da. of William ROGERS of St Anne's, Soho & sis. & heiress of Charles Rogers FRS., F.S.A (see D.N.B) m. by lic. St Geo., Southwark 1 Nov. 1755: d. 29 Jan. 1795

WILLIAM COTTON of Clapham F.S.A: Chief Clerk of Certificates in H.M. Customs b 20 June, bap L.P. 1759: d. 27 Oct. 1816: m, Lambeth, Surrey 16 Feb. 1792. — CATHERINE 2nd da. Rev. Wm SAVERY b. Rattery, Devon 19 May 1769: d. C. 18 Dec. 1803.

CHARLES COTTON b & d. 1757 MARY b. 1760: d. 1761 MICHELANGELO b. 1765: d. 1769 ROBERT COTTON. d. yng.

EDWARD COTTON b. at C 10 Nov 1803: educ. New Coll., Oxon: migrated to Victoria, Australia 7 Nov. 1841: m. a French wife & d.s.p. 13 Sep. 1860.

CHARLOTTE b at St L.P. 13 Jan. 1795 m. at Leatherhead, Surrey 1833 William Hall M.D. & d.s.p. 16 Sep. 1857.

MARY b at C 6 Aug 1800: m. at C. 11 Apr. 1837 Capt. Nath. Fred. Edwards J.P., R.N.(b. 6 Aug. 1800: d. 24 Jun. 13/8) & d. 12 Jan 1884 leaving issue 2s. & 1da.

MARIAN — CHARLES RYAN of Derriweit Heights, Macedon, Victoria.

ELIZA m. Alexander Mackenzie Cheyne M.D. & had issue 2s & 2da.

CAROLINE m.A.A.C. Le Souëf, Dir. Melbourne Zoo: Issue 5s & 5da.

MARY SUSANNAH m. W.J Meek: Issue 3s & 2da.

CATHERINE HELEN m. A.P. Wood: issue 2s & 1da.

Sir CHARLES RYAN Maj-Gen K.B.E., C.B. C.M.G., M.B., M.S (Edin) b. 1853: d. 1920 — ALICE da of Hon. Theo. SUMNER m. 1884: d. 1923

CECIL GODFREY RYAN b 1866. m. Audrey Lyla Colvin & d.s.p.

MARIAN ELLIS Flower painter b.1848. d. 1922 m. Capt F.C Rowan

ADA MARY b. 1855: d. 1943: m. 1883 Lord Charles T. M-D-Scott Adm G.C.B.

HENRY RYAN b. 1850 d. 1914 m. & had issue 3das

Hon. RUPERT SUMNER RYAN C.M.G., D.S.O. — ROSEMARY only da. of 21st Earl of 13 Errol

ETHEL MARIAN (MAIE) m. 1926 C.St.J. — RICHARD GARDINER CASEY, Lord Casey (Life Baron) K.G., P.C., G.C.M.G., C.H., D.S.O., M.C., K.St.J., LL.D. 1s.1da

BLANCHE ADELAIDE d. unm

MABEL HARTLEY. d. unm.

IN SEARCH OF ANCESTRY

Gerald Hamilton-Edwards

PHILLIMORE

First published in Great Britain by
MICHAEL JOSEPH LTD
1966

Second edition 1969 by
PHILLIMORE & CO. LTD.

Third edition 1974

Reprinted 1979

Fourth edition published by
PHILLIMORE & CO. LTD.
Chichester, Sussex, England
1983

ISBN 0 85033 494 2

Printed and bound in Great Britain by
R. J. ACFORD
Chichester, Sussex

CONTENTS

LIST OF ILLUSTRATIONS

Line drawings by Joan Harris

ACKNOWLEDGEMENTS

I am grateful to many people for their help in the writing of this book, to a number of officials, secretaries of societies and individuals for information willingly given.

Remembered with especial gratitude is Joan Harris for her delightful and amusing drawings and for her general help, especially in helping with the reading of the proofs of this book. Lady Henriques gave me valuable information about the Jews and Huguenots in Stepney and Alejandro Raimundez directed me to information about the Spanish registration. I am also pleased to mention for their help Anthony Camp, Director of the Society of Genealogists, London, L.W. Lawson Edwards, the Librarian there, Sybil Bach for help with information in the Public Record Office and elsewhere, Donald J. Steel for various contributions to my knowledge of family history, Michael E.B. Leader and Dr. I.A.P. Smythe-Wood for information about Irish records, Bill R. Linder of the National Archives of America, Washington, D.C., Lord Teviot for help and information from East India Company records, Donald Whyte, Chairman of the Scottish Record Society for help on Scottish records, Dr. Christopher W. Pugh for helping with xerox work, Ian F.W. McDowell for help in checking proofs of the bibliography, Peter Tonellato and Valerie Dismorr for their help in checking the index, Ann Chiswell, General Secretary of the Federation of Family History Societies, for information about the Federation and about the Guild of One Name Studies, and I should like to mention also the staff of the Bodleian Library, Oxford, for their expeditious production of many books and other material connected with this work.

Oxford
30 December 1982

GERALD HAMILTON-EDWARDS

Chapter One

DISCOVERING WHAT IS ALREADY KNOWN

Those of you who know Wilde's play, *The Importance of being Earnest,* may remember how annoyed Lady Bracknell was that Mr Worthing did not know the name of either of his parents. 'To lose one parent,' she declaimed emphatically, 'may be regarded as a misfortune; to lose both looks like carelessness!'

Few of us fortunately are likely to incur Lady Bracknell's displeasure through being in Mr Worthing's predicament. Nearly all of us know the names of our parents and usually quite a lot about them. Our grandparents, too, are usually familiar to us, though many do not know their christian names when it comes to the point, as we have always called them 'Grandpa' and 'Grandma'.

However, provided they were born in England or Wales or Scotland it is not too difficult a task to discover their full names and those of their parents and grandparents back to the time when civil registration began, which in England was in 1837 and in Scotland in 1855. Since those times there are general indexes in each country for all people who were born, married or died there.

But even this may be a very lengthy and slow business unless you go about it the right way. The first thing to do in this intriguing expedition into your past family history is to find out what is already known. You do not want to spend several years tracing back your family only to discover that 'Uncle Cuthbert worked all that out years ago'.

But before you make even these preliminary enquiries there is one question you should ask yourself, namely, why you are doing it at all. The answer may be that you just want to get on record for your family and future generations of it some information about it before such knowledge is forgotten and lost. This is in itself a perfectly good and praiseworthy reason for wanting to trace and write up your family history.

You will notice that I have added 'write up', because if you fail to record your work, even in some simple. form, such as a chart pedigree, you will probably only have succeeded in giving yourself some enjoyment and satisfaction and the value of your efforts will be greatly diminished. I shall later on have something to say on the best ways of recording your researches.

You may have other reasons. For instance your family may have played some small part at one time in a great national event and you may feel your work is a small contribution to history itself, as indeed it may be. For however humble and simple the lives of your ancestors may have been, their story is in itself a contribution to our

1

Uncle Cuthbert worked all that out
Years ago

knowledge of the past. Genealogists often discover in their searches interesting and delightful incidents which historians in their wider field might never come across, small incidents which reflect with great sincerity the life of the period.

Another question which you may like to have answered before you start on your task is, 'What are the chances of success?' This is a question which cannot be answered completely, because it depends so much on individual cases. Let me say straight away that any idea of tracing back to the time of William the Conqueror is almost certainly just a pipe dream. There has been a lot of nonsense talked by people claiming that their family came over with William the Conqueror. Naturally many of us are descended from the Normans who were present at Hastings or who came over later, when King William had established himself in England, but to prove it generation by generation from one of those who fought beside William at Hastings is a different matter. At the time of the Falaise Castle celebrations in 1931, when a bronze memorial was set up in Falaise Castle to the honour of the Conqueror and his companions in arms, a number of people claimed to be descended from the knights who fought with him at Hastings. More recently the nine hundredth anniversary of the battle of Hastings has produced a somewhat smaller number of claimants to such descents. But it appears that no living person is able to prove his descent step by step in the male line from a companion of the Conqueror at the battle of Hastings. This is the opinion among others of Mr G.H. White, editor of *The Complete Peerage*,[1] and also of the former Garter King of Arms, Sir Anthony Wagner.[2] As the latter explains, the Malets of Enmore came as near as anyone in being able to prove a direct descent in the male line from a companion of the Conqueror at Hastings, in their case from William Malet who fought at Hastings in 1066, but part of the descent in the early twelfth century is not clearly proved. As Sir Anthony has said 'could the early links but be made clear beyond all doubt the Malets would have the unique distinction of a proved male descent from a man who fought at Hastings'.

It is disappointing therefore that no man living today can prove satisfactorily a male descent from someone who fought at this famous battle. There are however a few families which can prove their pedigree beyond reasonable doubt to a holder of land in England at the time of Domesday. The Derbyshire family of Shirley are among those which have the rare distinction of being able to prove such a descent and Major John Shirley still owns the manor of Ettington in Warwickshire which his ancestor in the male line, Sewal, owned in 1086. This is probably a unique distinction. East Quantockshead in Somerset has been held since that time by only two families, the Paynels from 1086 to about 1200, and from that time by the Luttrell family, whose ancestor married the Paynel heiress.

There is one family which can even show a descent from pre-conquest times to the present day in unbroken male line. This is the family of Arden, which has a proved descent from Aelfwine, Sheriff of Warwickshire before the Conquest, down to Dr. George Arden, who is 27th in direct descent. It is considered probable, though it is not proved, that Mary Arden, the mother of William Shakespeare, was of this family. The Berkeley family of Berkeley Castle has a strong probability of a pre-conquest descent in the direct male line, but one of its generations is doubtful and the identification of its earliest ancestor is conjectural. Many of the male lines of Norman and Angevin baronies have died out or are not known to exist because the inheritance has descended through the female line and a great number of peers today come from families which a few generations ago belonged to the middle or lower classes.

Descent from such early times as those mentioned above are quite exceptional and in general the person who can trace his family back to the seventeenth century is fortunate. It is quite likely he will get back no further than the mid-eighteenth century. Success in this matter depends on a number of factors. Sir Anthony Wagner, in his *English Ancestry*, which is a shortened form of his *English Genealogy*, previously mentioned, both of which are recommended for reading, says that there are four main factors which govern the tracing of pedigree, namely, *status, record, name* and *continuity*.

By *status* is meant the position in the social structure. This may, of course, vary from generation to generation, but it will be apparent that it is easier to trace a prominent family than a more humble one. An hereditary peerage family is easy to trace as far back as the peerage goes, because the very essence of it is hereditary. But status is a wider term. It will be fairly easy to trace a professional family for instance which consisted mainly of clergymen, lawyers or officers in the army or navy. It will be less easy to trace a family lower down the social scale. But the pattern is often a changing one for, although class distinction was more marked in the past and people then for instance, did not so often marry outside their own social circle, yet they did so occasionally. Such a union was often the cause of rise or fall in status and, apart from marriage, it has always been possible in our country for men of ability to rise to high position. To realize this one has only to think of Cardinal Wolsey, said to have been a butcher's son, or Thomas Cromwell, a man of humble position who became Henry VIII's chancellor. This tendency to osmosis has

contd. on p. 6

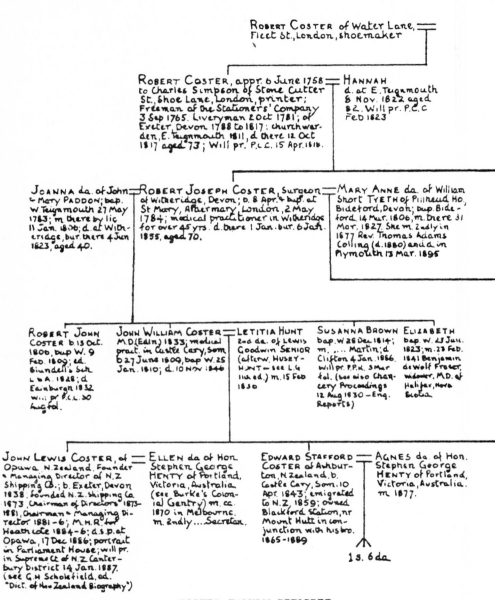

ROBERT COSTER of Water Lane, Fleet St., London, shoemaker

ROBERT COSTER, appr. 6 June 1758 to Charles Simpson of Stone Cutter St., Shoe Lane, London, printer; Freeman of the Stationers' Company 3 Sep 1765. Liveryman 20 Oct 1781; of Exeter, Devon 1788 to 1817; churchwarden, E. Teignmouth 1811, d. there 12 Oct 1817 aged 73; Will pr. P.C.C. 15 Apr. 1818. — HANNAH d. at E. Teignmouth 8 Nov. 1822 aged 82. Will pr. P.C.C Feb 1823

JOANNA da. of John & Mary PADDON; bap. W. Teignmouth 27 May 1783; m. there by lic 11 Jan. 1806; d. at Witheridge, bur. there 4 Jun 1823, aged 40. — ROBERT JOSEPH COSTER, Surgeon of Witheridge, Devon; b. 8 Apr. & bap. at St Mary, Aldermary, London, 2 May 1784; medical practitioner in Witheridge for over 45 yrs. d. there 1 Jan. bur. 6 Jan. 1855, aged 70. — MARY ANNE da. of William Short TYETH of Pillhead Ho., Bideford, Devon; bap. Bideford. 14 Mar. 1806, m. there 31 Mar. 1827. She m. 2dly in 1877 Rev. Thomas Adams Colling (d. 1880) and d. in Plymouth 13 Mar. 1895

ROBERT JOHN COSTER b 13 Oct. 1808, bap. W. 9 Feb. 1809; ed. Blundell's Sch L & A. 1828; d Edinburgh 1832 will pr P.C.C. 30 Aug fol.

JOHN WILLIAM COSTER M.D.(Edin) 1833; medical pract. in Castle Cary, Som b 27 June 1809, bap. W. 25 Jan. 1810; d. 10 Nov 1846 — LETITIA HUNT 2nd da. of Lewis Goodwin SENIOR (afterw. HUSEY-HUNT—see L.G 11th ed.) m. 15 Feb 1830

SUSANNA BROWN bap. W. 28 Dec 1814; m. .... Martin; d Clifton 4 Jan. 1866. will pr. P.P.K. 5 Mar fol. (see also Chancery Proceedings 12 Aug 1830 – Eng. Reports)

ELIZABETH bap. W. 23 Jun. 1823; m. 23 Feb. 1841 Benjamin de Wolf Fraser, widower, M.D. of Halifax, Nova Scotia

JOHN LEWIS COSTER, of Opawa, N. Zealand, Founder & Managing Director of N.Z Shipping Co.; b. Exeter, Devon 1838. founded N.Z. Shipping Co 1873. Chairman of Directors 1873–1881; Chairman & Managing Director 1881–6; M.H.R. for Heathcote 1884–6; d. s.p. at Opawa, 17 Dec 1886; portrait in Parliament House; will pr. in Supreme Ct of N.Z Canterbury District 14 Jan. 1887. (see G.H Scholefield, ed. "Dict. of New Zealand Biography") — ELLEN da of Hon. Stephen George HENTY of Portland, Victoria, Australia (see Burke's Colonial Gentry) m. cc. 1870 in Melbourne. m. 2ndly ....Secretan.

EDWARD STAFFORD COSTER of Ashburton, N Zealand, b. Castle Cary, Som. 10 Apr. 1843; emigrated to N.Z. 1859; owned Blackford Station, nr Mount Hutt in conjunction with his bro. 1865–1889 — AGNES da. of Hon. Stephen George HENTY of Portland, Victoria, Australia. m 1877.

1 s. 6 da.

COSTER FAMILY PEDIGREE

COSTER FAMILY PEDIGREE: An example of a chart pedigree, showing the kind of details which should be included if known.

This pedigree is also a good example of the changes in social status which occur in so many families. The earliest known ancestor is a shoemaker. His son, after apprenticeship, becomes a liveryman of the

JOHN WILLIAM COSTER — MARY A ... — MARY ANN m. by lic at W.T. 23 Sep. 1805
Master Mariner of Teign-   b. Bovey Tracey,   William Squarey and had issue (see Chan-
mouth; bap at Wolborough   Devon 1810/11   cery suit 12 Aug 1830, 14 Jan 1831, 1 Mar 1836 ¥
Devon, 4 Sep. 1785: d. 1 Jan 1859   English Law Reports v. 48 p. 252 etc)

JOHN WILLIAM   ROBERT COSTER   LAWRENCE HENRY   GEORGE FREDER-   ALFRED JOS-   4 da.
COSTER D 1840/41   b. 1841/2   COSTER b. 1842/3   ICK COSTER. b.   EPH COSTER
   1844/5   D 1845/6

WILLIAM TYETH — HARRIET   CHARLES   LUCY HANNAH   HELEN ELIZABETH — ROBERT WHITE STEVENS
COSTER M.R.C.S   CONNOR   HENRY   bap W. 29 Jun.   b 3 Sep. 1832, bap.   Author & Printer of Plymouth
(Eng) L.R.C.P. (Edin)   wid. of ....   COSTER   1831; m. Rev.   W. 7 Apr. 1836; m.   19 Oct. 1806; d. Ply. 28 May
L.S.A. of Hanwell,   Bradbury   Capt. in Marin.   Rich. Root Cnope,   there 30 Nov.   1870. He m. 1stly Eliza (d
Mx. bap. W. 22 Sep   d. at Rich-   Service; bap.   Vicar of St Augus-   1852; d at South-   1850) da. of Jacob Ginder.
1829; d. at Brent-   mond, Sur.   W. 7 Apr 1836;   tines, Kensington,   sea, Hants, 2 Dec
ford 12 Nov. 1870.   1 Feb. 1915   d unm. Will   London, and had   1916.
   aged 81   pr. Exeter 21.   issue.
   May 1907

OTHER   MARY LOUISA — ROBERT TYETH STEVENS   OTHER ISSUE
ISSUE   m. 22 Jan. 1881; d   Printer, Proprietor & ed "The   IS. 5 da.
   in Plymouth 3   Western Figaro" Col. in T.F.
   Dec 1886   b. Plymouth 10 June 1854; m.
   2ndly 30 Sep 1907 Mary Agnes
   2 S. 2. da.   da. of Wm. Brown, Land Agent
   of Linkinhorne, Cornwall. He d
   at Tring, Herts 29 Mar. 1920.

HELEN   ELIZABETH   EVA JANE
HUSEY   LETITIA   FRASER;
b Exeter   b Castle   m. .....
1837; m.   Cary, Som.   Miller.
... Marsh.   1841

W.T = West Teignmouth, Devon.
W. = Witheridge, Devon.
P.C.C. = Prerogative Court
   of Canterbury.
P.P.R. = Principal Probate
   Registry

Stationers Company and his elder son becomes a country doctor. The
latter's eldest surviving son is also a doctor and marries into one
of the county families of Dorset. His two sons migrate to New
Zealand, where they marry sisters, the daughters of a well known
Australian family. The elder brother founds a shipping company and
becomes a member of the New Zealand Parliament.

long been apparent in England. In the eighteenth century there were numerous examples of men who rose to positions of wealth and influence. Josiah Wedgwood, the great potter, started with nothing and died worth half a million. The Lombe family, who were sons of a Norwich worsted-weaver and who bought Thomas Cotchett's silk-throwing factory in Derby, made a great fortune and Thomas Lombe was able to provide a dowry of £60,000 for one of his daughters when she married the Earl of Lauderdale. Sir Richard Arkwright came from a poor family. After he invented the water frame in 1771 his fortunes increased and when he rode into Derby as High Sheriff of the county he was accompanied by, among others, thirty javelin men dressed in the richest liveries ever seen on such an occasion. Sir Winston Churchill, in his *Great Contemporaries* has emphasized how much this country owes to the middle classes and has pointed out how many of the great names of his own generation came from such a background.

This rise and fall in social status has always been a feature of English life and there have been recent examples of men created peers whose immediate ancestry has been quite humble but whose more distant ancestry was found to be armigerous and recorded as such in one or other of the Herald's visitations.

Record, the second factor mentioned, is of obvious importance. If the records have been lost or destroyed, as so many of the Irish records were in 1922 or the Devon and Cornwall wills at Exeter were during the last war, then a main source of information is gone. You may be unlucky in finding the very parish in which your ancestors lived has lost its parish registers. Fortunately this is not frequently so, for on the whole the British records have been well preserved and are one of our great heritages. It is really something of which the nation can be rather proud, that it has preserved in the majority of cases its parish registers often intact from the seventeenth century and even in some cases from the time they were first ordered to be kept in 1538, and that the wills of quite ordinary folk like farm labourers or of soldiers who may have fought at Agincourt, have been preserved from even the fourteenth century.

Name, the third factor, has great bearing on traceability. Surnames fortunately came into almost universal use in England as early as 1400. A great many names came from trades, such as Baker, Butcher, Stewart, Le Despenser and so forth. Another group came from nicknames, which are not always so apparent, such as Basset, which means 'short' and Blount, which is 'blond', and, rather more obvious, 'Longshanks'. A further group derived from the place where a person lived. Many of these at first bore the French 'de', which signified this, such names as 'De Montford', 'De Montmorency' and 'De Bohun'. In the course of time the 'de' was frequently dropped and few survive today, except in the French-speaking Channel Isles. Names like 'Atlee' (At Lee) and 'Atfield' (At the field) are also topographical in derivation. In the course of time these names often became corrupted and it is not always easy to derive the name in its present form.

A rare surname is a great help in tracing a family. When it is very rare you can collect all references to it you come across with some possibility, but depending on the derivation of the name, that their possessors may be related. Obviously there is no reason for the many people who took their name from their trade to be related. But those derived from a place are more likely to be, though in the course of time this relationship will in many cases be extremely distant. If you have a rare surname, there may be a one-name society of your surname which it may be well worth your while to join. For more details see Chapter 30 on "Development of Family History".

A common name can be a great bane. The name 'Smith' leaps to mind. This is the most common name in both England and Scotland and it is so because 'smith' was such a common trade. Apart from those descended from the village blacksmiths, many whose ancestors were goldsmiths, silversmiths or coppersmiths, received for brevity the shorter form 'Smith'. Even when other factors are favourable, when for instance, the family remained in one parish for many generations, the disadvantage of a common name soon becomes apparent. In one parish you may find two John and Mary Smiths having children baptized at the same period and it may not be possible to distinguish between them. Since the civil registration came in, the wife's maiden name is given in all birth certificates, but in the parish registers in England and Wales this was not done.

If you are unlucky in having a fairly common surname, nevertheless an uncommon christian name may be very helpful. Up to the last century people were very conservative about the christian names they gave their children and this is a great help to genealogists. In England it was rare for a child not to be called after some relation of the earlier generations, so that christian names were perpetuated throughout the centuries. Usually in England the eldest son was named after the father.

This name pattern may be very important and if, in a family where the names are Richard, Henry and William, you suddenly find a Walter or Stephen cropping up, his relationship must be suspect and needs strong confirmation. New names do sometimes come into families through the wife, especially among the younger sons and daughters. Sometimes, too, they are named after a godfather or a patron or a popular hero, like the boys named 'Horatio' or 'Nelson' at the time of Trafalgar, or those called 'Eugène' after Prince Eugène of Savoy who fought with Marlborough during the War of the Spanish Succession. It was often customary for naval officers serving in a ship to ask their captain to be a godfather to any son born during the commission and he was often named after his godfather. Then there are people named from some national event. In the Stoke Damerell, Plymouth, registers there is an instance of a boy being christened 'Nile' because he was born at the time of the great victory. A number of boys were called 'Redvers' after Sir Redvers Buller during the Boer War, and in more recent times the author knows of a boy called 'Rodney' because his father was at the time serving in H.M.S. *Rodney*.

An excellent article on 'The Descent of Christian Names' by D.J. Steel, is to be found in the June 1962 issue of the *Genealogists' Magazine*.

Continuity, the last of the four factors mentioned by Sir Anthony Wagner, relates to the continuation of a family for some generations either in one place or in one occupation or trade. Even quite an obscure family, one, say, of farm labourers, who have never, to use a modern phrase, 'hit the headlines' in any way, may, if living continuously in one parish where the registers are well preserved, be traceable as far back as these registers stretch, perhaps to Elizabethan times. Existing wills will help to confirm and expand the information given in the registers. This assumes another factor, which is really contained in the 'record' factor, namely that the family were Church of England, or Church of Scotland if in Scotland. If they were Roman Catholics or Nonconformists, then the problem will not be so easily solved.

Continuity in the same calling or trade can also be of great assistance. Records of apprenticeship, where they exist, may establish parentage, for often the father's name and occupation is recorded. In a higher social sphere a tradition of service in the church may make the tracing of a family fairly easy, for in the past clergymen of the Church of England, or clerks in Holy Orders, as they are officially called, were frequently graduates and their matriculation at Oxford or Cambridge, the only two universities existing in England and Wales until the nineteenth century, should reveal their father's name and probably their birthplace and other information. The registers of both these universities have been published.

From what I have said you will be able to a certain extent to assess your prospects and if, having done so, you decide to go ahead with your researches, then you should consider your plan of action.

It is of course possible to have your pedigree traced by professional genealogists. The College of Arms is mainly concerned with matters concerning armorial bearings, but individual officers of the college will privately undertake genealogical research. The Society of Genealogists will also undertake such research or they will give you the names of professional genealogists who undertake such work, though they will not recommend any particular individual. Most professional genealogists work on a time basis at so much an hour, as this is really the only practical way in which they can do work. It must be appreciated that a genealogist may spend many hours in searching for some detail without any success. You should satisfy yourself before employing a professional that he is both reliable and competent. Not all genealogists doing such work professionally are competent and an occasional one may even be a charlatan. You need therefore to check the qualifications and recommendations of any professional help you consider employing.

However, if you do employ such help you will be depriving yourself of a great deal of the interest and excitement in tracing your ancestors and the aim of this book is to show you how you can do it yourself. Also you will save yourself much money, for professional assistance is bound to be expensive. There may, however, be occasional phases in your searches where you come up against a particularly difficult patch and in that kind of situation it might be worth your while to get professional assistance to tide you over your particular difficulty. If you, for instance, were having great difficulty in tracking down a particular will it might be desirable to seek assistance of an experienced genealogist who would be more easily able to trace its existence, if existence it has. In some of the specialized fields, for instance if you discovered an ancestor in the East India Company, you might prefer to employ an expert in East India Company records, and might more quickly be able to obtain results. But if you have the time and opportunities I recommend that you do it yourself, as in doing so you will learn so much about records themselves and it will add greatly to the interest in tracing your ancestors.

Your first step then, in setting out to do your own searching, should be to make sure that no printed history of your family is already existing. It is true you will be lucky indeed if you find there is one, unless you come from a well-known family. Yet it is surprising how many such histories there are. There is a small bibliography of family histories by T.R. Thomson (2nd edition 1935) and there is a copy of it with MS additions at the Society of Genealogists. But the best way to make fairly sure there is no such history is to look in the British Library catalogue, as in this catalogue any history of a family is entered under the name of the family at the beginning of that name, besides, of course, being entered under the author. As the catalogue is kept reasonably up-to-date this will ensure that you have covered all but very recent publications, apart from privately printed histories which have not been put on sale and are therefore outside the requirements of the copyright acts by which the library can claim a copy of every book published. Even so a number of these privately printed family histories have been given by their authors to the library to ensure their preservation. Next best to seeing the current catalogue in the library itself is to look in the recently published printed catalogue of the library, which is to be found in many large reference libraries. This gives publication up to 1955. It is also possible that among the very large collection of manuscripts in the British Museum there is something throwing light on your family and it is worth while searching the catalogues of these.

Besides actual printed family histories as such, there are great numbers of pedigrees in various publications, such as the various editions of *Landed Gentry* from 1840 onwards and numerous publications, such as *The Genealogist, Miscellanea Genealogica et Heraldica* and *The Ancestor*. It would be a tall order to search through all these publications, or even their indexes, but fortunately this task is lightened for us by three valuable books, George Marshall's *Genealogists Guide*, the last edition of which was published in 1903, J.B. Whitmore's supplement to it, *A Genealogical Guide,* published in 1947 and Geoffrey B. Barrow's supplement since then, *The Genealogist's Guide*, 1977. In these publications it has been the aim of their compilers to record 'any descent of three generations in male line' which they have discovered in a very wide range of publications.

The next step, or perhaps a contemporary step, is to find out all you can about the family from other members of it. Naturally you will turn to the older generations of them and do not be too diffident in the way you approach them. There is often the feeling that you are being rather a nuisance, especially when particular members of the family do not seem very interested in it. This is often from a sense of false modesty. You must positively badger them and if necessary become quite a pest. I myself was far too diffident when young and I realize now that I might have discovered much from people of the older generation now no longer with us. Very often there is one particular member of the family who has taken some interest in it and you should make careful notes of all he or she tells you, trivial though these details may seem at the time, as it is surprising how pieces of information which seem unimportant at the time later turn out to be just the piece of information you need to confirm something.

Of course there are certain forms of information much more important than others. You should try to collect, or at any rate see and make copies of, any family documents, such as wills, marriage settlements, deeds of family arrangement, birth, marriage and death certificates. If you are lucky you may even find someone who has an old family Bible in which entries of baptism, marriage and burial have been made, as was the custom in the past, and naturally such a discovery is particularly fortunate. The information from it may allow you to construct a pedigree running back for several generations. It was the custom for the bride in past times to be given a family Bible on her marriage, in which she could enter the details of her own marriage and the baptisms, marriages and burials of her children. The eldest son would receive the family Bible of the father, and if he in turn was the eldest son of an eldest son, the entries in the Bible might go back for many generations. Family Bibles of younger children would not be so helpful, as they would only cover recent generations.

Besides visiting and questioning members of the family, it is quite a good idea, before doing so, to send out a questionnaire to all members who are likely to know anything about it. This can be either printed or duplicated. It will show that you are in earnest and will be more likely in consequence to win their co-operation, especially if accompanied by a tactful covering letter expressing hopes that they will do all they can to help! You will also get information in a more systematic form, and you will be saved repeating the questions to many people. A suggested form of questionnaire is given at Appendix A, but this of course may need modifying in accordance with a particular family's requirements.

This notice, having been sent out, will no doubt irritate, intrigue or bore the various members of the family, according to their individual characters, but will also stimulate some interest in the family, cause members of it to chat among themselves, with no doubt caustic remarks about your own sanity or peculiarity (What does he want to dig up all that stuff for? Much better left in the dust — all those old family quarrels and scandals!). In time you will get replies, some helpful, others less so, but the sum total will help you to build up quite a useful picture of the family background and will no doubt reveal information of which you had no idea. Often those members of the family who start off by saying they know absolutely nothing about it in the end provide a considerable amount of information. Remember that family traditions are always valuable, however absurd or exaggerated they may seem. There is nearly always some basis of truth in them, though they may have been much distorted in the course of time. Maiden aunts are inclined to push the social scale up a bit. 'He was something in the City,' they will tell you proudly, but that 'something' may turn out to have been some minor clerkship in a city firm, not the managing director of a world famous firm the name of which has escaped their memory, but which their tone so emphatically implied.

Your preliminaries are now concluded and in the next chapter I will discuss the methods of keeping your information.

---

[1] See *The Genealogists' Magazine* Vol VI, pp. 50-57 (March 1932) and Vol IX, pp. 416-28 (September 1944)

[2] A.R. Wagner, *English Genealogy*, p. 60.

Chapter Two

KEEPING YOUR RECORDS

A little forethought on the way you are going to record the information you discover will pay dividends in the future. When I started looking into my family history I rather haphazardly noted things down in an ordinary exercise book. As the material grew and I had to go into further books, I realized it would have been better to have had some kind of loose leaf note book, so that I could bring together notes referring to individuals or periods, as invariably when searching for one piece of information I came across something relating to another period or another person. My collection started off and for some time continued unsystematically, so that in time I found myself with some forty exercise books, the contents of which are contained solely and imperfectly in my memory.

I am now keeping my material far more systematically and I hope, on reading this, you will be led to do the same. Although a little more trouble, in the long run it certainly pays you handsomely.

There is no accepted system of indexing and filing genealogical information of which I know, but there is a very useful booklet by Dr J.E. Holmstrom, called *How to take, keep and use notes,* published by Aslib in 1947, which deals with the marshalling of information in a general way. The pamphlet is primarily concerned with collecting methodically information for use by writers and other research workers, but much of it is applicable to the kind of research done by genealogists.

Dr Holmstrom recommends the use of 8" × 5" card and cabinet, dismissing the smaller sizes as too small for use in gathering the type of information with which he is mainly dealing. For genealogists, however, who are frequently concerned in collecting small pieces of information, such as a single entry from a parish register, the smallest size has certain advantages. I recommend using both the 5" × 3" and the 8" × 5" sizes, using the former for small details such as I have suggested and the larger for longer material, such as extracts from wills and cumulative information about individuals from various sources. It is true you have the disadvantages of two separate arrangements, but I think the advantages outweigh the disadvantages.

In compiling the family history, if a larger card or slip is set aside for each member of it, with his or her surname, followed by christian names, clearly shown in block capitals along the top of it, this can be followed by standard details, such as date and place of birth, marriage and death. The lower half can contain additional information about his or her career and life which has been gleaned from various sources.

As Dr Holmstrom has pointed out, the larger size cards are the same size as the octavo pad, so that such pads can be conveniently used instead of cards. I personally prefer using slips of paper to cards, as they take up less room and, if reasonably strong, are quite suitable for ordinary purposes. It is convenient to have at any rate the larger slips in book form and this can be done by buying the full quarto exercise book (10″ × 8″) and asking a printer to cut it in half, wideways, or 'landscape', as the trade call it, with his guillotine. This gives you two booklets of 8″ × 5″. When you have filled up the booklet you can then separate the pages and file them in your cabinet in the correct place. I prefer narrow gauge lines on the cards or slips as these give you a bit more information on each. I have found an extract from a normal length will can be very conveniently recorded on such a slip, going over the page to use the back if necessary. Dr Holmstrom also suggests making envelopes by cutting in half old 10″ × 8″ envelopes. These are kind of envelopes in which you will have received brochures for Dutch bulbs, mergers of firms in which you may have a few shares, booksellers catalogues, sales of goods in which you have no interest from establishments of which you have never heard and other such matters which flow into your letter box. Apart from the satisfaction in making use of this otherwise often irritating literature, you can accumulate in these pockets newspaper and other cuttings, bits from relations' and other correspondents' letters and other matters which otherwise stray.

The most suitable way in which your material should be arranged in the trays needs careful thought. Dr Holmstrom suggests following a recognized classification in general outline and recommends the Universal Decimal Classification, which is an extension of the Dewey Decimal Classification used in most public libraries. For a genealogical collection, however, no classification is really detailed enough. Perhaps some librarian-genealogist will one day confer a boon on his fellow genealogists by developing and

Do not make yourself a slave to your own system

compiling a suitable one. The Library of Congress scheme is fuller than most, but the Dewey, with its simpler notation, seems more useful and practical. At any rate the main headings of this classification can be followed and, as genealogical material is particularly concerned with information about *people*, an alphabetical arrangement within the main headings of most of the material is a natural one. In fact, for the ordinary private collection, an alphabetical arrangement throughout, with cross references where necessary, rather like the dictionary catalogue found in many libraries, may prove most suitable. Third- or fifth-cut guides can be obtained on which the surnames or Dewey group can be inserted.

To be logical, as you are using two runs of slips, the 8″ × 5″ and the 5″ × 3″, you should make cross-references from the two series where necessary, but in practice, as it is you who will be making use of the collection, it is hardly necessary to do this. You will naturally look in each series of trays for information. Remember, this is your hobby, so do not make yourself a slave to your own system.

Making your Chart Pedigree

Early on you will find it useful to get out a chart or tabular pedigree, as this helps you to see things clearly. Here again it is advisable to adopt some consistency from the beginning. You want your pedigree to contain as much information as possible without losing its clarity. This obviously means you cannot include a great deal of detail. The amount will vary according to its importance. For instance, it is much more important to include the place of baptism, marriage and burial in entries before 1837, because these details cannot easily be found. Similarly, the existence of a will and where it was proved, prior to 1858, is very important.

Abbreviations must be used as much as possible. It is well to look at a publication like *Burke's Peerage* or *Landed Gentry* to see what abbreviations are used. Do not use 'b' for 'baptized', but 'bap', as 'b' should be reserved for 'born', which is already more or less an accepted practice. Always repeat the surname with each male entry. This may seem tiresome but leads to greater clarity. It is best not to repeat the surname of females. Use the equals sign for signifying marriage, inserting it between the names of the man and woman in question. From this sign draw your line showing descent. It is advisable to bring this line down to a point just above the level of the next generation, then horizontal just above the names. This is not only the clearest but allows the space above to be utilized. Ideally it would be nice to be able to show each generation in the same line, but this is not often practicable and lines may have to be brought round below or taken over, with suitable indication marks, to other pages. As long as it is quite clear whose children the next generation are, that is sufficient. Making a pedigree is a skilled job and only by guidance from experts and a certain amount of experimenting will you find the best arrangement. Study the lay-out of pedigrees in such works as Cussans' *History of Hertfordshire* or Ormerod's *History of the County and City of Cheshire*. Although these works were published in the last century the pedigrees they include are examples of good lay-out and also of the amount of detail which can fairly succinctly be included.

Personally, in making a pedigree, I work on the plan of exhausting in the early lines of descent those without issue or whose issue it is not intended to include, showing lower down those who have their issue inserted, and so on, generation by generation. The lay-out of a pedigree is bound to be to a certain extent a compromise, for you cannot show everything you would like to, and you do not want the pedigree to be too large and unwieldy. But British people are supposed to excel in compromise. You will soon find you need several copies of your pedigree. With A3 size paper and carbon and a ball pen you can get, with fairly thin paper, three or possibly four good copies, but it is better to plan to do your pedigree in black ink on a plastic drafting film such as is used by architects, from which they run off prints of their drawings. Such a plastic film is Ozalid. You should use a technical drawing pen, such as a Rotring or a Mars 700 (Stadler) and you should use with it the ink the makers recommend.

Manuscript writing is a skilled art, but you can make your pedigree reasonably presentable and clear if you obtain a sheet of graph paper (⅛ in. spacing is a good size) and place it on a suitable board slightly larger than A3 size.

If you are likely, as you may later be, to use the pedigree in a small booklet giving an account of your family, mark off carefully on the sheet of graph paper the size of A3 paper but rule off in the centre a space of about 2ins (1 in. each side of the centre). By doing this your pedigree will reproduce so that it forms two pages of A4 without any written matter in the fold of the book or booklet, though you should draw the lines across the space so that the continuation of the pedigree each side of the fold is clear. The A3 sheet of pedigree will then be able to be reduced to A4 size, thus forming two pages adjoining each other at a convenient place in the booklet of A5 size pages. The pedigrees in this book and in my *In Search of Scottish Ancestry* have all been done by this method. If you examine these I think it will make what I have said clearer.

The Rotring or Mars pens are very useful in making these pedigrees as they flow easily with jet black ink and do not cause ruled lines to blot. It is useful to use a transparent plastic ruler so that you can see through it exactly where your lines are going, and use a pen of about 75 mm for the pedigree lines, and for the details of each person use a thinner one, about 35 mm.

You need only have made the number of copies actually required at the time, as another advantage of the transparency method is that you can always have further copies made from the transparency and this can often be done while you wait or at any rate within a few hours. Most towns of any size have at least one place where dye-line prints are made and your local library or a stationer who sells mathematical instruments or stencils will no doubt be able to tell you where to find such a place.

Another advantage of this method is that it is easy to add further details to your pedigree as you find them and it is also not too difficult to make erasures and corrections. If you have made an error when the ink has only just dried you can wipe off the incorrect entry by using a slightly damped india rubber, but if the error has dried some time, then use the pencil-type eraser which will remove the offending word or words. Always write on the matt side of the plastic film.

You can have your pedigree reproduced by dye line in any firm which does this for architects. This method is a great time saver. It means that early on you can get out a pedigree and send copies of it to members of the family and others who may be able to help you. If you join the Society of Genealogists, which it is well worth your while to do, it is a good idea to send a copy of your pedigree to them as soon as possible, as it is possible that some other member may be interested in the family and may be able to give you information.

As regards the family, it will further help to stimulate their interest. It is surprising how people will tell you they know nothing, but when confronted with an actual pedigree will begin informing you of its inaccuracies and omissions. Your transparency can include drawings of any authorized armorial bearings, if the family should possess them, and also, a very useful adjunct, a sketch map of the district in which the family lived.

Xerox is a process of reproduction useful on many sides of genealogical work and also in the reproduction of pedigrees. This is one of the the benefits of our present age. Its reproduction qualities for written, typed or line-drawn material is about as good in reproduction as the original and it is a clean and dry process. There are many firms now which have A3 size xerox machines and in one of these you can have your pedigree on transparent film reproduced very easily, simply by placing an A3 sheet of blank paper behind it. But even if you cannot get an A3 xerox machine for your use, you can have your A3 pedigree reproduced in two halves, making sure that there is an overlap of about half-an-inch in the centre of them. You can then paste the two together carefully, so that the exact position of each sheet coincides with the other, then being able to reproduce any number of copies from your first copy, and this will be less expensive to do than reproducing many copies by dye line, as this has now increased in price.

For photographically-minded family historians the use of a camera with a suitable lens for fairly close-up work, or possibly with auxiliary lenses, can be very useful.

With this you can photograph tombstones, monumental inscriptions and also quickly and accurately record old family homes, the local church and any other interesting buildings or views of the countryside around, which may not have greatly changed from the period of your ancestors.

Chapter Three

CIVIL REGISTRATION

Having collected all the preliminary information you can from the family and other ready-made sources, you now start out on your adventure with your first practical investigations.

Naturally all possible aid must be taken from the civil registrations of births, marriages and deaths. Sometimes people have rather a shock when they learn that such registration only started in England and Wales in 1837 and that prior to that time there was no direct means of a person proving his birth, marriage or death except through church records, such as parish registers of baptism, marriage or burial, which are after all only records of religious ceremonies. The College of Arms did make an attempt as early as 1747 to institute a general register of births for the whole country, but mainly, it is said, through lack of publicity, the scheme eventually fell through.

In Scotland civil registration was introduced even later, in 1855, and in Ireland, although there was a registration of protestant marriages from 1845, the complete civil registration did not come in until 1864. As, however, Scotland and Ireland will be dealt with in later chapters, this one is concerned only with the registration in England and Wales.

These registers are kept at the General Register Office, St Catherine's House, 100 Kingsway, London, WC2B 6JB where there are general indexes covering the whole of England and Wales in one alphabetical arrangement in each quarterly volume, the indexes for births and marriages being here and those for deaths being at Alexandra House, across the road almost opposite. There are also district registers, kept in the District Registry of Births, Marriages and Deaths in each locality. If you are absolutely certain that your ancestors came from an area within the district registry it would be easier and quicker for you to search the local indexes, for these are far smaller and often contain perhaps five years or more in one index. However, if there is any doubt of the district in which your forebears were born, then it is necessary to go to the General Register Office, London.

You will have to work out, from the information you have accumulated, in which years to search for information. For instance, you may know the date of death of your grandfather, but not know his age and therefore when he was born. You can get his age from his death certificate in the General Registry and from this you can work out his approximate date of birth, remembering that the ages given by the informant at the time of death are by no means always accurate.

If your grandfather or other ancestor died after 1865 you may not need to get a copy of the death certificate to discover the age, as the age of the deceased is given in a column in the index. You may search all these indexes of death without fee and when you have examined the indexes of death, found the required age and worked out the year of birth, you can then, after filling in a form for a search for a birth, examine those indexes. It is advisable to cover a few years either side of the calculated dates as the age given at death is not always accurate; but start searching the index at the most likely year, as this may prove more economical of your time.

Covering, as they do, the whole of England and Wales, the indexes contain a great number of names and therefore each year is divided into quarters, marked on the back with the last month of the quarter. To cover one year you have, therefore, to search four volumes. People are often surprised at the size of the indexes, which must be about two feet by eighteen inches and even the more modern ones weigh about eleven pounds each and the earlier ones, being parchment, weigh approximately twenty-one pounds. Bearing in mind that you have to search twenty of these volumes for a five year period, pulling them out from their shelves and lifting them on to racks provided for the purpose, you will soon appreciate that genealogy is sometimes physically as well as mentally exhausting. After a few hours of searching there you will feel quite overwhelmed with fatigue. Discard, therefore, all heavy overcoats and similar trappings and approach the task in an athletic mood. I often feel that the correct dress for this work should be shorts and an open neck shirt! But we are a conventional race and few come there so sensibly habited.

Approach the task in athletic mood

If you are searching for an uncommon surname it may pay you to extract all entries of that surname which you find in the indexes. From these you will be able to work out likely brothers or sisters and the likely marriage of their parents. These you can confirm by obtaining essential certificates and save the expense of unnecessary certificates.

You may also feel somewhat depressed on your first encounter with these indexes to discover the number of people, not only of your surname, but also of the same christian name or names. It is sometimes, in fact, quite hard to identify an individual, especially if he has a common surname and a common christian name also. The area in which his birth took place will help, but there are cases where identification has been extremely difficult and has had to be supplemented from other sources, such as wills. Certainly people with unusual surnames have a great advantage and even an unusual christian name, as already mentioned, can be a great help, though it is unfortunate that earlier on people so seldom had more than one christian name.

However, assuming that you find in the index the entry which you are convinced is the right one for your particular ancestor, you then take the form down with the details filled in from the index and hand it to the official, paying a fee for the certificate. It is one of the annoyances to genealogists that it is necessary to obtain an actual certificate to get the information on it, as though you needed it for some legal purpose. Perhaps some day the authorities may be persuaded to allow genuine research workers to take copies of the entries without further payment for at any rate the earlier entries, say of a hundred years ago or more, in the same way that the census returns can now be consulted without fee at the Public Record Office up to and including the 1881 census. There have in fact been moves towards this being done.

The birth certificate gives the following information: place and date of birth; sex and names of the child; name and occupation of the father and the name and maiden name of the mother and finally the name, description and address of the informant.

The marriage certificate gives the place and date of the marriage, the names, ages, occupations, addresses amd marital status of both bride and bridegroom, together with the names and occupations of both bride and bridegroom's fathers, also the names of the witnesses. The witnesses may be very useful, as they are so often relatives. In the case of a marriage in church, the name of the officiating minister is also given. He is occasionally a relative, as, if there was a clergyman in the family, he was often called upon to perform the ceremony. The certificate also shows whether the marriage was by banns or licence.

The death certificate in England is not very informative. It only gives the place, date and cause of death, the name, sex, occupation and age of the deceased and the name, description and address of the informant. You will see that it does not even indicate whether the deceased was married or single. Nevertheless the small amount of information available from the certificate may prove useful in certain cases, but it is well to remember that if one only wants to discover the age and the rest of the information is known, then after 1865 the index will give you this and save you the expense of a certificate.

You can obtain these certificates by post and if you live far from London you may have to do this. But it is better to go personally if you can, as, apart from saving the handling charge for postal research you will be able to follow up clues on the spot, which the official searching for you will never do. For instance, in searching for one relative you may in the indexes come across another brother or sister, born within the five years you cover. You may not want a certificate at the time, but you can make a note of it in case you want to get one later. Similarly, if you do not find the entry within the five years you search, you can search further years on either side of this period. When known, both surnames in marriages can be checked.

There are certain other records at St Catherine's House in the General Register Office. These are the records of births and deaths at sea since 1st July 1837; certain army returns of birth, marriage and death of soldiers and their families as recorded in army registers, some extending back to 1761, similar R.A.F. records since 1920, and the consular returns of birth, marriage and death of British subjects in foreign countries which were recorded at the British consulates since 1849. It is possible, however, that some or all of these records may shortly be transferred to the Public Record Office.

You will see from the information given above that searching at the General Register Office will take some days, as you have to wait for the certificate which will give the information for the next step. You can either get these the next day personally, which is the quickest procedure, or else fill in an envelope with your name and address and have it posted to you. This may take some days, as they give priority to those being fetched.

At some period you will reach beyond the civil registration period and then you have to turn to other records. If you are lucky, though, you may find a great-grandfather or even a great-great-grandfather who was married just within the registration period, perhaps even in July 1837, the month in which the registration began. This will give his and his wife's father's name and occupation and so will take you back another generation.

Chapter Four

CENSUS RETURNS

At this stage it may be necessary to consider whether you should next examine the census returns or the parish registers. If you find, after the results of searching the civil registration that your family seem to have been established fairly firmly in one particular parish, then it might be best to search that parish register straight away. But even in that case it would be advisable to search the census returns also to gather the additional information which may be contained in them. In other cases, that is, in cases where it is not at all certain to what locality the people earlier belonged, the census returns may prove invaluable and certainly must be consulted. Remember, once civil registration is left behind, place is far more important than exact date, as there is no index covering the whole country, as in the civil registration, and to search the nine thousand odd parish registers would be an impossible task, taking several lifetimes.

It is unfortunate, from the genealogist's point of view at least, that no census was made in England until the nineteenth century. In 1753 a proposal came before Parliament to take a census, but it met with great opposition. Opponents of the idea said it would reveal England's weakness to possible enemies. Others opposed it on religious grounds, fearing it would provoke the wrath of God, quoting the Second Book of Samuel, the 24th Chapter. Parliament rejected the proposal and there was in consequence no census until 1801. The censuses since then have been made every ten years, except in 1941, during the Second World War. Those before 1841 however, if they had survived in detail, would have been of no use to genealogists, as they gave only the numbers in each household. The census of 1841 was the first to give the name of every person in the household with their approximate age (to the nearest five years below), their sex, occupation and whether they were born in the same county or not. It did not, unfortunately, give the relationship of each person to the head of the household, as the 1851 and later censuses did, but this can often be estimated with success. You will find, as you progress in your searches, that you must from time to time make intelligent guesses and your ability to do this is a great asset, but any such conjectures must, of course, be confirmed later with further evidence.

The 1851 census was far more valuable than that of 1841. This took each house, street by street, and gave the address, the names of all the people in that house the night of the census on the 30th March that year, their condition (single, married, widow, etc.), their exact age, their occupation and, perhaps most valuable of all, their exact place of birth. It also showed the head of the household and the relationship of each person to him, i.e. son, daughter, visitor, servant, apprentice. An annoying exception to the place of birth is of those born outside England and Wales, when the column will probably only say 'Scotland', Ireland' or 'France' etc.

The main problem in using the census returns is in finding the exact residence of the person concerned, but this usually works out to be easier than it sounds. You will probably find that one of the family was born somewhere around 1851, and this will show the address where the parents were living. Local directories may also be useful, though these often only gave the householders. There is a good collection of such directories in the Guildhall Library, London, and usually the library in the locality concerned has some local directories. In the larger towns, such as London, there is an index of street to the returns, so that you can discover easily in which volume of the returns your family will be found. In the case of smaller towns and villages there is probably no index, but at the beginning of each book will be shown the parish and the street and area covered. If your ancestor was born in a village you may only be able to discover the name of the village in which he lived and no address, but it is not a very long job to search the census of a whole village, which may only extend to three or four books. One's eye gets quite quick at picking out the name of the head of the family in each household. Apart from getting the genealogical information you will probably learn a good deal about the village in question, the main occupations of the inhabitants and so forth, and this should prove very valuable to you when you come to write up your family history. It will enable you to make it much more interesting if you can work in a little historical background rather than make your history just a bare recital of facts. Learning about your ancestors and the places where they lived is one of the fascinations in this family research, which makes it a living thing, not at all the dry-as-dust affair that so many people who know nothing about it are inclined to term it. Most of these census returns now have to be seen on microfilm.

There is always an element of luck in genealogy and the census returns may give you an unexpected piece of information which will be of great value. You may find, for instance, that there was an elderly maiden aunt or great-aunt living with the family. Such a relative may take the pedigree considerably further back. Take, for instance, someone aged eighty living then. The returns will give her birthplace and you will know she was born approximately in 1771. I say 'approximately' because you must be wary of taking these ages as absolutely correct. Sometimes these aged relatives were forgetful or did not want to reveal their real age. Sometimes the information was supplied by another member of the family or household, such as a niece-in-law, who would be unlikely to be very certain of the age of her husband's aunt, and may not have been very conscientious about finding out. On the whole, however, the returns seem to have been carefully made and are therefore particularly valuable. You will be able to go to the parish registers of the places of birth indicated and perhaps find the family has been in that parish for generations. I know of someone who was lucky in this way and was able to trace his family back to the middle of the sixteenth century in a matter of a few weeks and then, by use of wills, in which he was also fortunate, to get them back into the fifteenth century. But you must not expect such good fortune or you are likely to be disappointed, for such luck is exceptional.

You will of course keep carefully all the details you discover in the census return, including the visitors and servants, if any, for these can also prove valuable. For instance, families often got servants from their parents' or wife's parents' homes, and the birthplace of the servant may indicate where the family itself came from. Apprentices, who are often found living in the house of their master, were sometimes relations, and their birthplace may indicate a useful source.

Census returns up to 1881 are now available to be seen. These later ones are not so valuable as the earlier one, but in cases where the whereabouts of the family cannot be found in 1851 but is known for 1861, 1871 or 1881, then these returns will prove particularly useful. The information in them is similar to that given in the 1851 return. Unfortunately some of these later returns are in a far poorer physical condition than the predecessors.

All these returns are to be found in the Public Record Office census depository in Portugal Street, London and there is now no fee for inspecting them, but it is necessary to get a ticket to search there, a reasonable precaution to try to ensure that the people who search there are responsible people who will respect the value of these records and treat them with care. Generally today you can only search them on microfilm.

The information you glean from these returns will give you, if moderate fortune attends you, a considerable amount of further information about your family. Even with people of fifty years of age it will show you where they were born at the turn of the century and indicate further places of search for you. In the ordinary way this will be the parish registers and this valuable archive will be dealt with in the next chapter.

Chapter Five

PARISH REGISTERS

If your forbears belonged to the Church of England, then, having discovered the parish or likely parish from which your family came, from the census returns, from family information or other means, your next step is to search the parish registers.

Perhaps even earlier you should discover whether your parish has been included in the parishes of Great Britain which have been covered by the microfiche of the Latter Day Saints of Utah, U.S.A. These microfiches are very useful because they are arranged by counties and you get in alphabetical order names of people for the whole county for whatever parish registers or parts of parish registers have been included for that county. They cover mainly baptisms and marriages.

The booklet which will tell you the parishes, whether partly or in whole, which are covered by the L.D.S. microfiche is entitled *Parish and Vital Records List of the Genealogical Department of the Church of Jesus Christ of Latter Day Saints* prepared July 1977, with any additional supplements since then. This can be seen in many county record offices, large libraries, the Society of Genealogists, London, and the various tabernacles of the L.D.S. in Great Britain where they have copies of the microfiche which can be consulted. It is important to check that your parish is included for the period you wish to cover.

If you find your parish is not so included, then you should next enquire of the Family History Society of the county in which the parish is situated whether there is a transcribed copy of it for the period you need and if so where it is located. This will probably be the appropriate county record office, or possibly the reference section of the county library concerned. There is now in England a family history society for every county and it may well be worth your while joining it even if you do not live in the county where your ancestors did, as you will have the journal of the society sent to you and may receive other information. If there is a one-name society of your name you should also consider joining that.

If you find that the parish register for the period you want to search has not been transcribed and possibly indexed, by either the microfiche of the L.D.S. or by someone else, then you will have to search the original register.

You will probably find that your parish register has been transferred to the county record office of the county in which the parish is situated, as, with very few exceptions, this became obligatory under the Parochial Records Measure which came into force on 1 January 1979. By their transfer there they are not only made more accessible to searchers but they are kept under good conditions and are able to be repaired and restored where necessary and generally well looked after in conditions of good security.

You should get in touch with the appropriate county record office and make certain that the registers which you wish to consult are there for the necessary period you require. If you are unable to visit the county record office yourself they will be able to undertake this for you, but if you can manage to search the registers yourself this is desirable, as apart from its being more satisfactory you can then follow up any additional clues which may arise during your search.

You may find a hiatus in the parish registers during the Civil War in the seventeenth century. Also, during the Commonwealth in 1653, it was enacted that the births, marriages and deaths should be registered by 'some able and honest person' in a special book 'of good vellum or parchment'. This person was not the parish priest and this was really an attempt to set up a civil registration. You will notice it was the birth and death which was to be registered, not the baptism and burial. Unfortunately very few of these books survive. Fortunately in quite a number of cases the order was disregarded and the incumbent of the parish continued to record the baptisms, marriages and burials in his parish registers as before. But in other cases you may find an annoying gap, usually just at the period when you least want it!

It must also be borne in mind, when searching the earlier parish registers, that until 1st January 1752 the year began on the 25th March, the Feast of the Annunciation, so that before that date any dates in January and February and in March up to 24th came after December. People who have not realized this have been bewildered to discover a child born for instance in December 1750 baptized sometime in January or February 1750. Sometimes these dates are now written, in the form, '25th January 1734/5', signifying that the date was 25th January 1734 in the old style, but 25th January 1735 in the new style.

If the registers of the parish are missing or partly missing, its bishop's transcripts may survive. These are copies of the original registers which the incumbent had to send in annually to the diocesan registry. Many of them have now been transferred to the county record office or offices within the old diocesan boundaries. Here they can be consulted in comfort and usually without any fee. Those still in diocesan registers can be seen on application to the registrar and a fee may be required.

Unfortunately many of these transcripts have been lost or have survived in poor condition. The forwarding of them each year was an additional and irksome task and less conscientious incumbents were often careless in this duty. Furthermore their preservation in the registry was often in conditions far from ideal. The result is there are many gaps in these transcripts, particularly for the earlier periods, and those surviving, being on sheets of paper, are often torn or in a fragile condition. In copying them important details may have been omitted, although there are rare cases where details have been added which are not in the original registers.

For all these reasons, except the last mentioned, it is advisable to examine the original registers where they exist. Ideally it might be best to see both originals and transcripts.

It is best for you to take your extracts from the registers on the 8″ × 5″ slips I have suggested for the larger items. It is quicker this way, rather than attempting to use the smaller 6″ × 3″ slips for each individual entry. You can transfer each individual item to a smaller slip when you get home and, although this may seem rather a trouble, it is in the long run worth doing, as you then automatically bring together all your information about a particular individual.

When you examine your parish register you must be prepared for disappointments. You may have hoped to trace back your family for many generations, perhaps even to the beginning of the registers themselves. But, contrary to a widely held belief, families before the nineteenth century did not always remain in the same locality. Dr Peter Spufford of Jesus College, Cambridge, has studied this subject of Population Mobility, and has made it clear that even ordinary people moved about in the past far more than is usually realized.

Even the poorer people, although they probably did not move very far, seem to have moved about in the county, perhaps as work took them to neighbouring or more distant parishes. The higher class people may have moved further afield, unless they belonged to the county families and had a seat firmly fixed in the county. If you find your line dies out in the parish, then you may have to look around in the neighbouring parishes, but it depends on the individual circumstances. It is quite a good idea to look at an old map and see where the road from your village led to and where was the nearest inn. Villagers would often walk up the road in search of refreshment and change, and many a village lad met his future bride through first contacting her father or brother in the neighbouring 'local'.

If the name is a rare one, then it may be better to search the wills of the period, both in the local courts and in the Prerogative Courts. It also depends on the status and occupation of the family. If they were farmers or farm labourers then you may find them in the neighbouring parishes. Perhaps a son married a farmer's daughter from a nearby parish and he later took over the farm. Then there is always the difference between the movement of the farmer and the farm labourer. The labourer may move to a place where there is work in bad times. The movement into the towns in the late eighteenth and early nineteenth centuries must be borne in mind. You will find yourself learning a good deal of social history in your trail of searches and clues.

Although the parish registers may be no longer in the parish, you will no doubt want to go and look at the place. There are many reasons why you should do so. You will, for instance, have a chance to look around the church. There is always a possibility of some memorial inside it. Then there are the monumental inscriptions on the tombstones outside. Unfortunately, each year these are becoming less decipherable and today any prior to about 1800, unless they are on slate or else in a very sheltered part of the churchyard, are often impossible to read. It is worth enquiring if the inscriptions have ever been copied, as some parishes have copies of them made in the past and these can of course be very valuable, for the information on a stone is often far more informative than the bald entry of burial in the register.

Some stones which seem at first almost undecipherable can, after careful examination, be worked out. Sometimes they become quite clear when you look at them from a different angle. You can also clean the stone a little and it is worth while on such expeditions to arm yourself with a stiff, but not too stiff, brush. I hope none of you will have the experience which happened to one genealogist, who was carefully brushing the surface of a stone when the vicar came along. He was very nice and said he did not mind as long as it did not damage the stone. 'Oh, no,' the searcher assured him, 'I am very careful to rub gently,' and he gave an additional rub to show how gentle he was, but at that moment the whole face of the stone fell forward. However, the vicar had a sense of humour and they both laughed, so all ended happily.

Apart from the churchyard you may pick up local knowledge by wandering around the village. You may even hear something of your forbears over a glass of ale in the local pub. Names persist in localities even in these days of movement. A furniture remover recently told me that half his work was spent moving people back to the place in which they were born, after they had retired. It is a very human instinct to return to your native land in your old age. Some 'oldest inhabitant' may be able to give you some first- or second-hand information about your ancestors, if they were there not too far back. In the 1930s I heard in a Devonshire village something of the character of my great-grandfather who had been a doctor there and had died in 1856, some eighty years before. An old man did not remember him personally, but he had 'heard tell on him' and of his cheerful bedside manner. Not many counties are as fortunate as Gloucestershire, where Ralph Bigland, who was Garter King of Arms from 1780 to 1784, copied or had copied nearly all the inscriptions in most of the parishes in the county. They are contained in two huge folio volumes published at the end of the eighteenth and in the nineteenth centuries. Bigland was working at a time when the stones outside in the churchyard could be read even back to the time of Queen Elizabeth I. Would that all counties had had a Ralph Bigland!

When you visit the parish you may get a chance to meet the vicar, and if he has been there some years he may be able to tell you quite a bit about the history of the parish and even remember something about your ancestors who lived there. Vicars vary in their characters and personality as much as any other group of professional people, but most of them are helpful and kind and hospitable.

Most of them are helpful, kind and hospitable

When you get home after your day's search in your ancestor's parish you will return with perhaps varying emotions and certainly quite tired. Your forbears' village may not have fulfilled the image of it which you had built up in your mind. It may have been excessively modernized, so that little of it is left which your grandfather or great-grandfather would have recognized. Nevertheless it is bound to be interesting to you and no doubt you will have learnt a certain amount about it, even if not as much as you hoped.

Naturally a good map of the locality in which you discover your ancestors is invaluable. The 6″ to the mile and 25″ to the mile Ordnance maps of the earliest date available are desirable, but even more useful may be a copy of the tithe map for the parish, or of that part of it which covers your particular home. By the Tithe Commutation Act of 1836 tithes were changed to fixed charges on land and this necessitated a detailed survey, apportionment and valuation. This resulted in the best and most complete land record since Domesday was made. Each parish had its copy of the tithe map, which, in conjunction with the tithe apportionment lists, showed each field and house with its boundaries and the name of the owner. A second copy was sent to the Diocesan Registry and the third copy went to the central office of the Tithe Redemption Commission, now at 33 Finsbury Square, London, E.C.4. The parish copies have often been lost. The diocesan copy is more likely to be extant and probably now in the County Record Office. At the central authority you may be reasonably certain of finding a copy, their records being fairly perfect. A photostat copy of one of these together with the apportionment list applicable can be most valuable to you in your searches and enable you to visualize more easily your forbears' way of life.

"Very careful to rub gently"

Chapter Six

NONCONFORMIST RECORDS

It must be admitted at the start that the search for parentage of people not members of the established church is far more difficult. In the days when toleration of religious beliefs was not an accepted code, people who would not conform to the established church suffered many disabilities and even persecutions, and it was only their strong belief that their faith and conduct were right which sustained them.

After the breach with Rome in Henry VIII's time the Roman Catholics in England were hounded and persecuted and their religion, so to speak, went underground. Services and confessions were held in secret and the many priest holes in old houses in England confirm this. As a result Catholic registers were only able to be kept *sub rosa* and it is not surprising that few survived. Most of those that did were not included in the non-parochial registers which were handed over to the General Registry in accordance with the Act of 1840, as the Roman Catholic Church requested to be allowed to retain them. It is necessary therefore to ascertain from the Roman Catholic authorities whether any registers survive in the area where the people in question lived. The Catholic Record Society began publishing records in 1905 and have published some forty-eight volumes, which include a number of registers of baptism, marriage and burial. The baptisms often include the names of godparents. Those marriage registers which exist are mainly prior to 1754, because after the Hardwicke Marriage Act came into operation 25th March that year most Roman Catholics were married in the Church of England to ensure the legality of the marriage, though they may also have had a Roman Catholic marriage ceremony, which possibly went unrecorded. For the same reason many Nonconformists were married in the parish church because before 1806 this was the only legal way in which they could be married and it was necessary for such purposes as proving inheritance that the proof of marriage should be unassailable. For the same reason a number may have been baptized in the established church, though these were far fewer than the marriages. When it comes to burial, many of these sects had their own burial grounds and kept their own registers.

The Congregationalists are a very old body of Nonconformists and date from Reformation times. These earliest Congregationalists, or Independents, as they were often called, felt themselves unable to accept the idea of the sovereign being head of the established church and they also disagreed with the idea that anyone could be a member of the Church, and insisted that 'only people who were in earnest about their Christian discipleship and made open confession of their faith should be counted as members'. In Stuart times, when the kings tried to re-establish the Roman Catholic religion, the Congregationalists increased. Historically the name 'Puritan' is applied to all these early Independents and the Pilgrim Fathers belonged to the Independents.

The Congregationalists suffered under many acts of Parliament when Charles II was restored. Among them were the Corporation Act of 1661, which prevented them from holding office, the Act of Uniformity of the next year and the Conventicle Act of 1664 which forbade all religious meetings but those of the Anglican Church. The Five Mile Act of the next year brought even further disabilities, for this forbade Nonconformist ministers to teach in schools or to live within five miles of a corporate town. In 1673 the Test Act was passed, which ordered that all people holding office under the crown should take the sacrament according to the Anglican rites.

During the eighteenth century there was a gradual relaxation of these severe measures and they came to be more honoured in the breach than in the observance. Great Congregationalist preachers, like George Whitefield, stirred the conscience of many established church leaders. Although we sometimes think of the eighteenth century as one of great materialism and corruption, yet there were other elements sirring and a movement to humanitarianism and tolerance was spreading. By the nineteenth century many of the measures against Nonconformists had disappeared, though the Test Act did not go until 1828, in which year the Corporation Act was also repealed.

In 1749 it was decided to set up a general register of births of children of Protestant dissenters of the three denominations at Dr Williams Library in Red Cross Street. This continued until 1837 when the Civil Registration came in. The register was not limited to Londoners or even to Protestant Dissenters, but was open to anyone wishing to have the birth of their child registered, with the payment of a small fee for doing this, and the register was in fact used by other than members of the three denominations of Nonconformists, that is, the Presbyterians (including the Unitarians), the Independents (or Congregationalists) and the Baptists. This register is now in the Public Record Office (RG4).

Considerable thought was given to the form of the certificates so that they might be accepted as evidence and in 1806, in order to obviate any doubt in the certificates through a person being baptized and having his birth registered "at an advanced period of life", the certificate was re-worded to prevent this abuse. However, in 1821 the Master of the Rolls rejected a certificate from the registry as a proof of age, which led to the form being altered again and it received further modifications in 1826. The birth certificate was now dated and it clearly stated the exact date and place of the birth and was signed by the parents, or if they could not write, by a witness, preferably by a near relative.

Certificates had so far been on parchment, but at this date it was decided that they should be on paper. This register throughout its existence showed a high degree of accuracy.

Apart from the General Register at Dr Williams's Library and the individual registers on Nonconformist groups, births of dissenters were recorded in Church of England parish registers. This was under Acts of Parliament of 1695 and 1700.

Readers wanting to search Nonconformist registers are advised to consult the *National Index of Parish Registers, volume 2. Sources for Nonconformist Genealogy and Family History* by D.J. Steel (1973). This volume deals very fully with all Nonconformist registration, including the Society of Friends, or Quakers, the Moravians and a number of foreign churches, such as the Walloons and Huguenots, the Dutch Church, Lutherans, Swiss Churches and Greek Orthodox Churches, together with some information about some other denominations, including the Plymouth Brethren, the Universalists and the Irvingites or Catholic Apostolic Church.

Unfortunately many Nonconformist records have been destroyed. The National Union of Congregational Churches, founded in 1832, did a certain amount towards their preservation, more particularly in establishing, the year before, the Congregational Library, where many of the surviving records are today housed. The Congregational Historical Society has since 1901 published in its Transactions a number of early records.

The Congregational registers which survived were handed over under the 1840 Act to the General Register House and are now in the Public Record Office. Where they do survive the information in them is often fuller than that of the parish registers of the Church of England. For instance, a baptism of a child of John Harrison in Mount Street Independent Chapel, Plymouth Dock (now Devonport) in 1827 gives the dates of baptism and birth, the maiden name of the wife and their abode. The additional information of the mother's maiden name is particularly useful at a time when this would not have been recorded in the parish registers. But in general there are few registers before the late eighteenth century and these often have long gaps with no entries.

The Methodists are of later origin. The church came into being through the work of two brothers, both Anglican clergymen, John and Charles Wesley, who were dissatisfied with the lassitude and lack of driving force in the established church of their time. The Wesley brothers went around the country preaching, often meeting with great opposition. They never intended their followers to form a separate church but this gradually came about. Even in Wesley's lifetime the ministers of his following began to baptize, marry and bury their followers, though many other followers continued to be baptized and buried and particularly to be married in the established church.

But after the death of the two Wesley brothers, Charles dying in 1788 and John three years later, the Methodists began to form themselves into churches. There were also several offshoots from the main body, known as Wesleyan Methodists, such as the Methodist New Connection, formed in 1797, the Primitive Methodists (1807) the Bible Christians (1815), the Protestant Methodists (1827), the Wesleyan Methodist Associates (1835) and the Wesleyan Reformers (1849). After the end of the eighteenth century, however, there was a gradual progress towards unification again and today there are just the two bodies, the United Methodists and the Methodists.

In 1818 a Methodist Registry was opened for recording centrally the baptisms being performed in the various chapels throughout the country, and this register is now one of those in the Public Record Office. Wesley's own chapel in City Road, London, had its own graveyard and the registers of this ground start in 1779. Many other Methodist burial grounds have kept records, which are now at the Public Record Office. Besides the three large volumes of the Metropolitan Register there were 856 Methodist registers of baptisms, and burials handed over to the General Registry under the Act of 1840. These are now also at the Public Record Office. Marriages were not recorded in Methodist registers until after the Marriage Registration Act of 1837.

The official archives of the Methodist movement are kept in the Methodist Book Room, City Road, London. Information about individual Methodists who were active in the movement and about Methodist ministers can be gathered from the movement's magazine, which began as the *Arminian Magazine* in 1778, successively changing its title to *The Methodist* (1798-1821) and *The Wesleyan Methodist Magazine* (1822-1913). Nearly always there are obituaries of ministers. There is an index to these memoirs and to local histories from 1778-1839 published in the *Proceedings of the Wesley Historical Society,* Volume 7 (1909-10). The various branches of Methodism have also published their magazines.

The Quakers realized early the importance of keeping records of their baptisms, marriages and burials, and their records are on the whole well kept and also often well indexed. They date from their foundation by George Fox in the seventeenth century.

The Quaker records were handed over to the authorities in accordance with the 1840 Act, but before they did so they made digests of the information in them. These are held and carefully indexed at the Friends House, Euston Road, London, N.W.1. The digest entries are arranged geographically in the Quarterly Meeting areas, each of which had separate volumes for baptisms, marriages and burials. The form of dating is that peculiar to the Quakers, that is, January is 'First Month' and Sunday is 'First Day' and so forth. In each volume the entries are alphabetical as far as the initial letter and within each letter the entries are chronological. There are some eighty-five volumes, which contain approximately the following number of entries: births, 260,000; marriages, 40,000; deaths, 310,000. There is a description of these registers by J.S. Rowntree, *The Friends' Registers of Birth, Death and Marriage, 1650-1900.* The Scottish records are included in the digest at the Friends House, London, but the records of the Irish Friends are at their depository at 6, Eustace Street, Dublin. All these digests continue up to 1837 in England and Wales. There is a useful account of the archives of the Quakers by R.S. Mortimer in the *Amateur Historian,* Volume III, page 55.

As mentioned, in general Roman Catholic registers were not deposited under the 1840 Act. This was also so with the registers of the Jewish synagogues, as the Jews, like the Roman Catholics, asked to be exempted from the requirements of the Act, feeling that their registers were better kept with their own communities. There were also a number of Welsh Nonconformist chapel registers not deposited. These can only be consulted through the bodies concerned.

Recent work, particularly by family history societies, has included transcribing of nonconformist records.

Chapter Seven

WILLS AND ADMINISTRATIONS

Wills to the genealogist can be the most valuable and also at times the most frustrating of aids to information. The first difficulty is in finding them and then, when you have done so, you are often disappointed at the meagre information which they reveal.

On the more optimistic side, wills can reveal an enormous amount of information and one of their intriguing merits is that they may reveal all sorts of ancillary information which you never suspected and which you might never have lighted upon through other sources. Then in some cases inventories survive. These were lists of the goods of the deceased made by the administrators or executors after the person died. From these you can often glean a great deal about their lives. John West, in his delightful and informative book *Village Records,* published in 1962 (new edition by Phillimore 1982) has shown how you can even conjecture and reconstruct the house in which your forbears lived by means of these inventories.

Wills can reveal an enormous amount of information

A will, being a very personal document, adds body to the bare bones of your pedigree. You feel as you read through the winding legal phrasing that you are getting nearer to your ancestor and his ideas and thoughts. Sometimes there are strong human touches and often humour. I remember being much amused at the will of a late-eighteenth-century woman, who left her glasses to her sister Anne 'but if they do not suit her, then I leave them to my sister Mary'. I wonder what the ophthalmic surgeons of today would say about that kind of amateur prescribing!

Since 1858 wills and administrations in England and Wales present no difficulty, for from that time forward they were proved either in the Principal Registry of the Family Division, previously the Principal Probate Registry, at Somerset House, or else at one of the District Probate Registries which were set up at that time. But wherever they were proved, the printed will and administration calendars at Somerset House and at the District Registries list them. In other words you have an index in exact alphabetical order of all wills proved and administrations granted in England and Wales from 1858 to the present day. At Somerset House you can see either the original or a copy of any will or the details of any administration for a small fee. You may by now already know the date or approximate date of death of the person whose will you want to see, but in any case it is not a long job to look through, say, ten years of these calendars. In fact, if you do not know the date of death of someone and you are fairly certain he is likely to have left a will or enough estate to have had an administration if he died intestate (and most people do leave something, even if only a few pounds), then it is quicker to search the calendars here than to search the indexes to the deaths in the General Registry, as the indexes of death are divided into four quarters in a year while in the probate calendars you only have to search one index. The indexes of wills also give you far more information about the deceased and may save you from having to get a death certificate. They give you his description, address and place of death, his former place of residence if the will describes him as of somewhere else, the date of his death, the names of his executors or administrators and their address and description. The main item they do not give you which the death certificate does, is the age of the deceased. As far as intestates are concerned the information in the calendar is about as full as that given in the administration act, so there is no need to see it.

Having found the will in the calendar, you can then, as mentioned above, see either the original of it or a copy, according to whether it was proved at the Principal Registry in London or at one of the district registries. Recently there has been some relaxation of the rules which governed your copying extracts from wills, and now you are allowed to make short extracts, provided you write in pencil. But you can get a photo copy of a will for a small fee per page. A long will might be rather expensive, but you need not have a photo copy of the whole will. You can have photo copies of the pages you require, as often much of a long will is taken up with legal repetitions.

When we turn to wills prior to 1858, and these are the ones the genealogist will be principally concerned with, the situation is very different. Before that date the proving of administrations and wills was in the hands of the church. This may come as a surprise to you, but it is all bound up in our history and, just as the only way of proving the approximate date of a birth or death, or the date of a marriage prior to 1837 in England and Wales was through the baptism, marriage or burial registers in the church, so the recording of wills was left to the church. From early times a will was regarded as a rather

contd. on p. 36

AN OXFORDSHIRE YEOMAN MAKES HIS WILL: 'IN THE NAME OF GOD AMEN the Fourth day of February in the Fourth yeare of the reigne of our Sovereigne Lord and Lady William and Mary by the grace of God of England Scotland France and Ireland King and Queen Defendors of the Faith et Anno Dni 1692 I Nicolas Good of Great Hazeley in the County of Oxon yeoman being somewhat infirme in body but of sound and perfect mind and memory blessed bee God for the same and considering our fraile Estate under the condicon of mortallity how in the midst of life wee are in death Have thought good to make and accordingly I doe make this my last Will and Testament in manner and forme following hereby revoking and making void all former Wills whatsoever by mee heretofore made AND first and principally I commend my Soul into the hands of Almighty God my Creatour and most mercifull Father haveing an assured hopes by the meritts death and passion of my Blessed Lord and Savour Jesus Christ without any other meritts or meanes whatsoever to have full pardon and free remission for all my Sins and after this life to enjoy everlasting life and happiness in his heavenly Kingdome And my Body I comitt to the Earth from whence it came to bee buried in such place and in such decent manner as my Executrix herinafter named shall thinke fitt and convenient And for such Wordly Estate wherewith it hath pleased God of his great mercy and bounty to blesse mee which I doe acknowledge with all humble thankefulnes to have received by his providence and blessing and wherof it hath pleased him to give mee the Disposition that the same shall bee disposed off And accordingly I doe hereby give Devise bequeath and Dispose of the same as followeth . . .'

This will, with its elaborate preamble and pious hopes of salvation, is typical of the wills of the 16th, 17th and early 18th centuries. The testator goes on to leave to his 'Loving Wife Elizabeth the use of all and singular my household goods . . .' for her lifetime, and leaves the residue to his daughter 'Elizabeth Good of Rycott Lane in the said County of Oxon Spinster' and appoints her his sole executrix.

Nicolas Good signs by making his mark, as does one of the three witnesses whose names are at the bottom on the left. Below the testator's mark is the notification in Latin of the probate with the name of the registrar, Ben: Cooper, beneath it. This shows that the will was proved on 10th April, 1694 in the court of the Archdeacon of Oxford by Elizabeth Good, the daughter and sole executrix.

This is a particularly well-written and clear will of the period. Many of them are far more difficult to read.

MS WILLS. OXON 129, BODLEIAN LIBRARY

OXFORD

AN OXFORDSHIRE YEOMAN MAKES HIS WILL

sacred document and that is why in these early wills we nearly always find them starting with the words 'In the name of God, Amen', and continuing with hopes of salvation for their soul through the merits of Jesus Christ.

In theory, if a man died leaving a will and having land or property all in one archdeaconry, then his will would be proved in the particular archdeacon's court. If he had property in two or more archdeaconries in the same diocese, then his will would be proved in the bishop's court. If he had property in two or more dioceses, then his will would have to be proved in one of the archbishop's courts, the Prerogative Court of Canterbury or the Prerogative Court of York. Where a person had property in both provinces, although Canterbury appeared to have the right of prior probate, such wills were usually proved in the York province also.

Already you can see the picture getting complicated, for you would not know whether a man had property extending over two archdeaconries or two dioceses, so already your field of search is being extended. But this unfortunately is by no means the end of the story. Although a man having property in a particular archdeaconry *could* have his will proved in that archdeaconry, there was no bar to its being proved in a higher court and it often was. It is noticeable that up to the end of the eighteenth century people of any substance at all tended to have their wills proved in the Prerogative Court, particularly that of Canterbury. 'Men of substance' does not mean necessarily great landowners or local squires, but it includes people like farmers and tradesmen. Probably the wills of farm labourers and employed workers would only be proved in the archdeacon's court, for there were some additional expenses in proving in one of the higher courts, but their masters and employers might well do so. This may have been done, as is often maintained, because there was greater security in proving in a higher court. Perhaps the archdeacon's court was not always too efficiently run and there was more chance of a will getting lost in one of the smaller courts. But there is another possible contributory cause. Executors and the family may have felt there was more privacy in proving in a higher court, which was probably more distant. For people who proved their wills in the local archdeacon's court there may have been doubts about this. Junior clerks in the smaller courts, knowing the local people, may have been inclined to gossip about the contents of the wills. 'She never left Bob a penny — and him the eldest too — left it all to that "mummy's darling" Geoffrey!' Before 1858 proved wills were not normally open to inspection, but, even if they were, a person would have possessed an unusual curiosity to make an expensive and long journey to London, for instance, to see a will for no other purpose than idle inquisitiveness and even a trip to a local diocesan registry would not, in those days, be lightly undertaken if one lived the other side of the county from it.

After the end of the eighteenth century it is noticed that people did tend far more to prove wills in the archdeaconry courts. Perhaps by then they had become more efficient and were regarded as more reliable and discreet.

Then there are the 'peculiars'. These add further to the difficulties of finding where a will was proved. These 'peculiars', sometimes 'royal peculiars' were courts having special jurisdictions over certain areas. Thus if a person happened to have property in one of these districts, his executors would not be allowed to prove his will in the local archdeacon's court or even perhaps in the bishop's court, though he would always be able to prove it in the prerogative court. The origin and existence of these peculiars goes right back in our history and it is a subject in itself. In general one may say that they were a means of giving some extra emoluments to some offices and thus adding to the perquisites of some perhaps poorly paid positions. The King might grant a peculiar to some favourite, in the same way that the Stuart kings angered the nation by granting monopolies to certain favourites, so that only they could make or sell certain goods.

One such peculiar, as an example, is that area around Hurst and Wokingham, now in Berkshire, which was once part of Wiltshire, a little island of this county surrounded by Berkshire, to which geographically it should obviously have belonged. This was because that area was a peculiar of the Dean of Sarum, or Salisbury, and anyone happening to live in that area and have property in it had to have his will, when he died, proved in the Dean of Sarum's Court. This of course set up all sorts of confusion. Sometimes the peculiars were merely attached to a particular parish, where the rector or vicar benefited from the particular additional fees coming from this source.

It will be realized that the absence of any central index of wills and administrations means that the finding of a particular will may involve considerable research. The more obvious places are the archdeacon's, bishop's and archbishop's courts covering the locality of the person's home and death. It is not too difficult to check whether his locality lay within the jurisdiction of a peculiar and then you will, of course, search for the will or administration in that court. In the province of York the procedure was somewhat different. With the prominent exception of the great archdeaconry of Richmond, wills in this province were not normally proved in an archdeaconry, the local probate courts being those of the rural deans or surrogates acting under a commission from the commissary of the Exchequer Court of York.

In 1964 valuable consolidated indexes of wills and administrations covering the period 1796 to 1857 used by the Estate Duty Office were transferred to the Public Record Office. These indexes (in the Inland Revenue Section 27) are particularly useful in two ways, firstly because they cover wills and administrations in all the courts of England and Wales, not merely the P.C.C., and secondly because they are indexed in a more detailed way, as explained below, and not merely to the first letter, as with the P.C.C. wills. For these reasons no doubt genealogists and other research workers will use them more and more as their existence becomes known.

The indexes fall into two sections, those covering the period 1796 to 1811 and those covering the period 1812 to 1857.

In the period prior to 1812 the indexes are divided into three groups, namely (1) The P.C.C. Will Index (PRO Reference No. I.R. 27/1-16), divided into yearly parts, indexed in alphabetical order of surname in the year and month in which the will was proved, (2) P.C.C. Administrations Index (I.R. 27/17-20). Each volume contains details of administrations for a number of years, the entries being alphabetical, though not completely chronological. (3) The County Courts Indexes (I.R. 27/67-93) which cover both wills and administrations in the Prerogative Court of York, diocesan, archdeaconry and peculiar courts, each volume containing entries for several years and of more than one court.

After 1811 there are only two groups, namely the wills indexes and the administration indexes. Each group covers both P.C.C. and county courts.

The will indexes between 1812 and 1857 (I.R. 27/140-323) are divided into four annual parts, covering the names A-D, E-J, K-R, and S-Z. They give details of all wills proved each year in whichever court they were proved.

The Administrative Indexes from 1812 to 1857 are divided into two parts, namely (i) P.C.C. (I.R. 27/21-66) and (ii) County Courts (I.R. 27/94:139).

In the earlier period before 1812 the indexes are arranged under the first letter and the first vowel, thus there are five divisions, for the five vowels, within each initial letter. This means that the consonants following the initial letter are disregarded and it is the first vowel which fixes the name's position in the group. This may sound a little complicated but it is quite easy to follow when used a little. An example will make this clearer. Taking the names Carpenter, Chapman, Chaundy, Cheney, Chitty, Christian, Church, Clarke, Cross, Crozier, Cruse, Crawshaw, Creasey, those in the CA group would be: Carpenter, Chapman, Chaundy, Clarke, Crawshaw; those in the CE group would be Cheney, Creasey; those in CI, Chitty, Christian; those in CO, Cross, Crozier and those in CU, Church, Cruse.

From 1812 onwards the names included together are usually indicated by three letter groups, depending on the frequency of the names, for example HIG to HIK; HIL to HIM. In all cases with this index the existence of a will or administration proved or granted in England and Wales can be found in a matter of minutes, contrasted with the fifteen or twenty minutes taken to search each initial letter in the P.C.C. indexes.

From 1812 onwards the indexes for these wills are on the open shelves at the P.R.O. Therefore these can be consulted and you can quickly find your will and see in which court it was proved. If proved in the P.C.C. you will be able to see it at the P.R.O., but if it was proved in one of the county courts you will have either to see it there or else get a searcher to make extracts for you. Another alternative would be to ask the depository to send you a xerox copy of the will for which they will let you know the fee.

Indexes for the Estate Duty Office Administrations from 1812 onwards and for the abstracts of wills and administrations from 1796 to 1811 are not at present on the open shelves. It is therefore necessary to apply for these. Once again, if it is a P.C.C. admon. you will be able to see it at the P.R.O. but for county courts you will have to obtain the information from there as for the wills.

These indexes are particularly valuable not only because they cover the whole of England and Wales, and therefore direct a person straight away to the court in which the will is proved, but also because they give more detail than the normal calendar before 1858, namely the name of the testator, his residence, the names of the executors of the will and the court in which the will is proved. Copies of the wills themselves also existed in this office and this is fortunate, as it means that copies of those wills of the period covered which were destroyed during the Second World War at Exeter have been extracted and are now available at the County Record Offices at Exeter, Taunton and Truro. It is understood that the remainder of the wills in this office are being or have been destroyed on the grounds that other copies exist elsewhere. I hope it is correct that copies in every case do exist elsewhere. It seems a great pity in any case that these second copies of wills should be destroyed, as it is only too possible that individual wills have been lost in the various depositories throughout the country. However, it would appear that the Lord Chancellor has approved the destruction of these wills, presumably because their great bulk is causing housing difficulties.

Apart from these indexes there are also Death Duty Registers which are in I.R. 26. You may not normally want to consult these but they can prove useful in certain cases, particularly when a testator in his will has left property to "all my children in equal shares" or words to that effect, when he does not name the children. The Death Duty Register will give details of the distribution of the estate, mentioning the names of the people to whom the legacies were distributed and the amounts each beneficiary received.

Anthony Camp has written very fully on the Estate Duty Office wills and administrations in the *Genealogists' Magazine* of September 1967 (vol. 15, No. 11). In this he gives the complete indications of the exact references for applying for any of the indexes for the whole of the period from 1796 to 1857, after which the calendars to the civil registration of wills came in and can be seen at Somerset House. This will show you the references for any of the indexes which are not on the open shelves at the P.R.O. There are also two other articles on these wills and admons, one by D.M. Hawkins in June 1970 (vol. 16, No. 6), dealing with the copies of the wills from the Estate Duty Office which were used to replace the wills from 1812 to 1857 destroyed in the last war at Exeter which have been transferred to the Devon, Somerset and Truro record offices, and in the same magazine for December 1981 (Vol. 20 No. 8) by Jane Cox, entitled "A Note on the Death Duty Registers".

Indexes of wills proved in the Prerogative Court of Canterbury (P.C.C. for short) have been printed, mainly by the British Record Society, up to 1700, and the administrations have been covered to the mid-seventeenth century. Also there have been a number of indexes published, by this and other societies of local courts.

The Society of Genealogists has a slip index of all wills and administrations in the P.C.C. between 1750 and 1800, and they will search them for a small fee. Two volumes, covering names from A to CE have been published and the third volume is in progress.

An invaluable guide through the morass of difficulties in finding these wills is A.J. Camp's *Wills and their Whereabouts* 1974, a thorough revision and extension of B.G. Bouwens' work of the same title. It is a county by county survey, showing where the wills are to be found, and giving details of the various courts, the wills and administrations of which are now mostly transferred to the county record offices and other archive depositories. It also contains useful notes on testamentary procedure and hints on making will extracts, adapted from the notes made by B.G. Bouwens in his original work. For those particularly interested in north country wills and admons in the province of the Archbishop of York, see the account of these wills in the Borthwick Institute at York in Camp's work and also a brief account of its holdings in Chapter 26 of this book.

The situation today regarding the homes of the various wills is far better than in the immediate past, when they were in the custody of the various district probate registries, the officials of which, concerned with the day to day registration and probate of modern wills, were not always interested in these earlier wills and did not appreciate their value as historical and genealogical documents. Some no doubt were reasonably conscientious about their custody, but Bouwens records hearing of at least one registry where, when it was being closed, the wish was expressed that 'all the old stuff might get lost' and, as he remarks, 'the wish may be father to the deed'. Now that a great proportion of them have been transferred to other depositories, mainly to county record offices, they have come into the hands of people who appreciate their value, trained archivists who are anxious to make them available to research workers, and they can in consequence now be consulted in far more favourable and often more comfortable conditions.

It should be noted that during the period of the Commonwealth all the wills were proved centrally. This period is covered by the British Record Society indexes and this, among other advantages, is a very useful indication of the distribution of surnames in the middle of the seventeenth century. While one regrets the action of the Commonwealth government in instituting the civil registration of births, marriages and deaths, one rejoices in their action in instituting a central registration for wills and wishes it had been continued. There were, however, disadvantages. In times when travel was difficult it seems many wills failed ever to be registered.

It is hoped, however, that you will be successful in tracking down some of your family wills. As already suggested, it is best to take down details of wills on the 8″ × 5″ slips. The details you should record are as follows: (1) Name, as the heading. (2) Exact description of the person making the will, as given in the will itself. (3) Any note regarding place of burial, etc. (4) Bequests, amounts, to whom and any special provisos. (5) Any details of land held, being careful to note exact description and parish if mentioned. (6) Names of any trustees and conditions of trust. (7) Note of any family heirloom or articles to which there seems to have been special importance attached, such as tools of trade, which may indicate occupations. (8) Names of executors and any guardians of children. (9) Date of will. (10) Witnesses. (11) Details of any codicils, following the above pattern. (12) Details of probate. (13) Exact name of court in which proved, with reference. Below is given an example:

COSTER, Edward
Of the parish of St Martin Orgar, City of London 'oylman'
Bequests — to Daughter, Elizabeth Row
mentions late daughter, Mary Hardy
Grand-daughter, Elizabeth Mary Hardy
Executors, friends Wilfred Reed of Lower Thames St, 'oylman'; John Sawyer of St Martin's Lane, Cannon St, gent., and the testator's wife, Jane Coster.
Dated: 28th February 1787
Witnesses: Joshua Stafford Snr. Joshua Stafford Jun.
Proved: P.C.C. (66 Holman) 18 Feb. 1794 by Wilfred Reed and John Sawyer, surviving exors.

You will appreciate that from the above quite an amount of information about the family is gleaned. One of Edward Coster's daughters had evidently married someone called Row, and another daughter, who was dead in February 1787 when the will was made, had married a Mr Hardy and had a daughter living at that time. The wife was alive when the will was made but was dead before it was proved in 1794 because the executors who did so are described as 'surviving executors'. You also obtain the occupation of the deceased, namely 'oylman' and this will suggest other sources, because, as he was working in the City of London he may have been a freeman and a member of a city livery company. Thus the freedom rolls and the city livery company records may provide further information, including the important one of the name and occupation of the testator's father. If he in turn was a freeman, then you get his father's name and occupation and so on. In earlier times it was not possible to practice certain trades in the City unless you were a freeman, and the freedom rolls of other towns, where they have survived, are also very valuable in tracing parentage.

If you are searching for a name which is fairly uncommon and you have traced it down to a particular district, you should systematically make extracts of all wills and administrations of the name in that area. Then you can sit down and have the enjoyment of fitting it all together, rather like a jig-saw puzzle.

Rather like a jigsaw puzzle

Inventories, as already mentioned, where they survive, are often very helpful in piecing together something of the man's life and occupation, as if, for instance, he was a farmer it will indicate his farm stock, the value of his grain and so forth, or if the deceased was a tradesman or craftsman of some sort, this will probably be revealed by the inventory, probably listing his tools and materials. Inventories are often available for wills proved in the archdeaconry and diocesan courts. The inventories for the great collection of wills in the Prerogative Court of Canterbury were in 1964 transferred to the Public Record Office and are being indexed, but are not yet available for the public to see. W.G. Hoskins in his work *Local History in England* points out that these inventories contain an enormous amount of information of every kind about the upper strata of the population and emphasizes how necessary such information is for a good local history.

The indexing of this vast collection is a great task and will take a considerable time. But when it is completed it will be a most valuable tool to genealogists among others. It will in fact form an index to many of the P.C.C. wills, because where there is an inventory there should also be a will, though the reverse is not necessarily true and there may be a number of wills which have no inventory.

This search for wills may be just one of those occasions mentioned in Chapter 1 when you may prefer to employ a professional genealogist. As also mentioned in that chapter, the Society of Genealogists do this kind of research themselves or they will provide you with a list of professional genealogists. Some of these advertise in the Society's magazine and elsewhere. A professional genealogist has the advantage that he or she is experienced in this rather specialized and difficult field and may be useful to you in your initial search for wills, even if you continue with it later on. But as mentioned earlier, if you can spare the time it is better for you to do it yourself, because you will learn personally much more about your ancestors and will probably enjoy the searching and atmosphere of pursuit which attaches itself to the work, rather like a detective gradually unravelling clues.

After you have searched the wills, parish registers and census returns you have searched what may be termed the normal and direct sources. Your next step will be to examine more specialized records, which will depend on what you have discovered so far. The succeeding chapters will mainly deal with these.

Chapter Eight

MARRIAGE LICENCES

Marriage was often by banns, that is, notices of intention to marry called out three times during the Sunday services in the parish church or churches in which the bride and bridegroom lived, in one of which the two people intended to marry. When for some reason the people concerned wanted to dispense with this requirement they could do so by being married by licence. Such an occasion might be when the couple wanted to be married quickly because the future husband was perhaps going abroad with his regiment. But licences cost more money than banns, so that nearly always the poorest classes if possible were married by banns.

Probably for that very reason it became to a certain extent what would today be called a 'status symbol' to be married by licence. It was thought rather ordinary or common to be married by banns and so in the past everyone who could afford it was married by licence, even though there was plenty of time to have the banns called in the parish church. There was probably another reason why banns were disliked by the upper classes. They did not enjoy having their names called out in church for all and sundry to hear. They felt this revelation of their intentions in such a personal matter as marriage was rather vulgar and they did not wish to see the village yokels gaping with curiosity at hearing about their squire's daughter's matrimonial future. Such things were considered private family affairs and not the concern of the villagers.

Of course there were others who thought differently and a good country squire might have been happy to feel that the villagers, who were probably mostly his tenants and employees, took an interest in his daughter's marriage, but even so he would probably have followed the convention and had her married by licence.

Of course, as always happens in history, the habits of the upper classes were copied by those of lower social status and so all down the classes people got married by licence if possible, until it came down to the man who really could not afford the higher fees, the ordinary workman, who would perhaps in any case have been thought presumptuous at marrying by licence and laughed at by his fellow workers as having ideas above his station.

So it was not merely the upper classes, as is sometimes thought, who were married by licence, but most farmers, yeomen, merchants and clerks in city offices did so and it was generally only the great mass of what have in the past been called the lower classes who had their banns called out.

The village yokels gaping with curiosity

All this is very useful to the genealogist, for not only is it a little easier to trace a marriage if it was made by licence, but also some additonal information will be gleaned about the bride and bridegroom.

There were several kinds of licence. If both people lived in the same diocese, then they could get the licence from the bishop of that diocese, but if they were in different dioceses, then they had to go to the archbishop's office for it. These came from the archbishop's vicar-general and so were known as vicar-general licences. But it might happen that the two people wanting to get married lived in two ecclesiastical provinces, in which case they had to go to the office of the Master of Faculties of the Archbishop of Canterbury as Primate of all England and so these were known as Faculty Office Licences. There were also certain deàns and chapters, archdeacons and holders of peculiars who had the right to grant these licences. You will probably already be noticing a similarity to the method for obtaining probate of wills, and the various jurisdictions were in fact similar.

The actual licence was given to the people who were being married, but the allegation, which was a kind of statement made by the bride and bridegroom, was kept at the diocesan registry, together with the bonds, which were assurances by the bondsmen, who went surety for the couple about to be married. These bondsmen were usually friends and sometimes relatives.

Information from the allegations and bonds varies in different dioceses, but the allegation usually gives the name and status of the bride and bridegroom, that is, whether the man was a bachelor or widower and the woman a spinster or widow, and it often gave the occupation of the bridegroom. It would also indicate the place or possible places where the marriage could take place. If one or both of the people were under age, then the name or names of the parents giving their consent would be given and this is, of course, particularly valuable information.

THE DIOCESES AND ARCHDEACONRIES OF ENGLAND IN 1797: This map, published by John Andrews on 18th November that year shows the diocesan boundaries and the general localities of the archdeaconries. It is therefore useful in indicating not only where a person's will is likely to have been proved, but also, for people married by licence, under whose authority that licence is likely to have been granted. The table at the side shows that the total number of churches in England and Wales at that time was 9083, and that there were 26 deaneries and 60 archdeaconries.

BODLEIAN LIBRARY, OXFORD

These allegations and bonds were kept in the diocesan registry, where some still remain today. Their consultation may be hedged with difficulties and in some dioceses you can only have them consulted by an agent, usually the diocesan registrar, who is generally a solicitor. This involves fees which may be rather high. In other cases you are allowed to consult the indexes yourself and the necessary documents will be produced, again for a fee which is not always light. However, most dioceses have now handed over their records to the local County Record Office, which becomes also the Diocesan Record Office. Here the records are under the care of trained archivists and are available for consultation, usually without any fee and the staff are usually very helpful.

A number of marriage licences have been published by the Harleian Society and other bodies, such as county record societies. Others have been indexed in manuscript and some copies exist in typescript. The Society of Genealogists, for instance, has many MS copies. It has published *Abstracts and Indexes* of these, compiled by Lydia Collins, 1981, and the Federation of Family History Societies has published (with Bishops Transcripts) *Marriage Licences, Bonds and allegations* a Guide to their location and indexes, compiled by J.S.W. Gibson, 1981. A number of Family History Societies have compiled lists of these in their area. Information on marriage licences is also contained in the *National Index of Parish Registers.* The Devon and Cornwall Record Society has TS indexes and extracts of marriage licences for Devon and Cornwall from 1523 to 1631 by Vivian, indexed by Mann and Pershouse; from 1631 to 1762 by Mann and from 1734 to 1837 by C.A.T. Fursdon. These are in the Devon and Cornwall collection in Exeter City Library. There are copies of the Vivian and Mann series in the Society of Genealogists.

There is often at the registry a calendar of the licences, arranged chronologically under the various licensing authorities, such as the archdeacons surrogated for the granting of licences. This means going through them page by page, but in some cases there is a rough index, to the first initial letter, of the licences. This index may only cover a portion of the period. Towards the end of the eighteenth century the authorities seem to have got more index-conscious and sometimes these indexes start around 1780. But even then they are usually only under the bridegroom's name and they may also prove rather unreliable, even though they do save time. It is hoped that soon all the marriage licences for the different dioceses may be properly indexed and that this source of information, so valuable, not only to genealogists, but to all searchers seeking biographical and sociological information, may be more easily available.

Chapter Nine

SOME PRINTED SOURCES

In the first chapter brief reference was made to the necessity for making sure that your family has not already been written up. Therefore you will by now, I hope, have made certain that there is no printed history of it available and no MS or TS account of it lurking among the old papers of relatives. But there are a number of other printed sources which may have some reference to your family and contribute to part of its history. The chances of your finding such printed assistance may not be great, but you should at any rate make sure that no one has already done part of your work for you.

Naturally the finding of printed material of major importance will depend on the status of your family in the past. This may have varied at different periods, for, as I have pointed out in the first chapter, one of the refreshing aspects of British history is that people of ability and character have always been able to rise in the social scale. Equally it must be admitted and realized that families as easily fall in the social scale. There is a lot in that old Lancashire proverb 'There's nobbut three generations between clog and clog'. There have been so many examples of industrialists during the nineteenth century making fortunes, which have been quickly dissipated by their sons, brought up in a different social environment far from their father's industry, perhaps put into the army with a commission in a crack and expensive cavalry regiment to raise the social strata of the family.

Therefore, whatever your family's position today it need not have been in that position years ago. Consequently it is not to be ruled out that your family has links with the peerage, even if this does not seem likely to you. One of the best known peerages is the *Complete Peerage,* edited by G.E. Cokayne and others, in thirteen volumes, which has only just been completed. This is a monumental and accurate historical account of every holder of a peerage as far as can be gathered throughout our history. But to the genealogist it is only useful when information is wanted about the actual peer or his wife, as the antecedents and the children, other than the successor, are not included.

One of the most useful peerages for the genealogist is Collin's *Peerage of England,* and the most useful edition of it is that edited by Sir Egerton Bridges and published in 1812. It can be found in a number of larger reference libraries. This gives a very full account of the peerage families, attempting to trace their origins as far back as possible and giving the descent of younger sons and daughters and often their descendants to several generations. The ninth volume contains a reasonably full index, which is, of course, particularly valuable. There are, as may be expected in a great work like this full of factual matter and one compiled in days when means and methods of research were more limited, a number of errors and some of the early generations of families are suspect, but on the whole the work is reasonably accurate for its period. This peerage, as its title implies, does not include Scottish and Irish peerages, but as far as Scotland is concerned there is *The Scots Peerage* by Sir James Balfour Paul, a former Lyon King of Arms, the nine volumes of which are a mine of information, dealing with the peer's antecedents and a great number of collaterals. The last volume is an excellent index to the whole work.

The two principal current peerages are *Burke's Peerage* and *Debrett's Peerage*. Debrett's is the older, having been first published in 1803, and, perhaps for that reason, always seems to be referred to by the press as the ultimate authority on matters concerning the peerage. One connects it with old saws like 'if your name's in Debrett don't say "serviette"', and so forth, but from the genealogist's point of view Burke's peerage is far more useful, as it shows the pedigree of the peer and his family as far back as it is known. Some people at first find the manner in which the descents are shown confusing, but once the ingenious lay-out is mastered it becomes very clear and concise.

It is really a pity that there should be these two peerages in what is a limited field and if only they would pool their resources, retaining the more-satisfactory Burke style of lay-out, then perhaps they could produce a really outstanding work, combining to include a full index, which at present is such a dire need to make the work really complete. The index could be a separate volume and it would not be necessary to produce one with every issue. An index of the editions at ten year intervals or even twenty year intervals would be a great assistance.

Another valuable publication, already mentioned earlier, is *Burke's Landed Gentry*, which has been published at various intervals since 1836. Its first edition, which was not arranged alphabetically, was called *The History of the Commoners* and is in four volumes. There has been an index to the families in it, but not a full index to everyone mentioned in it though each volume has an index. The second edition, published in three volumes between 1846 and 1849, contains an index of some 311 pages, with references to some 100,000 names. This makes it a particularly useful edition. From the second edition until the ninth edition (1898) the title was *The Landed Gentry of Great Britain and Ireland,* but in 1899 the first separate edition of *The Landed Gentry of Ireland* was brought out, subsequent editions of the Irish volume being 1904, 1912 and 1958. In 1976 a volume was published by Burke on Irish families under the new title of *Irish Family Records*. The main work after 1898 became known as *The Landed Gentry of Great Britain* and this had an Irish Supplement in 1937 and an American Supplement in 1939.

The peerages of both Burke and Debrett contain baronets, and there is also the *Complete Baronetage,* edited by G.E. Cokayne, published in five volumes from 1900 to 1906. This, like the *Complete Peerage* is mainly useful for the holders of the title and their wives and does not otherwise give the history of their families. *Walford's County Families,* published at various intervals between 1864 and 1920, is a useful work often overlooked. It, however, does not give the ancestry of the families, but only details of living people belonging to such families, usually the head of the family. It is somewhat similar to the modern *Kelly's Handbook to the Titled, Landed and Official Classes,* 1880 to 1979, published originally (1875) as *The Upper Ten Thousand,* Walford gives more genealogical detail, mentioning usually the eldest son or heir. It is perhaps more confined in its scope, but both publications include all county magistrates.

If you are fortunate enough to have a prominent individual in your pedigree you will get much reliable information about him from the *Dictionary of National Biography*. The present edition of the main work of this reference tool, known for short as the D.N.B., is in twenty-two volumes, taking its scope from the beginning of England's history up to 1900. It is particularly inclusive of literary and clerical people, but is often criticized for its failure to include distinguished engineers and business men. This fault is not so prevalent in the supplements, known as the *Twentieth Century D.N.B.* published at intervals since 1900, the last volume of which brings the work down to 1970. Unfortunately, for financial reasons, although these supplements are better balanced in the fields of activity they cover, they are not so inclusive as the main work and for that reason many distinguished people who would have been in the main work have not been able to be included in the supplements.

This work really supplants most of the earlier biographical works, drawing upon and correcting them as necessary and including many more people. There is however one work which is not as well known as it deserves to be and which has brief notices of many people who died between 1851 and 1900 not included in the D.N.B. This is *Modern English Biography* by Frederick Boase, which, with its supplements, runs into six volumes and contains over 30,000 biographies. It was originally published between 1892 and 1921 and was reprinted in 1965. It has a good subject index which includes lists of pseudonyms. It fills a gap before such works as *Who's Who* came into existence, though there is also *People of the Period,* which is useful to a limited extent.

The best way to make use of *Who's Who* in genealogy is to use the *Who Was Who* volumes which cover nearly all those who have been in *Who's Who* and who have died between the years covered by each volume. These cover from the beginning of the work in 1897 to 1960 and in recent years have been published for every ten-year interval.

Kelly's Handbook, mentioned above, includes some people not to be found in *Who's Who* and vice versa. There is today a plethora of *Who's Who* in particular fields, such as Art, The Theatre, Sport, Librarianship, Municipal Government, but as these are nearly all of recent date their value to the genealogist is not so great.

If you discover that any of your family owned property or were in any way prominent in some particular locality, then the county histories of that locality should be examined. Some counties have been far more fortunate in their historians than others. One could wish that all counties had had such works as Blomefield's *Norfolk* or Bateson's *Northumberland*, Ormerod's *Cheshire* or Cussan's *Hertfordshire*. Ralph Bigland's history of *Gloucestershire,* which fulfils the genealogist's dream, has already been mentioned

One of the greatest works in this field is the *Victoria County History*. Unfortunately in so many of the counties the work has never been completed, but counties are at present in many cases making valiant efforts, some far more than others, and hardly a year goes by now without at least one volume of the work being published by some county or other. This is a very full and excellent work, tracing the history of each manor in each parish, and it is well indexed, so that where the work has been completed, as, for instance, in Hampshire and Berkshire, it is a valuable work to consult.

Chapter Ten

PERIODICALS AND NEWSPAPERS

One of the most useful genealogical tools is the *Gentleman's Magazine,* which was first published in 1731 and continued into this century, though for genealogical purposes it is only useful to 1868, after which it ceased to give those valuable notices of birth, marriage and death, which it had done from its commencement.

Do not be misled by its title into thinking that these notices only refer to the upper classes. Even from its earliest times it included notices of merchants and other middle-class citizens and, as it developed, these notices increased. They are to be found at the end of each monthly issue and there are also longer obituary notices of more prominent people. Naturally, distinguished people, nobles and outstanding personalities are given fuller notice. One nearly always finds the clergy well covered and not only do you get the marriages and deaths of most of these but you can also trace their appointments in the preferments lists. Notices relating to officers in the Army and Royal Navy are plentiful. The volumes are not much use in tracing persons in the lower social strata, such as farmers, artisans or labourers, though these may be mentioned, particularly in obituary notices, if there was something of special interest in their lives or if they lived to a great age.

Each volume of the magazine is indexed under various headings and for the genealogist's purpose the most useful of these is, of course, the index of names. Unfortunately this index is a poor one in that it only lists the surnames and gives no christian names or even, until the nineteenth century, initials. This means one has usually to look up every reference to the surname in the hope of finding one you want. This may not be a very heavy task if one is dealing with a rare surname, but when you come to such common names as Smith, Jones or Robinson, you will appreciate that the task is a formidable one.

In addition to the indexes for each volume there are cumulative indexes, from 1731 to 1786 and from 1786 to 1819, but unfortunately these again only list the surnames, so when confronted with 'Smith' you have before your eyes a sea of volume and page numbers. For many years genealogists have been hoping for a comprehensive index of the whole work. The College of Arms have a slip index, not open to the public, and some years ago there was a project in conjunction with the Society of Genealogists for this to be typed, so that copies could be available at the society and in other places. This, however, fell through, but since then the Church of the Latter Day Saints, generally known as the

Mormon Church, have made a typescript copy of this index. Unfortunately there is no copy of this at the Society of Genealogists, but it is hoped that there may be one there at some time in the not-too-distant future, or at any rate a microfilm of this index may be available there.

The Mormon's interest in genealogy is a religious one. They are anxious to trace their forbears so that they can baptize them by proxy into their church. Their genealogical researches are therefore prompted by a motive which differs from that of the ordinary genealogist. This American religious body has spent very large sums of money in having records in Great Britain and in Europe copied, often by microfilm, and their genealogical library in Salt Lake City, Utah, which is their headquarters, contains a vast amount of genealogical material which has been gathered from all over the world. They are using many modern methods, including punched card computers and electrical sorting machines, to assist in the vast work of indexing the material which they have on hand.

More details of the microfiche and other records which the Genealogical Society of Utah have published will be found in Chapter 5, "Parish Registers".

Meanwhile there are partial indexes which are very useful. There is Edward Alexander Fry's *Index to the Marriages in the Gentleman's Magazine, 1731-1768,* published in 1922, and there is the *Index to the Biographical and Obituary Notices . . . 1731-1780,* published by the British Records Society in 1891, revised by Mr Fry. Another useful help is *Musgrave's Obituary,* published by the Harleian Society, which lists many deaths in the eighteenth century of which notices appeared not only in the *Gentleman's Magazine* but also in other contemporary publications, such as the *London Magazine.*

Runaway marriages at Gretna Green

In the earlier volumes of the *Gentleman's Magazine* the editor probably depended largely on sources which were sometimes rather inaccurate and doubtful, but, though the entries must be accepted with caution, yet there are often little pieces of information in them which are quite correct and which are amusing and help to infuse your skeleton pedigree with life. Some relate to runaway marriages at Gretna Green or elsewhere, such as the notice in June 1795 'at Gretna Green, Mr Wm Coster, clothier, of Salisbury to Miss Savage, a natural born daughter of Edward, late Duke of Somerset, about 19 years of age, with a fortune of 5000l.' In those more calculating days they were fond of mentioning a bride's dowry. The magazine is rich in local colour and history and you feel, as you turn over the pages that you are seeing almost at first hand the life of the time.

The *Gentleman's Magazine* also used current newspapers for its notices of birth, marriage and death. You will see on its title page a number of newspapers listed and these were no doubt the ones on which it drew. Sometimes the notice in the newspaper is fuller than that in the magazine and it is worth while tracking it down. This is not as difficult as it sounds if you live in or can visit London. The British Museum Library has a fine collection of early newspapers called the *Burney Collection*. One advantage of this collection is that the papers are arranged chronologically and not by separate newpapers. Thus you find the various papers together for the same day or week. In the eighteenth century there were a number of newspapers, many of them weekly or bi-weekly, but some were dailies, such as the *Daily Courant,* the *Daily Journal* and the *St James's Evening Post.* The provinces were not so well supplied, but there were papers like the *Bath Chronicle* which in the eighteenth century covered notices not only of local people but also of people throughout the country. It also covered lists of arrivals in the city, but these were mainly people in the social world. There is an index of names mentioned in it for a considerable period in the Bath Public Library (Reference Library).

The two older universities have good collections of early newspapers and there is a useful *Catalogue of English Newspapers and Periodicals in the Bodleian Library, 1622-1800,* published in 1936, by R.T. Milford and D.M. Sutherland.

There are articles on the genealogical value of early English newspapers by Mr C.D.P. Nicholson in the *Genealogists' Magazine* in the March 1929 and successive issues. From these you will see the kind of additional information you may obtain from a newspaper entry. It must be observed, though, that the majority of these entries relate to comparatively well-known people and many entries of lesser people in the *Gentleman's Magazine* have no notice at all in the newspapers. There is a useful article in the *Amateur Historian* by G.R. Mellor on 'History from Newspapers' (Volume II, 97, 1955) and another article in the *Proceedings of the Leeds Philosophical Society,* Volume VIII (1957), by Donald Read on 'North of England Newspapers *c.* 1700-*c.* 1900 and their value to Historians'.

Notices of marriage and death were always more numerous than those of birth and in the early issues of periodicals like the *Gentleman's Magazine* only very prominent people had notices of the birth of a child. Even *The Times*, which later became such a medium for the announcement of such events, from the time it began in 1788 until well into the nineteenth century had very few notices of birth. This paper, however, has the advantage over other papers in having been indexed from its commencement, first by *Palmer's Index* and later by its own official index. These indexes do not include the notices of birth, marriage and death, but they do include obituary notices (very sparse in early numbers) and such wills as were reported.

The number of periodicals relating to particular counties is very great. Many counties have record societies in the publications of which are often information about families connected with those counties. Many of them, like the Devon and Cornwall Record Society, have also fine MS collections.

The *Annual Register* began life in 1758 and has been published every year since then. It is very useful for providing information about events in any particular year but from a genealogical point of view it is not nearly as useful as the *Gentleman's Magazine*. Its lists of births, marriages and deaths are far more limited, referring only to well-known people. Their obituary notices include many people who would not be found in the *Dictionary of National Biography,* but they are still more exclusive than those for whom obituaries would appear in *The Times* of more recent years.

But it is not always realized that for a considerable time there were two *Annual Registers* being published. The original *Annual Register* was started by R. Dobson and published by his publishing house from 1758 to 1790, when the stock and the copyright were sold, the copyright being purchased by Messrs Rivington, the publishers, and the stock by a man called Otridge, and some others. From then onwards each of these continued publication separately. This is mentioned particularly because one of the two, that continued by Rivington, had a general index from 1758 to 1819 (published in 1826). It is divided into the main general index and six sections, on births, marriages, promotions, deaths, poetry and titles of books. Be wary, however, of the abbreviations used: a = army, Fr. a = French army, m means Marines, M.P.I. indicates Members of the Irish Parliament, merchant means merchant service, not just a merchant, and mil = militia, n = navy, rev. indicates revenue service, not the ecclesiastical gentleman, and vol = volunteer, not volume.

There are also many periodicals devoted to particular interests, such as the *United Services Magazine,* which began life as the *United Service Journal and Naval and Military Magazine* in 1829 and was later known as *Colbourn's United Service Magazine.* It contains notices of birth, marriage and death and obituaries, sometimes quite extensive, of officers of the Navy and Army. Unfortunately, as so often with these magazines, it is not indexed, so you need a good idea of the date of the event to be able to find it without lengthy search. Fortunately it is not difficult to find the date of death of an officer in either service as you can search the army or navy lists and see when the name disappears and probably find the exact date in the report on deaths since the last publication. There is also a very useful MS index to naval obituaries which appeared in the *Naval and Military Gazette* in the Admiralty Library at Earl's Court, London. This only covers naval obituaries.

If you happen to be dealing with a surname which is not further down the alphabet than 'Alexander', then there is a particularly useful index by Joseph Foster, that prolific painstaking collector and writer to whom genealogists owe so much. It is unfortunate it never reached completion as its compiler intended. It must have been completed in MS for it to be published as far as 'Alexander'. The discovery of the rest of the MS, if it survives, would be most welcome to genealogists. It includes notices of all marriages in the *Gentleman's Magazine* and the *Historical Register* and also all marriages in *The Times* from 1865 to 1880. It also includes marriages from Westminster Abbey registers. It was published in *Collectanea Genealogica* 1881-85, as 'Marriages of the Nobility and Gentry, 1650-1880'.

E.L.C. Mullins' *Texts and calendars: an analytical guide to serial publications,* published by the R. Hist. Society in 1958, is particularly useful in giving lists of the publications of societies like the British Record Society, Harleian Society and the various county record societies.

Chapter Eleven

RECORDS OF CLERGYMEN

Before Durham University began life in 1832 and London University some four years later, the only universities in England and Wales were the two ancient foundations of Oxford and Cambridge. As, in the past, many clergymen had a university education it is a comparatively easy matter to trace the parentage of the clergy, because the matriculation registers of the university concerned will give the father's name and usually the place of residence when the son was born, and these registers have been published for both Oxford and Cambridge. The Oxford registers, called *Alumni Oxonienses,* edited by Joseph Foster, are in two series, the earlier in four volumes covering the matriculations from 1500 to 1714, and the second covering from 1715 to 1886. There are also two additional volumes, published in 1893, also edited by Foster, called *Oxford Men and their Colleges,* the second volume of which gives the matriculations from 1880 to 1892. These registers often give biographical details beyond the university career, particularly for clergy, the dates of their successive livings and of their death. Ordination papers too are particularly valuable in the case of non-graduate clergy, as these include a certified copy of the ordinand's baptismal entry. Today they are usually held by county record offices, which have also been appointed Diocesan Registries.

The Cambridge registers, the *Alumni Cantabrigienses,* are also in two series, the first, edited by John Venn and J.A. Venn, covering from the earliest times to 1751 and the second, edited by J.A. Venn alone, from 1752 to 1900. The biographical details given in the Cambridge *Alumni* are rather fuller than those in the Oxford one, particularly in the second series. They may, for instance, include the name of the wife. Both these publications try to link up the person with any other relations at the university and sometimes you can trace a man's pedigree back several generations if his forbears were also university men.

There are lists of clergy in the early 19th century which give varying details, usually brief.

It should be remembered that clergymen are officially described as 'clerks in holy orders' and this is frequently abbreviated to 'clerk', so that if you come across someone so described he was probably an ordained member of the Church of England and not a 'pen-pusher' in an office. Information can also be found about clergy from Crockford's *Clerical Directory,* first published in 1858, and from earlier clergy lists. A useful book, as far as it goes, is Joseph Foster's *Index Ecclesiasticus,* which gives clerical appointments for the period 1800 to 1840. Short notices of the death (and sometimes the marriage) of clergy usually appear in *The Gentleman's Magazine*.

Information about ministers of other denominations is more difficult to trace. There are lists of such clergy for many of them, but they do not go back very far in most cases. The Methodists have indexed the biographical notices of their ministers from 1778 to 1839, of whom obituary notices appear in their Arminian and Methodist magazines, as mentioned in Chapter 6. The Congregational Union of England and Wales have obituaries of their ministers in their Year Book and these are often quite full, but they do not go back far. Information about Jewish rabbis and Huguenot ministers will be dealt with in a later chapter and likewise records of Scottish and Irish clergy will be referred to in later chapters on those countries.

Roman Catholics suffered for many years under disabilities and were not allowed to conduct services. Information on some of their priests can be traced in the publications of the Catholic Record Society and there have been biographical dictionaries of some of the orders, such as H.N. Birt's *Obit Book of the English Benedictines from 1600 to 1912*, published in 1913, and W. Gumbley's *Obituary Notices of the English Dominicans from 1555 to 1952*. In general, information about Roman Catholic priests is best sought through the authorities of the church.

Chapter Twelve

LAWYERS, DOCTORS AND OTHERS

In England and Wales men in the legal profession divide into two groups, barristers and solicitors. A solicitor cannot be a member of the bar and a barrister cannot be enrolled as a solicitor.

To become a barrister you must be admitted through one of the inns of court, which are today, Lincoln's Inn, which is particularly linked with Chancery practice, the Middle Temple, the Inner Temple and Gray's Inn. When men enter these inns certain particulars about them are recorded, including their parentage, usually a description of their father's occupation or status and his place of residence. All the inns except the Inner Temple have published fairly complete admission registers, so that information from these is easily obtainable. In the case of the Inner Temple only admissions for the period 1547 to 1660 have been published. For later admissions it is necessary to write to the Librarian for information. This inn suffered some loss of its records during the Second World War, but their admission registers survive.

Parentage of solicitors, formerly called attorneys, can be traced through their articles of clerkship, which from 1730 to 1838 are in the Public Record Office in Chancery Lane (C.P. 5). Although these are arranged by the date of entry into articles, there is a MS alphabetical index to the names. There are also Admission Books 1729 to 1848 and 1838 to 1860 (C.P. 8).

In the period 1710 to 1760 you may also find these articled clerks in the Apprentices' Indexes at the Society of Genealogists, as they were regarded as apprenticed to attorneys in a similar way as others were to other trades. This will give the father's name and profession or occupation, and the name of the attorney to whom they were apprenticed and the fee paid. Solicitors' names and the place where they practised can be traced through the law lists and by going through these you can usually discover when a solicitor died, and you would normally expect, in view of his profession, that he would leave a properly drawn up will, but this is not always the case. Not all solicitors seem to practice what they preach.

Judges of all courts are appointed from the barristers, so that their parentage is traced from the same sources, and judges of the higher courts, being prominent people, are easily traceable in such works as Foster's *Judges of England,* but many of them in any case will be found in the *D.N.B.*

Magistrates, or justices of the peace, are laymen. They are appointed by the Lord Chancellor and their record of appointment will be among the Lord Chancellor's records, but many county record offices have lists of J.P.s for various periods and they can also be traced during the nineteenth century from directories of their locality. Some information about officials of the various law courts may be traced in such works as the *Royal Calendar* which exists from the late eighteenth century.

Medical men, if they are graduates in medicine, can be traced through the university records, which will give their parentage. It may be more difficult to trace others.

The medical world in earlier times had divided itself into two main divisions, the physicians and the surgeons. The physicians were of higher status, often university men with degrees in medicine or members of the College of Physicians. The surgeons until 1745 were in London linked with the barbers in the Surgeons and Barbers Company, one of the livery companies. After that date their status began to improve, particularly after 1800 when the Royal College of Surgeons was founded. Nevertheless even in the early nineteenth century surgeons stood well below the position of physicians. The term then did not indicate the function they have today. They did not specialize in surgery but had the simpler functions of a general practitioner of medicine and dentistry, the setting of bones, pulling out of teeth and serving as general medical advisers and apothecaries. Socially they stood somewhere between the tradesman and the professional man. Even physicians were not regarded socially as much above attorneys. There were no doubt those among the upper classes who would have exclaimed disdainfully, as Bertram did when being forced to marry Helena in *All's Well that Ends Well,* 'She had her breeding at my father's charge, a poor physician's daughter my wife! — Disdain rather corrupt me ever.' It must also be remembered that the law about medical practice and medical practitioners was far more lax in the past and men could practice and call themselves doctors with little or no medical qualifications. A young boy might be apprenticed, as the poet John Keats was, to the local surgeon for five years. If this was during the early and mid-eighteenth century his parentage may be found in the apprentices index already mentioned. If he was a member of the Royal College of Surgeons or of the Royal College of Physicians, then information about him may be traced from their records. Many doctors in early times were Licenciates of the Society of Apothecaries (L.S.A.) and that body, from the late eighteenth century, has detailed records of people admitted. These records, which are now in the Guildhall Library, London, are very useful, as they give not only the name and occupation of the father, but also other details, such as the names of referees and include a certificate from someone verifying that the applicant is over twenty-one years of age. As sometimes the applicant obtained his reference from his local vicar or rector, this often indicates where he came from.

Monk's Roll of Physicians should not be overlooked, though this only covers a few better-known medical men. Medical directories began to come out in the early nineteenth century and these will tell you where a practitioner was in practice and in the volume of the year after he died you may even find a short obituary of him. Some of the later directories give a brief account of those entered, at least indicating their qualifications.

Many English doctors qualified in Scotland or Ireland or abroad. Leyden in Holland was at one time a popular place to do so and a list of English students there has been published. All four of the Scottish universities are of old foundation. Glasgow and Aberdeen have each published some details of their matriculations, Glasgow being the fuller. It must be remembered that Aberdeen was divided between King's College and Marischal College and it is necessary to look in the records of each. St Andrews has only partial lists of matriculations and Edinburgh has not published any of its matriculations, but only lists of graduates. In some cases the information in the matriculation registers is disappointing and one will not necessarily discover the names of the parents from them. Many English medical men qualified in Ireland at Trinity College, Dublin, and the matriculation registers of this college have been published.

Medical men in the Army and Navy and in the East India Company service can be traced in the records of these services. As in civil life, surgeons in the services in the past had a lower status. In the Navy they were not commissioned officers but only warrant officers and their status in the Army was not much better until the mid-nineteenth century.

The sources for information about other professions are very varied and extensive. It is only possible to give here briefly some of these. Tradition is a strong thread in many occupations and in none, perhaps , is it stronger than in the theatrical profession. One thinks of the Forbes-Robertsons, the Terry's, the Keans, the Lanes, the Gielguds and the Redgraves. Theatrical families, as you can see looking through *Who's Who in the Theatre*, tend to marry among themselves, so that you get a great number of links between them all. A lecture by Dr J.M. Bulloch on 'Theatrical Families' is published in the *Genealogists' Magazine'* in Volume 6, p. 337 (Dec. 1933).

The well-known *Dictionary of Music and Musicians* published originally in four volumes under the editorship of Sir George Grove, now in its sixth edition, expanded to 20 volumes, will give information about distinguished musicians. A valuable work on architects is H.M. Colvin's *Biographical Dictionary of English Architects 1660-1840* and in an allied field mention may be made of an article on 'County Masons' in the *Genealogists' Magazine,* Volume 9, p. 274 (Dec. 1952) by Frederick Burgess. From the eighteenth century details of careers of men who served in the customs and excise services, either in London or throughout the British Isles, may be gathered from the establishment records at the Public Record Office. These begin in 1683 but there are a number of gaps. The run is good from 1700 to 1763, after which there is a gap until 1770 when they continue to 1829, the period from 1813 to 1829 being a good one. A good article on these records by Rupert C. Jarvis is in the *Genealogists' Magazine* for September 1948 (Volume 10, p. 221).

When the History of Parliament now being compiled is completed it will be a great source of biographical information. The three volumes by Sir Lewis Namier and John Brooke covering the House of Commons 1754-1790 and Romney Sedgwick's two volumes *The House of Commons 1715-1754* (1970), are an indication of this. In each case a considerable portion of the matter in the volumes is devoted to biographies of all the members covered in the period. There are earlier published collective biographies of members, such as Joshua Wilson's *The Present House of Commons*, dealing with the house at the time of Trafalgar in 1805.

Artists are covered by Samuel Redgrave's *Dictionary of Artists of the English School*, first published in 1874, and by M.H. Grant's *Dictionary of British Etchers* and his *Dictionary of British Sculptors*. Authors are covered by a number of publications and their career can be traced to a certain extent by noting their publications in the British Museum catalogue.

Chapter Thirteen

NAVAL ANCESTORS

In a seafaring nation like Great Britain most families can expect to find one or more ancestors of its line in the Royal Navy and such ancestors can usually be traced with some success for, as those who have served in one or other of the forces will well know, these services have a habit of wanting returns in triplicate of all sorts of details and this paper-work, irritating at times, comes in good stead when you want to trace something about someone. Unfortunately in the past they were not always as thorough or as demanding as the present day service departments.

Nevertheless service records are prolific and the Navy has as good records as any service. Naturally it is easier to trace information about an officer than a rating, but even so in the MS records far more can be discovered about a rating than about a man in a comparable position in civilian life.

The main MS sources are among the Admiralty records in the Public Record Office, but before dealing with them I will first mention some of the printed sources. These in general refer only to officers.

Earliest among them is John Charnock's *Biographia Navalis, or, Memoirs of the Officers of the Navy from 1600,* which was published in 1794 in four volumes. John Campbell's *Lives of British Admirals,* also in four volumes, was published in 1779 and, as its title implies, is confined to Flag Officers. *The Naval Biography of Great Britain,* by James Ralfe, published in 1828 is a rare work which includes some officers not in other works. John Marshall's *Royal Naval Biography,* which, with its supplements, runs into twelve volumes, covers all officers who reached the rank of commander and who were living, or had only recently died, during the period from 1823 to 1830. All these works give details of the officer's career, particulars of any actions in which he may have taken part and often his parentage.

The most comprehensive printed work is W.R. O'Byrne's *Naval Biographical Dictionary,* published in 1849 and including every officer of the rank of lieutenant and above, serving or retired, who was living in the year 1845. It includes notices of nearly 5,000 officers. O'Byrne mentions in many cases the father of the officer and frequently any other relatives who were serving or had served in the navy. In addition, the original MSS of this great work are easily accessible, being in the British Museum MS Department (Additional MS 38039-54) and these MSS, include in most cases the completed forms which were sent out to the officers concerned, together with any letters the officer may have written and these often give far more information than is contained in the printed volume.

The Sailor's Home Journal, afterwards the *Naval Chronicle* edited successively by W.R. O'Byrne and by his brother Robert, during the years 1853 to 1863, contains many obituary notices of naval officers which supplement the information in the dictionary.

O'Byrne brought out a second edition of his work and this was more comprehensive because it included also all Royal Marine officers, surgeons, chaplains and pursers. Unfortunately it was never completed but only reached the name 'H.S.C. Giles'. It is difficult to come across copies of this edition, but there is one in the British Library and in certain naval libraries and clubs.

An officer's career can be traced through successive navy lists. Steel's *Navy List* was first published in 1772. It was succeeded in 1814 by the official *Navy List,* while Joseph Allen's *New Navy List* was published for many years during the nineteenth century. In 1954 the National Maritime Museum published *The Commissioned Sea Officers of the Royal Navy,* the three volumes of which include brief dates of promotion of the officers from the earliest times until 1815.

A useful list of MS and printed lists of naval officers is contained in R. Sims' *Manual for the Genealogist, Topographer, Antiquary and Legal Professor,* 1856.

Turning to MS records, the Admiralty Records at the P.R.O. seem at first sight rather overwhelming. They are described in Volume 2 of the 1963 edition of the *Guide to the Public Record Office* and they are listed in the *Public Record Office Lists and Indexes XVIII* (H.M.S.O. 1904) to which there is a supplementary typescript list on the shelves of the Record Office at Kew. A very useful little book is Gerald Fothergill's *Records of Naval Men* published in 1910. It is designed to be read in conjunction with the official list and explains the type of information found in the various records.

In seeking the parentage of an officer one of the best sources is the series of Lieutenants' Passing Certificates, as from 1789 onwards, with a few earlier ones from 1777, the Navy Board copies of these have filed with them the baptismal certificate which the candidate had to produce to prove that he was at least twenty years of age. In the Record Office at Kew there are two MS indexes to these certificates. One was compiled by Miss E.H.B. Fairbrother and covers the year 1777 to 1832 and includes the information from the baptismal certificates. The other, compiled by Miss P. Schrader, covers the years from 1789 to 1818.

Administration of the Royal Navy was, prior to 1832, divided between the Admiralty and the Navy Board, each jealous of its own·particular provinces, which to a considerable extent overlapped. Because of this dual control we find also a series of Passing Certificates in the Secretary of the Admiralty's records, but these do not contain the baptismal certificates and are only useful for the other information contained in them should the Navy Board copy be missing.

If your ancestor was prominent in any sea action you will be able to trace information about him in various reports and letters, such as the Admirals' Despatches or Captains' Letters in the Secretary's Department. There is also a possibility he may be mentioned in one of the naval histories, in particular in Sir William Clowes' *Royal Naval History,* the eight volumes of which contain reference to hundreds of naval officers and men. There is no general index, but each volume is well indexed and does not take long to consult.

If a forbear was unfortunate enough to be wounded or court martialled, then his misfortune is, in your search for information about him, your good fortune. An instance of the former in my own family may help to illustrate the kind of information you may find in these cases.

Thomas Ambrose Edwards, when a lieutenant, was wounded in 1807. At that time officers and men did not automatically get a pension for wounds. The wounded man had to submit a petition, or 'memorial', to the King, asking that a pension might be granted to him. In order to back his claim he would give an account of his career and show how he came to be wounded. Thomas Ambrose Edwards therefore submitted such a petition in 1810, which came before the Prince Regent.

'Your Memorialist,' it reads, 'entered the Service as a Midshipman on board His Majesty's Ship *Hyaena,* commanded by the Honble. C. Boyle, in the Year 1798, and accompanied Captn. Boyle into the *Cormorant,* which ship was wrecked on the Coast of Agypt [sic] in 1800, when your Memorialist was made a Prisoner by the French and was severely afflicted with the Ophthalmia while in Egypt. Your Memorialist, on being liberated, joined *La Diane* and continued in her until that ship was paid off in 1802.

At the commencement of the present War, Your Memorialist joined the *Pompee,* Sir W. Sidney Smith, and after the capture of the Island of Capri, was sent to a signal Duty on shore; the *Pompee* being ordered home your Memorialist was directed to leave the Island of Capri and join her, and was proceeding from Malta to Gibraltar, on board the transport ship *Monarch* when she was attacked off Tunis on the 11th Aug. 1807 by the French Privateer *Prince Jerome* and later engaged in a severe action of half-an-hour during which Your Memorialist received a Grapeshot and a Musket ball in the left thigh, that broke and splintered the bone, and occasioned a considerable contusion of the thigh, with lameness.

In June 1809 your Memorialist was promoted to the rank of Lieutenant and appointed to the *Pandora* Sloop of War, and when assisting the embarkation of Troops at Deal on the 18th July 1809 he was thrown from the bow of a boat on the beach at Deal and, falling on the side that was before wounded, he received a violent contusion that occasioned the wound to break out and which has not since healed and ultimately rendered your Memorialist incapable of doing his duty, and obliged him to be invalided from the *Pandora.* A Certificate from Captn. H.H. Spence to this effect is enclosed, and as your Memorialist, owing to the wound and hurts he has received in His Majesty's Service is (and will be always) afflicted with extreme lameness, so as to render him unable to serve on board a Ship, he humbly hopes his case will be taken into consideration, and a Pension allowed to him. And your Memorialist as in duty bound will ever pray.

THOMAS AMBROSE EDWARDS

No 1 Charlotte St.,

Bloomsbury Square.

Decr 27th 1810.'

The memorial was presented to the Prince Regent in Council at Carlton House on the 8th February 1811 and was referred by His Royal Highness to the Lords Commissioners of the Admiralty. They on the 14th March following reported that they found the allegations to be true and that 'the College of Surgeons by whom the

Memorialist had been surveyed, have reported to us that the Injury his Thigh-Bone has received is in its effect of equal prejudice to the habit of Body with the Loss of a Limb'. Their Lordships, therefore, recommended 'a Pension of Two Shillings and six pence a day be settled on the Memorialist'.

Courts martial will often reveal details about the person tried. Usually information of at any rate part of his career comes out and often the statement in mitigation will give an outline of the accused's service. Often too, letters written to the Admiralty after an officer had been sentenced may reveal much. In one such letter or petition to be reinstated after dismissal a young midshipman revealed that he had four brothers in the 'Service of the Army and Navy, one an old and wounded officer, a Lieut. in the Navy . . . two in the regular Army and another younger than himself still in the Navy' and that there had been another 'who had lost his life in the service of the country'. This last fact, in this particular case, revealed something which was not known from any other source.

Probably the next most valuable direct source of information to the Passing Certificates for officers are the various returns of services. That of 1817 includes all officers serving. It is of particular value because from it can be gleaned the whole of the officer's naval career to that date. Where the baptismal certificate is missing from the passing certificate, as it sometimes is, especially if the officer was examined abroad, then his place of birth can be discovered from the muster rolls of any ship in which he was serving before his promotion to lieutenant. His place of birth is also mentioned in some of the returns of midshipmen's services.

The ship's musters list all the officers and ratings on board and in the case of the ratings give the birthplace. Midshipmen and Volunteers (later Cadets) were not commissioned officers and were therefore technically ratings and thus their birthplace was given. So, by tracing back an officer's career to when he was a midshipman you can then, through his ship's muster, find the place of his birth. It must be mentioned, however, that many of these places of birth are inaccurate and also that there are examples of forged baptismal certificates among the passing certificates. There are stories of how men sat outside the dockyards when the midshipmen were taking their examinations for lieutenant, prepared for a small fee to issue bogus baptismal certificates to show that the midshipman was over twenty years of age, as required by the regulations. Ages as stated on returns are also often wrong. Both Nelson and Collingwood provide examples of false ages in their records.

Among other useful returns are the 'List of Acting Lieutenants, Masters, Mates, Midshipmen, whose qualifications have been admitted at an examination' of 1816 and 1818, which contain the place of birth and age of those who passed in those years. The 'Return of Midshipmen's Services' for 1814 also gives the place of birth.

The 'Register of Lieutenants Soliciting for Employment' from 1799 onwards is another example of a valuable source, for this gives the applicant's address. It must be remembered that in earlier times the Navy was not a continuous service as today and officers were commissioned anew each time a ship was commissioned. In theory they were civilians in between commissions, when they were left on shore.

The 'Bounty Papers', which cover the period 1675 to 1822, give the name and address of the relation to whom the bounty is to be paid in the case of seamen killed in action or dying, and also certificates of baptism of the next-of-kin and often parents' marriage certificates to prove relationship. These series include both officers and men.

[commission document in cursive handwriting, partially legible]

Commission, Nathaniel Frederick Edwards to be Lieutenant of H. M. Sloop the *Beaver*. 10 February 1827. At this period commissioned officers in the Royal Navy received a separate commission each time they were appointed to a new ship.

The persons signing this commission are as under:

Robert Saunders Dundas, 2nd Viscount Melville (1771-1851), First Lord of the Admiralty 1812-1827, in which office he showed considerable administrative talent. He was re-appointed to the Admiralty by the Duke of Wellington in 1828 and remained in it until 1830.

Sir William Johnstone Hope (1766-1851), Vice-Admiral, G.C.B. Member of the Board of Admiralty or of the Council of the Lord High Admiral 1820 to 1828.

John Wilson Croker (1780-1857). One of the most outstanding Secretaries of the Admiralty, which office he held for 22 years until 1830.

Men sat outside the dockyards ... prepared for a small fee to issue bogus baptismal certificates

Most of the records, it will be noticed, belong to the period starting towards the end of the eighteenth century. Early records are less prolific. Nevertheless they are quite considerable and the difficulty lies more in tracing where the information is. These earlier records are seldom well indexed. There is however, a great deal of information about the Navy of the Restoration period and this is mostly due to the diarist Samuel Pepys who, it will be remembered, was Secretary of the Navy. The collection itself is at Magdalene College, Cambridge, and is not accessible to the general public, but there is available Dr Tanner's *Catalogue of Pepsyian MSS,* really a calendar of these papers, which cover the proceedings of the Admiralty and the Navy Board from 1673 to 1679. Pepys' 'List of Commissioned Officers' is particularly valuable in giving the name with the rank and ship of almost every officer who was serving between the years 1660 and 1688. These names have been included in the *Commissioned Sea Officers* published by the National Maritime Museum referred to earlier.

The 'Captains' Letters' in the Secretary's Department cover a very wide range and are often very valuable. You never quite know what you are going to find in them and it is a rather exciting kind of lucky dip. I found, for instance, a letter written by the same Thomas Ambrose Edwards who was wounded, writing when a captain to ask for an appointment for his youngest midshipman brother Nathaniel Frederick. Applications for appointments of relations were quite common in days when influence was used quite openly.

These captains' letters are kept in bundles or groups of years and then alphabetical under the captain's name. They are indexed.

'Lieutenants' Letters' often contain applications for appointment to ships and they usually give the home address of the officer. There are similar series for officers of the Royal Marines.

The series of letters entitled 'Promiscuous' may be on almost any conceivable subject, from an irate uncle seeking the whereabouts of his nephew to a creditor that of his debtor. They are in bundles arranged alphabetically and chronologically. The letters from the Royal Naval College, Portsmouth, beginning in 1773, are useful in giving reports of the scholars' progress, usually mentioning the parents' name and giving the date and reason for discharge.

Another valuable source is contained in that whole and voluminous series of letters, papers and registers covering Greenwich Hospital. The old Greenwich Hospital stood roughly in the same relation to the Royal Navy as Chelsea Hospital does to the Army, but the naval hospital was wider in scope, covering both in and out pensioners, the school and apprenticeship of children of seamen, and such matters as the children at Clarence House, Paddington Green. They are invaluable for information about anyone admitted to this foundation, whether officer, seaman or child.

All the 'Secretary's In Letters' series can best be consulted through either the digests, which are subject indexes commencing in 1762 and more detailed after 1792, or by the indexes proper. A useful account of the subject headings and catch letters and abbreviations used in the digests and indexes is given in Fothergill's textbook. These headings and the abbreviations used for them are also given fully in a P.R.O. typescript which can be obtained from the P.R.O. at Kew. This is entitled "A Guide to the Admiralty Index and Digest (ADM 12)". This gives a great deal of other useful information regarding the indexes and digests of the Admiralty Records in the P.R.O. at Kew. A number of the indexes and digests are on the shelves of the Record Office.

The Record Office staff are helpful and co-operative and will even answer queries by post which do not involve much research, but you cannot expect them to give time to anything approaching an extensive search. They do keep lists of searchers who are willing to undertake such work on payment, should you wish to employ one rather than do the research yourself.

It is always useful in genealogical research to have a background knowledge of the social circle with which you are dealing. Clowes' History has already been mentioned. A shorter useful book is Michael Lewis' *The Navy of Britain* and his *England's Sea Officers* is valuable in its specialist field. But one of the best books to read about the social life of the Navy during the period indicated is the last mentioned author's *Social History of the Navy, 1793-1815* published in 1960. Drawing considerably on Marshall's *Royal Naval Biography* and O'Byrne's *Naval Biographical Dictionary,* the author has made a valuable analysis of the social background of the naval officer of the period. From this one gleans such information that 19 per cent of the officers from the landed-gentry families reached the rank of post-captain; and that, though few working class men could hope to attain commissioned rank at all, of those that did so over 13 per cent reached post rank and even 2 per cent reached flag rank. It also makes clear those intricacies of entry into the Navy before 1794, when there were 'Captain's servants' who were actual servants and 'Captain's servants' who were protégés of the captain, young gentlemen belonging to the quarter-deck, who after 1794 were to be termed 'First Class Volunteers' and later still 'Cadets'.

The excellent account of lower deck life is also useful. The genealogist can learn, for instance, that there is a 23 per cent chance a seaman ancestor during the French Wars was a volunteer and that 15 per cent of a ship's complement were foreigners.

The author also emphasizes the point made earlier of the unreliability of ages in naval records. He records how Admiral Sir George Elliot related that 'a crown-piece handed to the porter at the Navy office as one went in to be examined produced a certificate showing one to be of any age one liked to mention'.

The book also brings out the importance to the genealogist of the captain of a future officer's first ship, for he is likely to be at any rate a friend of the family and possibly a relation, for this was an age when influence or 'interest' was widespread and of paramount importance.

Warrant Officers

Returns of services of warrant officers are in ADM/29/1. It must remembered that at this time the only executive officers were the fighting sea officers. All those providing a service in the navy were warrant officers, including chaplains, surgeons, pursers, gunners, boatswains, carpenters. The warrant officers' returns of service give their complete service from the time they received their warrant rank, giving their date of entry and the departure of each ship in which they served. From this you can get further details from the ships' logs and muster rolls as to where they served and any actions in which they took part.

Being warrant officers, you will not get for them their place of birth, but in the muster roll of the earliest ship to which they were promoted when promoted to warrant officer, if the roll survives, you should be able to get on the date of entry as warrant officer, the ship from which he came, and if this muster roll survives you can trace his career back through that to the date of his entry to the ship, when his place of birth should be given and his age.

There may be alphabetical indexes to the volumes in this group to the names of persons whose returns of services are recorded in the volume, but you must be aware that these indexes may not be complete or always absolutely accurate. In a volume dealing with pursers' services of the Nelson period, two of the warrant officers being searched for were not found, but it was then noticed that the pages in the volume were only numbered up to 314 and it was realized that those recorded after that page were not in the index. On searching them both the warrant officers being sought were found.

Midshipmen Additional Information

The great value of passing certificates in discovering the parentage of officers who passed for lieutenant has been mentioned already. But some midshipmen never passed this examination nor reached the rank of lieutenant.

Information about them can be found from various other returns. A return in Adm 6/182 gives a survey of those serving as midshipmen in December 1814 and this gives their place of birth and age. Another return in Adm 6/176-180, "A list of Masters' Mates, Midshipmen and others, Candidates for promotion," although it only gives the age and not the place of birth, is particularly interesting in giving a report on the character of the young man by the captain of the ship in which he is serving. These reports can be frank and terse. One midshipman, aged 18, in H.M.S. *Tigre*, was reported on as "an heavy stupid young man. Captain Halliday is of opinion that he is not likely to do credit to the service". In another case on William P. Williams, aged 22, it says "William P. Williams, aged 22, seven years [length of service] M's Mate. Passed. Has been with his present captain 18 months and has conducted himself perfectly to his satisfaction. His letter of 14th February 1815 transmits certificates of his good conduct from Captains Cunningham and Elliot. *Captain* Elliot, Crocodile, 4th May 1814." and against it is written "promoted".

This return has the disadvantage of having no index to the names, but if the ship in which he was serving between 1814 and 1816 is known, and this is not too difficult to discover from other sources, then the entry sought can be found fairly quickly.

A return in Adm 11/23-25, of five volumes covering midshipmen, mates, volunteers, gives a useful account of their services and ranges over the years 1815-1832. There is a typed index to the names in these volumes on the shelves at the P.R.O. at Kew.

Ratings

Finding out the place of birth of seamen can best be done through the muster rolls of any ship in which the man served. It is therefore necessary to know this, otherwise the hunt for his parentage is more difficult. It is often known in a family that an ancestor was in a certain ship in the Royal Navy, or perhaps that he was in the Baltic Campaign, in the Crimean War, or in some other campaign. In that case it narrows the search down to a number of ships, and sometimes if you know he was more likely to have been in a Plymouth ship than a Portsmouth ship or Chatham one, that may narrow it down further.

If he was in the Baltic Campaign, it may have been in 1854 or 1855, so that it will be necessary to check the muster rolls of all ships in both years. Eventually you will find him, and in tracing backwards through the muster roll to the date when he joined the ship you should then find on his first entry, his age and place of birth recorded and also the ship from which he came. You will then be able to seek his parentage from the parish registers of his birthplace. Apart from this you will be able to discover from the ship's log where he sailed in this ship and any actions in which he may have taken part. Also you can then trace his career both backwards and forwards, as when he leaves the ship it will show to which he went, and so the muster roll of that ship will give his entry and again his age and place of birth, and the log will show where the ship went and again any action which took place and so on. When he is discharged, you will get the next ship to which he was posted.

In the same way you can trace him backwards until you reach back to his first ship. In this way you will learn quite a bit about his career in the navy.

Seamen's Effects

Possibly searching through the muster rolls forwards, you may come across the entry "DD", which means "discharged dead". The log for this date should show how he died, such as "died from sickness" or "through enemy action" and so forth. This will link you with another record, which will also give you his birthplace and the name of the person who claimed whatever effects he left, including pay due to him. Seamen's Effect Papers are in Adm 44/1. When you find his name in this return you should find possibly a letter from the "correspondent", who will be the person who claims his effects, that is his next-of-kin, perhaps his father, or if married his wife or a son or daughter, if the wife was dead. There will also, it is hoped, be a baptismal certificate to prove the relationship, and if married, the marriage certificate. This should be a copy certified by the rector or vicar of the parish. There should also be a certification by a magistrate or other reliable person that this was a true copy.

Royal Marines

The records of the Royal Marines are now at the Public Record Office. They were only transferred there in 1960 and it is unfortunate they were not handed over earlier as it appears a number of their records, notably some of the 'Description Books' (Adm. 158), have been lost. However, the material surviving is good and fairly comprehensive. They are described briefly in the 1963 edition of the *Guide to the Public Record Office.*

The information in the Royal Marine records is similar to that found for the Army. The 'Attestation Forms' (Adm 157), 1790-1883, give the age, birthplace, trade and physical characteristics of each recruit, with details of his enlistment and attestation. There are also summaries of service and details of discharge. These are arranged alphabetically under the year of attestation or of discharge.

The 'Description Books' (Adm. 158) referred to above are probably the more convenient source for the genealogist. There are 283 volumes of them surviving, covering the period 1750 to 1888. These are in book form and summarize in alphabetical order the information given in the attestation forms. Rather less valuable, because of their later date, are the more modern 'Registers of Service' (Adm. 159), which cover from 1842 to 1905 in 70 volumes. These give similar information to that found in the Attestation Forms and some additional information.

The Royal Marines have an official Corps Historian, who has his office at Eastney Barracks, Southsea, Hants, and is helpful in providing any information he can about the Corps. He is usually able to provide a record of officers' services of more recent times and it may be advisable to discover from him what he has available before visiting the P.R.O.

Chapter Fourteen

MERCHANT NAVY RECORDS

In comparison with records of the Royal Navy, those of the merchant service are far less prolific and start at a later period. This is understandable when you consider that the term "merchant service" embraces a greatly varying service of individual or small company shipowners which had no particular reason for co-ordination until recent times. Thus the records of this service are mainly the records of seamen and ships resulting from legislation brought in by governments to have some control over, and information on, conditions at sea of crews and some registration of ships and their owners.

Many of these records were held by the Registrar of Shipping and Seamen, and these records are now more accessible for search since they have recently been brought into the Public Record Office at Kew.

Other records survive mainly in some of the custom offices throughout the United Kingdom. These are mainly of ships of some of the ports in question and these records give only information on the ships, their masters, the owner or owners, changes of ownership and the history of the ship in particular.

Muster rolls of merchant ships were kept from 1747. These gave the names of officers, seamen and other people employed on board, their usual place of residence, date of joining and name of their last ship. It is unfortunate that these rolls survive only for one port from 1747, namely Shields, and only from three other ports from earlier than 1800, namely for Dartmouth, Liverpool and Plymouth.

A full and detailed article by Nicolas Cox, "The Records of the Registrar-General of Shipping and Seamen", was published in the journal *Sources for Maritime History,* Vol. 2 No 2 (Sept, 1972), and a five page leaflet "Records of the Registrar General of Shipping and Seamen" was issued by the Public Record Office in 1973, giving details of their holdings. This chapter aims at giving information of the main records in the article and the leaflet and some other information from other sources.

The two main categories of records at the Public Record Office are the Transcripts and Transactions of ships with a deck and of more than 15 tons burden which were registered with custom officers, who forwarded a copy of these details to the Custom House in London or in Edinburgh. This was done under an Act of 1786, a later Act of 1825 bringing in some further regulations. Details of ownership in the latter act were fuller and were required to be held in the traditional 64th shares. The certificates of registry had to be endorsed with details of the owners and masters and any changes of these. Copies, known as Transcripts and Transactions, are contained in the Series I (BT 07). They give the name of the ship, her home port, place of registration and date, the names, addresses and occupations of the owners, the masters' names, place where the ship was built and the date, unless it was a prize capture, details of the ship herself, such as her length, breadth, number of decks and masts.

Unfortunately the serious fire at the Port of London Custom House in 1814 destroyed all the copies forwarded there. William Cotton, whose father William Cotton was at that time Clerk of the Certificates in the Customs House and therefore in charge of these certificates, states in his MS *Reminiscences* "Feb. 12. The Custom House was destroyed by fire: my father lost all his office books and papers, but no private property."

As a result the series there now only begins from later that year. The Port of London Registration Books, 1786-1814, are, however, still available to see.

The Merchant Shipping Act of 1854 was mainly an act consolidating the previous laws concerning shipping, but a new form was drawn up, which provided some additional information, such as names and addresses of the builders and details of the ship's engines, which is an indication of the growth of steam-driven ships. After this act all ships on registration were given an official number. These Transcripts and Transactions are known as Series II: Transcripts (BT 108) and the indexes to them are BT III. The separate forms used from 1854 are in Transcripts and Transactions: Series III, Transactions (BT 109). This system continued until 1889, after which all ships papers were kept together and filed away at the date when the closure of the ship on the register took place. The approximate date of this can be found from Lloyd's register or from the Mercantile Navy List, or, if necessary, from the Registrar-General of Shipping and Seamen.

The act of 1854 required customs officers to send in to the Registrar-General annual lists of ships which had been registered in their port. This return had been made voluntarily since 1786. These lists comprise the Annual List of Ships Registered (BT 164).

Agreements and Crew Lists

As mentioned earlier muster rolls were kept from 1747 but unfortunately nearly all of these early rolls have been lost. However an Act of 1835 brought in the Agreements and Crew Lists. This act required a written agreement to be carried for every man. This included the man's wages, his type of service and the nature of the voyage.

Original agreements, with a list of all men on board during the voyage had to be delivered by the master to the Registrar-General of Shipping. Until 1860 these forms are fairly complete and are in "Agreements and Crew Lists: Series I (BT 98)", but after that date, because the Census Returns for 1861 and onwards recorded names and details of all those on board British merchant ships, only a 10% sample was kept (BT 144).

There were special arrangements made for fishing boats under 80 tons by an act of 1883, but only a 10% sample was kept for these also (BT 114).

A special series of the "Agreements and Crew Lists" for more recent times has been kept for such well-known ships as the *Titanic, Lusitania, Discovery* and *Great Britain.* These are in Series III (BT 100).

The registers relating to ships and their owners and masters will particularly interest persons searching for information on shipowners and masters, but for those anxious to collect information about an ancestor who was a serving seaman the Register of Seamen's Service will be of paramount interest, while at a few ports the earlier muster rolls instituted in 1747 survive from 1800. The Act of 1835 provided for the first time for a registration of seamen. The first register under this act exists from 1835 to 1839, when it was mainly superceded by the "Register of Seamen: Series II (BT 112)" which covered the period 1835 to 1844 and in which register the names are arranged numerically, but individual seamen can be traced by the "Alphabetical Index of Seamen (BT 119)". The registers themselves give the information about the men in a coded form.

In 1844, because of difficulties in identification, a further act determined that all British seamen should be given a Register Ticket, which recorded useful information such as his place and date of birth, and his service, including any in the Royal Navy. These were recorded in BT 113, to which there is an alphabetical index in BT 114, which gives the ticket number and place of birth. There is also a separate "Register of Masters' Tickets (BT 115)". But this ticket system was unpopular and only lasted until 1854. Thereafter a new register was begun (BT 116) which listed the seamen alphabetically and gave their age, place of birth, details of voyages, names of ships and the ports from which they left. This, however, was discontinued in 1856, as it was decided it was not required as the "Crew Lists" fulfilled the need for it.

Masters and Mates

In 1845 the Board of Trade instituted a voluntary examination for masters and mates for foreign-going British merchant ships, and this was made compulsory under the Mercantile Marine Act of 1850, extended by a later act of 1854 to home-trading ships. These are found in BT 124 for Foreign Trade and for the Home Trade in BT 125 and BT 126.

These series give, in numerical order, the name, place and date of birth, any registered ticket number, rank for which examined and the place and date of the certificate granted. Names of ships with details of voyages are also given, in yearly columns, and notification of deaths, injuries and retirements.

Reference to these series are given in "index to Registers (BT 127)". This gives place and date with certificate number.

Lloyds also published a volume entitled *Lloyd's Captains' Register, comprising the names and services of certificated masters of the British Mercantile Marine now afloat, compiled from the records of the Registrar-General of Seamen,* 1869. This is now a rare book, but there is a copy at the Society of Genealogists, London. It does not include those who during the five years prior to publication have not been afloat, but gives the full names of masters (including those so qualified but serving as mates), place and date of birth, port at which examined, date of examination and details of ships served in since receiving master's certificate.

The examination for competence as engineers in 1862 indicates the development of steam ships. These certificates are in BT 139 and the certificates of service of engineers are in BT 142, with an index to both in BT 141.

Similar certificates were instituted for skippers and mates of fishing boats in 1883 (BT 129, BT 130, with index in BT 138). Officers examined in colonial ports were registered separately (BT 128 and BT 140). The indexes for these are in BT 127 and BT 141.

Apprentices

Indentured apprentices under the 1834 Act can be found in the Index of Apprentices (BT 150), but only a percentage of specimen copies of these have been preserved.

Deaths on board

Masters were required to hand over any wages and effects of seamen dying during a voyage. A register of these exists from 1851 in BT 153. With other details this records the cause of death, name and port of the ship, date and place of payment of wages and the master's name. The Index to the Seamen's Names (BT 155) give page references to the registers. There are nine MS registers of half-yearly lists of deaths covering the years 1882-1888, classified under Cause of Death in BT 157.

Births and Marriages at Sea

From 1854 registers of births, marriages and deaths at sea were compiled from the ships' logs. These are recorded until 1883, births and deaths only from 1883 to 1887 and deaths only from 1888. These are in BT 158.

Masters were also required by an Act of 1874 to report births and deaths on board to the Registrar-General of Shipping. Births were entered in BT 160 and deaths in BT 159.

The Royal Naval Reserve, under an Act of 1859, provided reservists for the Royal Navy of 30,000 men from serving merchant seamen and fishermen. Records of these are preserved in BT 164.

In addition to all these records of the Registrar-General of Shipping and Seamen in the P.R.O. at Kew, there are certain records in the Custom Houses of some ports in Great Britain. These are mainly of ships registered at these ports since about 1820. Such records usually give the names of the ships, the owner or owners (in 64th parts), changes of owners and masters, and the career of the ship while she remained at sea.

An example of such records is given below from the Custom House registers of Plymouth:

1824 Reg of Shipping, Custom House, Plymouth p. 14.

No 14 Port of Plymouth. Dated 28 May 1824.
Name Dutchess of Somerset. Burthen 10891/94 tons. William Joly *master*.

Was built at Bridgetown in the Port of Dartmouth in the County of Devon in the Year 1802 which appears by a former Register granted here the 31st Octer,. 1822.
No 32, now delivered up to be Cancelled agreable to the Act of George 4 Cap. 41.

Name of Surveying Officer P. Curgenven Tide Surveyor.

One *Deck* Five *Masts length* 68ft 4ins. Breadth taken above the Wales 19f 3ins. Depth in the Hold 10ft 3ins.
Schooner Rigged with a standing Bowsprit. Square sterned Carvel built No Galleries No Head.
Admeasured Aground Keel for Tonnage fifty five feet three ins & half.
Subscribing Owners John Stevens of Plymouth in the County of Devon Coal Merchant.
Shares J. Stevens 64/64ths.
Wm Lockyer Comp. John Arthur Col.
Other Owners
Custom House, Plymouth. 8 July 1829. Walter Prideaux of Plymouth in the County of Devon, Banker, and Henry McKeever of the same Place Sailmaker, assignees of the Estate and Effects of John Stevens of Plymouth aforesaid owner a Bankrupt have transferred by Bill of Sale dated the 6th July 1829 Sixty four Sixtyfourth Shares unto Samuel Jinkin of the Parish of Stoke Damerell in the County of Devon Merchant. [in red] Register Cancelled & Registered De Novo at Plymouth the 11th July 1829 No 27 to Property being Charged—

Custom House, Liverpool 6 Jany 1826
Francis Hickes has now become Master
Custom House, London, 12th Dec. 1826.
John Hickes has now become Master.

11 July 1829
Sub. Owner Samuel Jinkin pa. Stoke Damerell, Mercht
18 Feb. 1831 transferred to Wm White Ridley in sd Co Mercht.
Reg, Cancelled & Reg de Novo at Plymouth 22 Feby 1831 No 8.
No 200 (22 Feby 1831)
Sub Owner William White Ridley of Plymouth Mercht.

Reg. Cancelled — Vessel Wrecked at Padstow
nite [sic] of December 1832

Custom House 22 March 1833.

Another later example is given below. It will be noticed that both these ships sank at sea, which is an indication of the fate of so many ships in the time of sail.

Bk 3 No 13 Plymouth dtd 5th May 1831 p. 105.

Name Fury *Burthen* 117 45/94 Tons Thomas Moon *Master*

Built at Hayle, St Ives 1802

Main and Qtr Decks 2 masts 1.68ft b. above main Wales 21.2″ Dept 12ft 10 ins. Brig Rigged with a standing Bowsprit Haglboat sterned. Carvel built No galleries No figure.
Subs. Owners
Thomas Vivian, Grocer of Plymouth
Thomas Stevens, Coal Merchant of Plymouth
Thomas Moon, Mariner of Stonehouse,
all in co. of Devon 16/64ths each
Other Owners
Robert Moon, Mariner, of Stonehouse afsd 8/64ths
Edward Moon, '   '   '   ' 8/64ths

Abandoned, being in Sinking state in the North Sea 8th Nov 1831, leaving behind the Register & all Ships Papers

affidavit 19 Dec. 1831.

Chapter Fifteen

ARMY RECORDS

As in the case of the Navy, the main bulk of the Army records are held at the Public Record Office and, like the Admiralty records, they are very extensive. Regimental records, however, are now held at Army Records Offices in various parts of the country.

As with the senior service, the tracing of an officer's career is naturally easier than that of someone in the ranks. There are no collective biographies of army officers as a whole, like Marshall's *Royal Naval Biography* or O'Byrne's great work. Had a work been produced, say, about 1820, it would have included all those who had survived Waterloo and would have been most valuable. Lieutenant-General Henry George Hart, the compiler of Hart's Army List, worked on an army biographical dictionary which was much advertised and was hoped to be published in 1850. This unfortunately never happened. However his MS is now in the Public Record Office at Kew in W.O. 211/2-6. This contains detailed biographical accounts of the General and Field Officers compiled by him for his projected Army Biographical Dictionary.

There are, however, a great many regimental histories, varying greatly in quality. The best of these are very good and often give accounts of officers' services. An early series of regimental histories are those edited by F. Cannon, but many later histories are more accurate and more comprehensive. There is also the work of the Institute of Army Historical Research, which publishes a journal, the volumes of which contain a great amount of information about regiments and their officers and men.

The Regiment or Corps is the key to information in the Army. An officer can be traced fairly easily through the army lists. There are MS lists among the army records at the P.R.O. from 1702 onwards (W.O. 64) and the lists have been printed annually since 1754, though there is an isolated issue of 1740. There is also Charles Dalton's *English Army Lists and Commission Registers, 1661-1714,* in 6 volumes and his *George I's Army.* The 13 volumes of Sir John W. Fortescue's *History of the British Army* are well indexed and contain references to hundreds of officers and men.

The earlier printed Army lists are not always indexed, but by the end of the eighteenth century they are regularly so and it is therefore not a long task to trace an officer through the successive volumes, noting his promotions and finally his disappearance from the lists. This may be because of his death, in which case you will find notification of it in the pages of casualties. He may, on the other hand, have sold his commission, in which case you may find a reference to that also.

To trace an officer this way you naturally want to use a library where there is a good run of the lists on open access. The P.R.O. has a nearly complete set of them. The Society of Genealogists has a good run of them and some of the military clubs, like the Army and Navy club, have good runs, and also the National Army Museum, Chelsea.

At the P.R.O. there are valuable returns of services for officers at various periods. These do not unfortunately start very early, but the 1828 returns of officers retired on full pay and half-pay and the 1829 active list full-pay returns are especially valuable for the detailed information they give.

The 1828 (half-pay) return (W.O. 25) gives, among other details, the age on first appointment, the date of the latter and the regiment in which commissioned; the successive promotions and dates, whether placed on half-pay by reduction or by the purchase of a half-pay commission, etc., if desirous of further service; the total length of service on full pay and half-pay; whether married and, if so, the date and place of marriage, and the general place of residence during the last five years.

The 1829 (full-pay) return (W.O. 25 and W.O. 76) gives all the above details with some important additional ones, namely, the place and date of birth; whether first commission obtained by purchase or otherwise, details of any campaigns in which the officer has taken part; an account of service abroad; if married, details of place and date and name of wife and indication if she is still alive, names of legitimate children, with their date of birth and place of baptism; total service, divided into time abroad and time at home.

In both the above returns you get the signature of the officer making it.

The returns of services of officers retired on full pay and half-pay of 1847, being more recent and referring only to retired or half-pay officers, is not for those reasons so valuable. Nevertheless it may prove very useful in filling gaps and in giving a succinct account of an officer's service.

This return gives the following information: name, rank and regiment; full christian names and surname; age at time of the return and on entering the service; dates of the various commissions held; date of last retirement or entry on to the half-pay list and cause of retirement (whether arising from reduction, the decision of a medical board, at own request or in consequence of regimental proceedings); if under sixty, whether fit to serve again or under any disability and also whether engaged in any employment which would interefere with serving permanently or temporarily on full pay and also, if under sixty, the number and ages of family and how many of them are capable of maintaining themselves; finally, the place of residence, parish and nearest post town, and the officer's signature.

In the early nineteenth century the War Office issued instructions that officers were to report their marriages and these reports give the officer's age on marriage, the name and age of the bride, the place and date of the ceremony and the names of the officiating clergyman and witnesses. These returns are to be found in W.O. 25 at the P.R.O.

There are also card indexes there for the half-pay returns of 1828 and for the Reports of Officers' Marriages from about 1810 and there is a card index in progress for the Records of Officers' Services from 1829 onwards (W.O. 25 and W.O. 76).

Another valuable source of information about officers' careers is the Commander-in-Chief's Memoranda (W.O. series 31). In earlier times there was no Royal Military

Academy to enter by competitive examination or possibility of being selected from the ranks to go to an O.C.T.U. Officers had to be recommended by persons in influential position and approved by the colonel of the regiment into which they aspired to obtain a commission. They could be recommended for a commission either with or without purchase. There has been much nonsense talked about the purchase of commissions. Some people seem to think that you were just able to go along to some army agent and buy a commission, like buying a pound of tea at the grocer's. The purchase of a commission was only part of the procedure. It was really a kind of payment down as an indemnity, rather like the caution money at Oxford and Cambridge colleges. It was returnable to you when you gave up your commission in that you could then sell it to some other approved purchaser. The same happened when promotion occurred. You had to pay the difference between the purchase money of that rank and the value of your own commission. Higher ranks were more expensive, of course, and also prices varied according to the regiment. A cavalry commission was more expensive, as being more exclusive, than an infantry regiment, and such famous regiments as the Life Guards or Horse Guards, which formed the Household Cavalry, were the most expensive of all. Promotion was, of course, dependant on vacancies, and the sad thing was when a perfectly efficient and otherwise eligible officer could not raise the money for his next step in promotion and had to let it pass and see the officer below him buy it and step up above him. The system had many faults, but not nearly as many as some people allege it had. There were always ways of granting promotion to really outstanding officers without purchase and there are many examples of people like Major-General James Wolfe, who reached high rank without either influence or wealth.

Genealogically, however, these Commander-in-Chief's Memoranda are most interesting. You will often find in the bundle concerned the letters of recommendation and will learn from them a great deal about the young man anxious to obtain a commission. You will discover, for instance, the names of the people who recommended him. These will probably be friends or at least acquaintances and their letters will also often indicate where the applicant was living. There will also be a letter of application, probably with the applicant's home address, mentioning the regiment in which he desires to be commissioned, and possibly giving reasons why. Perhaps he has had relatives who have served in it, and these may be mentioned by name.

By the end of the eighteenth century the price to be paid for commissions in the various regiments had been regulated. There were, in fact, printed forms and the future officer had to declare and certify 'upon the Word and Honour of an Officer and Gentleman, That I will not, either now or at any future Time, give by any Means, or in any Shape whatever, directly or indirectly, any more than the Sum of . . . being the full Value of the said Commission as the same is limited and fixed by His Majesty's Regulation'. The colonel of the regiment also, in making his recommendation, had to state, 'I veritably believe the established Regulations with regard to Price is intended to be strictly complied with, and that no Clandestine Bargain subsists between the Parties concerned'. These Memoranda papers (W.O. Series 31) begin in 1793.

When an officer sold his full-pay commission and purchased a half-pay commission he went on to the Half-Pay Register. If he died while still holding such a commission, there would probably be some small balance of pay due to him and this had to be disposed of, so that in the Half-Pay Warrants you should find details of this, giving probably the date on which the officer died and either the name of the executors or, if the officer died intestate, the person to whom Letters of Administration were granted. These wills or administrations were nearly always proved or taken out in the P.C.C. and further useful information may be derived from consulting them.

The Royal Military Academy at Woolwich opened in 1741 and records of entry exist for 1799 to 1805 and from 1820 to 1839 and then on with some gaps until its closure. The Royal Military College (now the Royal Military Academy), Sandhurst, opened in 1812 and admission records exist from that date onwards. The registers for Sandhurst give for each cadet the date of admission, age on admission, height, his father's name and rank or occupation, and the date of his leaving the college, with remarks as appropriate. Similar details are given in the registers of the Royal Military Academy, Woolwich. These details can be obtained from the Librarian, Central Library, Royal Military Academy, Sandhurst, Surrey GU15 4PQ.

Officers' records are mostly at the P.R.O. and recently a number of *Records of Officers Services* held at varous Army Record Offices throughout the country have been transferred to the P.R.O. Unfortunately a number of these, mainly of the cavalry, are missing.

The surviving records of all regular 'other ranks' prior to 1901, previously held at these Army Record Offices, have also now been moved to the P.R.O. It is unfortunate that the records of non-pensioners before 1883 were many years ago accidentally destroyed by fire, but in such cases some idea of a man's service can usually be made up from the Muster Rolls.

A great deal of information can be discovered about a man who served in the ranks of the Army. The first need is to discover in which regiment he served. This is not as difficult as it sounds. Usually there is some idea in the family, some old cap badge retained or some tradition remembered. If you do not know which regiment your ancestor was in but know that he was stationed in a certain place at a certain time, then the Monthly Returns (W.O. 17), which cover the period from 1759 to 1865, give the distribution of each regiment at home and abroad, and from this you can find which regiments were stationed in the particular place at the time. This will reduce the search to the muster rolls of perhaps two or three regiments.

If none of these methods are able to be used, there is yet another way you can discover the regiment your ancestor was serving in during the period of the early nineteenth century, though it is a somewhat lengthy process. In the Registers Various (W.O. 25) there are two returns. One (W.O. 25, Service Return No. 1) is a statement of periods of service of all NCOs and men, liable to serve abroad on 24 June 1806, and the other (W.O. 25/1125ff, Service Return No. 3) is a return of NCOs and men who were discharged or ceased to belong to their respective corps between 1783 and 1810.

Both these returns are arranged in alphabetical order within their regiments. Thus you are faced with searching every regiment of the army at the time but as the names are in alphabetical order this search is not as lengthy as you might imagine.

It may, however, take some time to search these two lists until you find the name you are seeking. But when you have found your man and discovered the regiment in which he was serving, then you can search the muster roll of his regiment and hopefully find his place of birth and age. If, however, the name is a common one, there may be other men of the same christian and surname. Therefore if the details on the muster roll do not agree with your own known facts, you will have to search on until you find a man of identical names where the facts on the muster roll of his regiment agree with your own.

I learnt of these two returns from a review by Dr. Christopher Watts, who is also the author, with his brother Michael J. Watts, of an interesting article in the *Genealogists' Magazine* for December 1977, entitled "In Search of a Soldier Ancestor".

If a family had an ancestor serving in the army around the time of Waterloo, so often he will be linked with the battle and the tradition will come down in the family that he was at Waterloo.

The Watts brothers had a tradition that one of their ancestors fought in a Norfolk regiment at Waterloo. The article gives an account of the prolonged search to discover whether this tradition was true. It was found, as in many other such cases, not to be, but the search discovered a great deal of information about their soldier ancestor, John Watts, and that he was not in a Norfolk regiment but in the 99th and 6th Foot and that he served in the retreat to Corunna and in the ill-fated Walcheren expedition. In their search the brothers found a great deal of information about him in the various sources they explored. But it took one or other of them a year-and-a-half of Saturday mornings to do so and almost another year of these mornings to read and note all which they had covered. Persistence is certainly a valuable quality in family history searching!

The muster rolls usually start towards the end of the eighteenth century, though the Royal Artillery has muster rolls going back to 1719 and quite a number of units and regiments have records from the mid-eighteenth century.

These muster rolls are arranged by ranks, officers, sergeants, corporals, drummers, privates, casuals, etc., and within each group they are entered in the order in which the men joined. From 1790 onwards they are usually in bound books. The muster will usually show on the man's first muster on joining, his place of birth and age on enlistment and sometimes an indication of his trade.

Starting from a somewhat later date are the Description Books, which give fuller information about each man, not to help future genealogists, but so that he could be traced if he ever deserted. They give usually the date and place of enlistment, age, perhaps the trade, height, colour of eyes and hair and description of his complexion. Some of these Description Books go back to 1795. It is quite a remarkable thing that you may be able to discover the colour of your ancestor's eyes and hair, an ancestor who was serving perhaps at Waterloo as a private soldier.

The Chaplains Returns usually cover only stations abroad. They record details of birth and baptism, marriage and death and burial of men in the Army and their families between 1796 and 1880. These records are, however, at the General Register Office. There is a comprehensive index of these returns covering the whole period. A small fee is charged for search in it.

There is also at the General Register Office a series of registers of regiments stationed both at home and abroad, which has records of births, baptisms, marriages, deaths and burials both of officers and other ranks, and their families. These registers go back to 1790 and there is an index of births and baptisms but not for the marriages, deaths and burials. Here again these can be consulted for a small fee.

There are Records of Service for the Royal Artillery at the P.R.O. which cover both officers and men for the period 1756 to 1917. These records give the name, description, place of birth, trade, length of service, details of promotion, discharge or death.

There are also a series of returns of Widows' Pensions for the period 1735 to 1912; pensions for Wounds and Superannuation, 1814 to 1920 (P.M.G. 9); Pension Returns of the Royal Hospital, Chelsea (W.O. 116), 1842 to 1883; Miscellaneous Pensions, 1795 to 1856 and some other similar returns. The Casualty Returns (Index for 1797-1817 W.O. 25/1220 etc) are valuable where you know an ancestor was killed in battle. As in the case of the Navy, the courts martial records can give much information about ancestors who have gone astray. They cover the period 1684 to 1847.

Fuller details of the records of Chelsea Hospital and of those at the sister institution at Kilmainham, near Dublin, together with fuller accounts of Army records in general, will be found in the author's *In Search of Army Ancestry* (1977).

National Army Museum

The new home of the National Army Museum in the Royal Hospital Road near Chelsea Hospital was opened by H.M. The Queen in November 1971.

The Museum's literary research material, now under the Department of Records, consists of four main collections, namely books, manuscripts, prints and photographs, all of which are now housed at Chelsea. To use the reading room you must apply to the Director for a reader's ticket.

In the Reading Room on the open shelves you will find a complete set of the Army Lists, nearly every regimental history of both British and Indian forces, together with a number of standard reference books. The collection includes a great number of campaign histories, regimental journals and biographies. There is a card index to the MS material and items in it can be produced without undue delay.

Among its several genealogical sources is the Hodson Index, covering information about officers of the armies, maritime services and civil services of the three Presidencies of Bengal, Madras, Bombay and the East India Company dependencies, up to 1845. The continuation of this index was carried on by the late Lieut-Colonel H.K. Percy-Smith, with the assistance of a number of voluntary helpers. His first task was to complete the index to 1860, adding some details of officers in the medical services. There is also among the MS a great deal of papers of great commanders, such as Field Marshals Lord Roberts and Viscount Gough, and the whole of the military MS collection from the Royal United Service Institute which was transferred to the National Army Museum in 1968, apart from a few items post-1914 which went to the Imperial War Museum. The collection is particularly strong in material on the eighteenth and nineteenth centuries. Fuller details of the National Army Museum archives are given in an article of that title by Boris Mollo, the Keeper of the Records of the Museum, in the *Genealogists' Magazine* for June 1974.

Chapter Sixteen

THE EAST INDIA COMPANY

This great company, sometimes known as 'The Hon John Company' founded in 1601 as a trading company, became one of the greatest administrative units the world has known. Its trade grew and grew and many of our great families of today owe their rise in the social world to the wealth which their ancestors in this company brought back with them when, after their profitable years abroad, they retired to England.

The returning 'nabobs' became a feature of English life in the eighteenth and early nineteenth centuries. They often entered Parliament and usually settled in pleasant and large estates, suitable to their new fortunes and status, often regarded by their older-established neighbours as *nouveau riche* but gradually living this down and becoming absorbed, through the osmotic trend which has always been a feature of English society, into the aristocracy or landed gentry. One can think of families like that of the Kennaways of Escot, Devon, whose ancestor, Sir John Kennaway, concluded with the Nizam of Hyderabad a treaty of alliance against Tippoo Sultan, for which service he was in 1791 created a baronet. He married a daughter of James Amyatt, sometime M.P. for Totnes and Southampton and a former free merchant and sea-captain in the service of the company. These Anglo-Indian families frequently intermarried and this was notably so in the military service, as can be seen from that valuable work by Brigadier V.C.P. Hodson, *Officers of the Bengal Army,* of paramount use from a genealogical point of view.

It must not be thought, however, that most of the British who went out to India returned wealthy men. Quite the contrary; the majority either died out there or returned with very little or even nothing on which to enjoy the retirement to which they had looked forward.

The East India Company's records are among the finest in the world. This material is now available in the India Office Records, Orbit House, Blackfriars Road, S.E.1, which is a true gold mine for the historian and researcher. The India Office Library, a separate institution, is also here.

In 1771 an official was appointed by the company to take charge of the records and from that time forward they are remarkably good. But even the earlier records, though they had no single official responsible for their preservation, have been well looked after and much work has been done and is being done towards publishing them. It is interesting that, although India and Pakistan are today republics, both these countries, especially India, have done much work on these records and the publishing of them.

The company was a trading company and its ancillary forces, its army and navy, only came into existence as forces for protection against attack by natives or by some other country. As early as 1606 this 'civil service', as it became called from about 1750, was organized in grades, such as merchants, factors, writers and cadets. The careers of these early civilians can only be traced through the *Court Minutes, Original Correspondence, Factory Records, Consultations* and so forth. But from the mid-eighteenth century more information can be discovered from the *Writers' Petitions,* beginning in 1749 and continuing until 1805. In the early years they may be scanty or missing but in general they should give you information regarding parentage and place and date of birth. From 1806 to 1856 similar information can be obtained from the 70 volumes called *Committee of College Reference*, the college being the old East India Company College, now Haileybury College. There is a two-volumed index covering the whole period from 1749 to 1857.

Persons applying for a writership had to submit a certificate from a teacher stating that the applicant was competent in the elementary general principles of mercantile accounts and had also to forward a copy of a baptismal or birth certificate the former duly certified by the incumbent and the two churchwardens. A number of the company's civil servants had in addition to provide a bond in the sum of £500 with two people as securities. These could be friends or possibly relations and so are a useful clue. Registers for the civil servants abroad exist from 1741 and are indexed. There are also bonds starting in 1788 for those employed at home, such as the clerks at East India House in London.

Apart from the MS returns relating to the three main stations of Bengal, Madras and Bombay, which in the case of Bengal start in the early eighteenth century, there are the three printed volumes by Dodwell and Miles covering the period 1780 to 1838 for the three stations and the *Register of Bengal Civil Servants 1790-1842,* by H.T. Prinsep, and a *Record of Services of Madras Civilians, 1741-1858,* by C.C. Prinsep.

There are good records of officers who served in the company's army from 1790, when applications for cadetship are recorded in a series of 147 volumes called *Cadet Papers.* These contain among other details certificates of baptism and are well indexed in ten volumes, so the parentage of a military officer is not difficult to ascertain in the period from 1790 to 1860, during which some 20,000 young gentlemen entered the company's service. From 1809 the papers record, or should record if properly filled in, the school at which the applicant was educated and also the profession, situation and residence of the parents or next-of-kin. It is interesting to note that in the twenty-five years from the time this detail was recorded, that is, from 1809 to 1834, Charterhouse sent more young men into the service than any other of the principal English public schools, followed closely by Westminster and then, in order, Rugby, Eton, Winchester, Harrow, Blundell's, Shrewsbury and Merchant Taylors.

There are numerous sources through which an officer's career can be traced, though it may require patience and considerable labour. However, if you are fortunate, you may find your officer among the limited number in some MS volumes called 'Service Army Lists' in the Military Record Department. This series, which appears to have been compiled about 1839 in England from details forwarded from India and then continued to 1859, will give details of the officer's career and service. They are divided into the three main presidencies, Bengal having 48 volumes, Madras 29, and Bombay 16, each presidency being well indexed. There are also numerous MS army lists for the eighteenth century and printed ones by the time the nineteenth century had begun. Then there are the valuable series from 1803 of *East India Registers* which, among other matters, contain lists of army officers.

Prior to about 1790, when the cadet papers start, the appointment of military officers can only be traced through the *Court Minutes, Despatches or Proceedings*. Although this is cumbersome and lengthy, nevertheless the material is mostly there, and these are among the records which the Republic of India are continually publishing.

Embarkation Lists, from 1753 to 1860, give details of all ranks embarking for India and also details of civilians, such as free merchants and their wives.

Lord Clive's Fund gives useful information about recipients of this bounty, such as widows or orphans of officers and others. Beginning in 1770 it often discloses information of families not otherwise easily discovered.

The Medical Services of the company have been well covered by two published works, which largely save further research. These are Lieut.-Colonel D.G. Crawford's *History of the I.M.S.,* 2 vols., 1914, and his later work, *Roll of the I.M.S. 1615 to 1859.*

The Veterinary Service has a volume of certificates covering the period 1826 to 1859.

The company had both a naval and a merchant navy service. Genealogical details of sea-officers in these services are less easy to trace. There are three volumes of baptismal certificates of some officers, covering the period 1780 to 1830, mentioned in Section III of the *List of Marine Records,* under 'Miscellaneous'. Fuller details of the marine records will be found in the *List of Marine Records of the late East India Company,* published in 1896. From about 1702 ships' logs are fairly complete and there are some accounts of earlier voyages from 1605. The logs have also, sometimes, in separate books, lists of officers, crew and passengers on board. The published list of ships' logs indicates if there is any list of the officers and crew surviving. There may also be a pay book in which you may get your ancestor's signature for his pay. A printed list, *Register of Ships employed in the Service of the Hon. the United E.I. Co.,* compiled by Charles Hardy was published in 1798 and his son Horatio C. Hardy compiled two supplementary volumes, which bring the work down to 1812. From then onwards the *East India Register* gives similar information. C.R. Low's *History of the Indian Navy, 1613-1863,* should also be consulted.

There were certain employees of the company known as 'Uncovenanted Civilians', who were only available for subordinate appointments, and were sometimes known as 'Monthly Writers'. There are various lists of these, the earliest being in 1774 of some of them employed under the Calcutta Committee of Revenue. Another, of 1783, is in the *Bengal Public Consultations* of the 29th May that year.

From the earliest times of the company until 1834 no one was allowed to go to India unless he had the company's permission, nor could he live there without a licence. A considerable body of such people were the 'Free Merchants', that is, people trading in India who were not employees of the company. Naturally there were many anxious to go out there, as fortunes were to be made particularly in the early days, so permission was a privilege not casually granted. Applications appear in the *Court Minutes* and permission may be granted in these records and an announcement made in the *Despatches*. Free merchants had to obtain securities, and the names of the people acting as such will also be given in the *Court Minutes*. The usual security was provided by two people, to cover £2,000. In later times lists of persons in India not servants of the company are shown in a special series, commencing in Madras in 1702, in Bombay in 1719 and in

Bengal in 1794. The *East India Register* from 1803 to 1837 contains similar lists. There are also twenty-five volumes (1766-1829) covering Europeans who were not employees of the company and who had been accused of misconduct.

There is a large series of more than 800 volumes, entitled 'Home Miscellaneous', covering a multitude of matters. A detailed catalogue of these, with a good index, was compiled by S.C. Hill and published by the India Office in 1927.

From early times chaplains at the various factories or stations forwarded home copies of their baptismal, marriage and burial registers, so that even where the originals have been lost, as those of St Anne's, Calcutta were during the time of the 'Black Hole' and siege, certified copies are available. These cover the periods, Bengal from 1713, Madras from 1698 and Bombay from 1709. There are also Roman Catholic registers for Bengal and Madras from 1836 and Bombay from 1842. A great many of the registers have been published and also many of the inscriptions on European tombs in India. In addition to this there are many MS copies of registers and monumental inscriptions at the Society of Genealogists. The wills and inventories of early company servants are sometimes recorded in the *Consultations*; there are, for instance, a number of copies of eighteenth-century wills in the St Helena *Consultations*, and in the *Factory Miscellaneous* series there is a volume for the years 1618-1620 and 1657-1725. In the Ecclesiastical Record Department at the India Library there is a MS alphabetical list of wills and administrations covered by the Mayor's Court for the following years: Bengal, 1704-1779; Madras, 1753-1779; Bombay, 1728-1783, and there is also a register of all wills proved in the three presidencies for the following years, namely, Bengal from 1728; Madras from 1736 and Bombay from 1723 onwards. Then there are records of grants of probate and of administrations from 1780; inventories and accounts from the same date. Bombay: wills and administrations from 1783; inventories and accounts from 1798. Each of the presidencies has an index and it is therefore a simple task to trace a particular name.

There are many printed sources, particularly for the later period, the late eighteenth century and nineteenth century. One can only indicate a small number in this very large field. There is, for instance, S.C. Hill's *Bengal in 1756,* and his list of Europeans and others in the English Factories in Bengal at the time of the siege of Calcutta in that year, a most detailed and useful list, giving sources of information and references. There is Prebendary H.B. Hyde's *The Parish of Bengal* and *The Parochial Annals of Bengal*; the valuable *Guide to the India Office Records, 1600 to 1858,* by Sir William Foster, the *Court Minutes of the East India Company,* published in a number of volumes covering the period from 1601 to the mid-seventeenth century. Then there are the many periodicals, like the *Asiatic Journal,* which began publication in 1816, the earlier *Asiatic Annual Register,* unfortunately unindexed, which covered the first dozen years of the nineteenth century and last, and undoubtedly the most valuable and already frequently referred to in this chapter, the *East India Register and Army List,* which was issued twice yearly from 1803 to 1860 and covers such matters as casualties, notices of births, marriages and deaths, lists of Europeans not in the company's service and shareholders of East India stock, with their place of residence. As previously mentioned, it also gives lists of ships with the names of owners, commanders and principal officers.

The National Army Museum, London, has also much information about East India Company officers, including the Hodson Index, which is complete for officers of the armies, maritime services and civil services of the Bengal, Madras and Bombay

Presidencies. It also holds some of the indexes of the late Lt.-Col. H.K. Percy-Smith.

The Central Library at Poplar, London E.14, has some records relating to the East India Company's hospital there, which was demolished in 1866.

You will see that, if you had an ancestor in this great and unique company, there is plenty of material for you to search for information about him and, as so large a number of families were connected with this company, the chances are that you will sooner or later come across one of your own ancestors so connected.

Ian A. Baxter's *Brief Guide to Biographical Sources* (1979) is a valuable guide to the many sources of biographical interest scattered among the India Office Library and Records.

Chapter Seventeen

JEWS, HUGUENOTS AND OTHER IMMIGRANTS

The Romans invaded and conquered Britain in 55 B.C. and occupied it for many years. But they eventually returned to Rome, though no doubt some soldiers, having married British wives, stayed behind and became farmers and there must be diminutive portions of Roman blood in British descendants living today. The Anglo-Saxons invaded, conquered and stayed, eventually intermingling with the Britons, so that today we regard ourselves as an Anglo-Saxon race, though the Norman conquest in 1066 brought in its turn much French blood into our veins.

The Normans were the last invaders, but England has long been the refuge for the persecuted and homeless and among these one particularly remembers the Jews and Huguenots.

The Jews for many generations in England suffered oppression and restrictions on their liberty and it was not until the last century that their final disabilities, such as their right to stand for parliament, to be Lord Mayor of London, or to be even a freeman of that city, were finally removed.

From earliest times there had been settlements of Jews in England until they were expelled from the country by King Edward I in 1290. From then until Cromwell's time they were not allowed to settle in England, but in 1655 the Protector allowed them to return and a number came over, particularly during Charles II's reign, when Dr Fernando Mendes, a Portuguese Jew, was appointed physician in ordinary to Queen Catherine of Braganza.

The Jews who came to England during the late seventeenth century were of two kinds, the Iberian or Sephardim, and the Eastern European or Ashkenazim. The former, whose numbers in London in 1680 are said to have been about 2,000, descended from the refugees of Spanish oppression in the fifteenth century who had fled to Portugal and while there were forced by Manuel I to take the Christian faith and be baptized. But not unnaturally they always secretly maintained their faith and came to England when the opportunity occurred, to escape further oppression. Some of them came via other parts of the Continent, particularly the Low Countries. Among those that came from Holland was a Henriques, ancestor of the late Sir Basil Henriques, who did so much for the Jews in the East End of London and founded the Bernard Baron St George's Jewish Settlement in the street which is now named after him, and whose work was carried on so ably by the late Lady Henriques, his widow.

These Sephardic Jews had earlier intermarried with the Spanish, many with the aristocracy and had been on the whole wealthy, mainly merchants or bankers, and they were a helpful influence in England's commercial life. Although they were at first, and are even today, a closely-knit community, intermarrying within their own religion, some gradually infiltrated into other spheres through marriage with Christians or through becoming Christians. Many people therefore in investigating their ancestry may discover, perhaps to their surprise, that they have Jewish forbears.

The Sephardic Jews are fairly easy to trace, for they have distinctive surnames and tended because of their interest in commerce, to be centred in London. Their synagogue was the great synagogue in Bevis Marks, and their marriages, published in 1949, are particularly useful in giving the parentage of both bride and bridegroom. The birth and burial registers of this community can also be seen.

Some of these Jews kept their names and the coats of arms to which many of them were entitled. Mr W.S. Samuel, in an interesting lecture to the Society of Genealogists, delivered in March 1932 and published in the *Genealogists' Magazine* that year, gives the example of Dr Fernando Mendes, who was a court physician, and Senhor Alvaro da Costa, who, when they came to London after the Restoration, kept their names and coats of arms, making no outward show of their religion 'although subsequently the synagogue records refer to these two Portuguese gentlemen as Moses Mendes and Jacob da Costa'.

More often it was thought prudent to discard the ancestral name and take a Jewish name for the purposes of the faith but adopt a commercial pseudonym. Thus Abraham Israel de Sequeira of Bury Street traded there under the name of Gomez Rodriguez and his son, Isaac Israel de Sequeira, as Alphonso Rodriguez. Other sons of this Abraham took other surnames. They included Symon Henriques (who was sometimes called also Symon Rodriguez) and Pantaleon Rodriguez Mogadouro. Isaac Haim Pereira was known outside Jewish circles as Manuel Lopes Pereira and also, for trade purposes, as Manuel de Velasquez and also again as Jacques Vandepeere. One of the difficulties in tracing back these Jewish families is the fluidity of their surnames. However, once these Portuguese Jews were settled in England they retained the same surnames, though they might use another name for trade purposes, a custom which persists today just as much among non-Jewish as among Jewish people. In the course of time some of these Sephardim surnames became anglicized, Martinez becomes Martins, Rodriguez becoming Rogers, Benhamo, Benham, and Londo, Lindon.

The Sephardic Jews were regarded as the aristocracy of the Jewish world. The Ashkenazim were often poor refugees from oppression in Russia, Poland and Rumania. They came later than the Sephardim. A number came over during the eighteenth and early nineteenth century, but from 1880 onwards they came in increasing numbers, fleeing from the pogroms of inhospitable countries. Many arrived over here penniless and many settled in the East End of London, because the Anglo-Jewish community there went out of their way to welcome them, setting up in Whitechapel a board of guardians to look after their welfare, and also because there already existed in Stepney some synagogues and also opportunities for keeping the Jewish dietry laws. This accounts for the large Jewish population which Stepney possesses even today. Many of these Jews were tailors, cabinet makers, cigar makers, old clothes dealers or pedlars, but at the same time some were learned rabbis who had to earn their living by working at some trade.

These Jews, at any rate during their early days in England, tended to keep Jewish customs and retain their form of name, being known as son (ben) of their father. This was rather like the custom in England before surnames were adopted, such surnames from personal names, as Johnson, deriving from 'John's son', and Robertson, from 'Robert's son'. Thus Isaac, a son of Israel, would be called Isaac ben Israel. Alternatively they were often known by the name of their birthplace. Samuel gives an example of this in Mordecai, the son of Moses, who came to London from Hamburg at the end of the seventeenth century and was known as Mordecai Hamburger, though among gentiles he was known as Marcus Moses, and his eldest son, among Jews, was known as Moses ben Mordecai, but in general circles as Moses Marcus, the name Marcus being a variant of the biblical Mordecai. These Ashkenazim Jews who settled in England tended to alter their names, which in due course became the surnames of their descendants. Thus Jews called Zevi, which in Hebrew means 'a stag', became by Teutonic translation 'Hirsch', or 'Hirschel', which sometimes became anglicized into 'Hart' and even developed into 'Harris'. 'Ben Uri' became 'Phillips' and 'Ben David', 'Davis'. Another example of name-change is found in the well-known Jewish family of Lopez. Sir Massey Lopes, created a baronet in 1805, from whose sister the present Lord Roborough descends, was originally called Menasseh Lopez.

Jewish records of birth, marriage and burial exist in the various synagogues throughout England and there have been publications of some of these by the Jewish Historical Society in their Transactions. Some notice of them is made in 'Jewish Ancestors and where to find them', an article by Edgar R. Samuel, a son of W.S. Samuel, in the *Genealogists' Magazine,* XI, 412 (December 1953). The works of Cecil Roth and of A.M. Hyamson should also be consulted. There are also great collections of Anglo-Jewish genealogies, like that of the late Sir Thomas Colyer-Fergusson, which he bequeathed to the Jewish Historical Society of England and which are now housed in the Jewish Museum at Woburn House, London W.C.1.

There is a valuable alphabetical index by Arthur Arnold of all the ascertainable wills and administrations of Jews proved in the P.C.C. This is contained in *Anglo-Jewish Notabilities,* published by the Jewish Historical Society of England in 1949, and this same volume also contains a brief biographical dictionary and a list of Anglo-Jewish coats of arms.

In general the amount of matter available relating to Jewish families is quite considerable and because they were a closely knit community their ancestry sometimes, for that very reason, is more easily revealed than that of the main English population. This applies equally to the next great community to be considered.

The Huguenots

The main wave of Huguenot refugees came to this country during the latter part of the seventeenth century following the revocation of the Edict of Nantes in 1685. These French Protestants, fleeing from religious persecution, set up their own churches in this country and for several generations continued to use their native tongue, though they soon learnt English.

Many Huguenots settled in London, mainly in the area around Spitalfields and here there are still a few of their houses to be seen with their long extra-wide top floor windows which were designed to allow maximum light for their silk-weaving looms. There are still street names which bring them to memory, streets such as Fleur-de-Lys Street and Fournier Street. Other Huguenots settled further outside at Wandsworth, or in provincial towns like Norwich, Southampton, Bristol, Exeter and Plymouth.

Gradually they became absorbed in the life of this country, though still looking with lingering nostalgia back to their homeland. Today nearly all the French churches have disappeared and the Huguenots worship in English churches, and in many cases their names have been anglicized, so that people are often unaware of their Huguenot origins. The Huguenot Society has published a number of their records and several of their genealogies are well documented. Ths society was founded in 1885 for the purpose, among other matters, of publishing Huguenot archives and literature. Among these have been many of the Huguenot church registers and the Returns of Aliens and Certificates of Denization (or naturalization). In England there are three libraries devoted to Huguenot archives and records. These are the libraries of the Dutch church of Austin Friars and L'Eglise de Londres, better known as the Threadneedle Street church, and the joint library of the French Hospital and the Huguenot Society. The manuscripts of the Dutch church have recently been deposited on permanent loan in the Guildhall Library. Some of their records have been published, edited by J.H. Hessels.

The Threadneedle Street Church Library, which is next to the French Protestant church in Soho Square, has records not only of its own church but also of several other London churches, and its collection has been described in the *Proceedings of the Huguenot Society* XIV and XVIII. The same proceedings, XIII, give an account of the third library, the combined one of the French Hospital and the Huguenot Society itself. This library is now housed at University College, Gower Street, London. In addition a number of other libraries have collections of Huguenot archives, among them the two university libraries at Oxford and Cambridge, the Guildhall Library, Dr Williams Library and that at Lambeth Palace.

Huguenot records are on the whole well kept and many of their church registers date from the late seventeenth century, or from the time these Huguenot churches were first established in these islands. Some thirty volumes of these registers have been published. A number of original registers are at the Public Record Office. Among other records churches often have lists of congregations at various periods.

Among the most valuable publications of the Huguenot Society are those concerning denization, naturalization and returns of aliens. They cover the period from 1523 to 1800 and cover other races beside the Huguenots themselves, such as the Jews.

There are also many purely genealogical records held by the Society. C.E. Lart's valuable MS collection was given to the Hospital Library by his daughter after his death. This is a very large collection by a specialist in Huguenot genealogy and also in French *noblesse*. They include seventeenth and eighteenth century French armorials. Then there is the Wagner collection of pedigrees, which are listed in Volume XIII of the *Proceedings* and for which there is also a card index at the Hospital Library, which includes some additions to the collection. There are also abstracts by the same compiler of Huguenot wills at Somerset House.

While some Huguenot surnames, like Bosanquet and Minet, continue in their French form, others, as mentioned, have been severely anglicized, which is rather sad and unfortunate. For instance 'Chapuis' has become 'Shoppee', some Beaumonts are now Beemans and Batteleurs have lost their French identity in 'Butler'. These have at least some semblance of their former structure. Much more difficult to connect are those which have been translated into their English equivalent. 'Le Blanc' has become 'White', 'De la Rue' been transformed into 'Street'. These are, unfortunately, often difficult to trace, because no record may have been made of the change.

Not all Huguenots came direct to this country. Some may have emigrated first to Switzerland, Holland or one of the German states, and then later emigrated to England. The whole history of these people is a fascinating one and many of us in our pursuit of ancestors, in discovering Huguenots among them, may thus be introduced to another intriguing facet of our history.

Other Immigrants

As a country with a reputation for giving sanctuary to people escaping oppression, England has naturally in the course of its history attracted many such people. Among them were those who came here to escape from the terrors of the French Revolution in 1789. Some of these were aristocrats, many of whom eked out an existence by teaching dancing in places like Cheltenham and Bath. The majority of them returned to France when the restoration came, but a few married English wives or husbands and settled down in this country. Many of these French immigrants were in distressed circumstances. Some account of them can sometimes be traced in the grants in aid of the 'French Emigrés in England', which are recorded in the Bouillon Papers in the P.R.O., the Prince de Bouillon having been appointed the administrator of the help given to these refugees by the British Government. A good general account of them is given in *The French Exiles* by Margery Weiner, published in 1960. William Cotton, donor of the Cottonian Collection at Plymouth, in his MS *Reminiscences* mentions "The Marquis and Marchioness de Thuisy, refugees from the French revolution, occupied a house on the Green [at Richmond, Surrey] near the theatre, having formerly lived in one of my father's houses in Kew lane and received many kindnesses from him, which they always gratefully acknowledged."

There were lesser influxes after the second and third French revolutions, but there were some refugees from European countries following the year of revolution, 1848. Then there have been the immigrants from the Russian Revolution after the First World War and those from Poland after the Second World War. Many of the latter have changed their names, some unfortunately to prevent retaliatory action being taken against their relatives in their home country. It is particularly important and desirable that their ancestry should be recorded, even if this is kept from publication, so that their links with their former country may not be lost and that their descendants may know their true origin.

Chapter Eighteen

SCOTTISH RECORDS I

The Scottish people have always been interested in their forbears and, being an exact and legally-minded race, have kept careful records. So that, apart from some haphazard destruction during their troubled times, such as the destruction of the Brechin Burgess records during the '45, their records are rich in genealogical material, far richer in most ways than those of England.

Civil registration of births, marriages and deaths began later in Scotland. It was not until 1855 that Scottish law required such registration. But when it started it was greatly superior to that of England or Ireland, in fact the first year of that registration may be called the *annus mirabilis* for genealogical searchers in Scotland, for the amount of detail in all the certificates is quite astonishing. Unfortunately they attempted something a little too thorough and found the difficulties in obtaining such full details too great to keep up. Therefore a modified certificate came out in 1856 and this was again slightly modified and improved upon in 1861 and the marriage certificate only was again a little altered in 1922.

This year 1855, this *annus mirabilis,* gives the following details.

Birth Certificate
The name and baptismal name if different; sex; year, date of month and hour of birth; place of birth (if in lodgings, so stated); father's name, rank, profession or occupation, his age and birthplace, when and where he was married and his other issue, both living and deceased; the mother's name and maiden name, her age and birthplace; the signature of the father or mother or other informant, and residence if out of the house in which the birth occurs; when and where registered and the signature of the Registrar.

The 1855 *Marriage Certificate* gives for bride and bridegroom:
the date and place of the marriage and in what form the marriage took place; the present and the usual residence; age, rank or profession and, if related, the relationship of the parties; status (widow or widower and if so whether second or third marriage and the number of children by each former marriage, living and dead); birthplace, and when and where registered; the names with the rank, profession or occupation of both the parents in each case; if a regular marriage, the signature of the officiating minister and of the witnesses, or if irregular, the date of the extract, sentence of conviction or decree of declarator and in what court pronounced; the date and place of registration and signature of the Registrar.

The 1855 *Death Certificate* gives the following information:

Name, rank, profession or occupation; sex and age; place of birth and length of time in the district; names, rank, profession or occupation of both parents; if married, wife's name; issue in order of birth, their names and ages; year, date of month and hour of death; place of death; cause and how long the disease continued, medical attendant certifying, and when he last saw the deceased; burial place and name of undertaker certifying it; signature of informant (usually mentioning relationship if related); date and place of registration and signature of the Registrar.

You will notice the valuable additional information over the English certificates; for instance, in the birth certificate the mention of the parents' age and place of birth and the place and date of their marriage; in the marriage certificates the details of any former marriages, with issue if any, and the birthplace of the parties; in the death certificate the place of birth of the deceased, the names of the deceased's parents and the details of any marriage and any issue of it. This is infinitely superior to any corresponding certificate in England and Wales or in Ireland and is probably not excelled by any of the certificates in the dominions, many of which are very full.

But even the curtailed form of certificates gives more valuable information than the corresponding certificates in England and probably in most other places. In the birth certificates 1856-60, the age and birthplace of the parents is omitted and also details of their marriage and of any other issue; but in the certificates from 1861 onwards the date and place of parents' marriage is restored.

In the marriage certificates 1856-60 the heading 'Residence' is substituted for 'Residence, Present, Usual', and details of any former marriage and issue and the birthplace of the parties are omitted: from 1861 onwards the information is substantially the same, the heading 'Residence' being altered to the more useful 'Usual Residence'. In the 1922 certificates the information is also similar, except that the names of the parties, in addition to their signatures, are given in full, the only information being omitted is the relationship, if any, of the bride and bridegroom.

The death certificates from 1856 to 1860 omit the deceased's place of birth and details of any marriage and its issue. From 1861 onwards the information is in effect the same, except that the burial place and the undertaker's certification are not included.

It will be seen therefore that even in these curtailed certificates the value of information is greatly superior to that given in the English certificates. These advantages may be summarized as follows: in the *Birth Certificate* (except for 1856-60) the date and place of parents' marriage; in the *Marriage Certificate* the name and maiden surname of the mother of each party, and, in the *Death Certificate*, the deceased's condition (married, single, widower, widow), his parents' names and the rank, profession or occupation of his father. There are of course occasions when columns will be marked 'unknown' or left blank, particularly in the death certificate when, for instance, the deceased died in lodgings and the lodging-house keeper did not know the names of his parents. On the whole, however, they have been completed fully, the Scottish being a conscientious race regarding ancestry.

Both the Civil Registration records and the Old Parochial Registers are at the General Register Office, New Register House, Princes Street, Edinburgh 2. There are general indexes for the whole of Scotland, year by year, for the Civil Registration. The Old Parochial Registers, apart from a few cases, are unindexed.

The Civil Registration and the Old Parochial Register can be searched at the General Register House for fees varying according to the length of time and whether in a particular register or a general search. Search days have to be successive. Under a General Search you are permitted to make notes of relevant entries. The office is open from 10 a.m. to 4 p.m., Mondays to Fridays, and library facilities are available for researchers.

Parish Registers

The old parish registers in Scotland were often badly kept and probably far more of them have been lost than in England. Sometimes all that survives seems to be a rough notebook of the parish clerk, which may have been used to copy the entries into the actual register, which has subsequently been lost. Few of the registers, except in the larger towns, start before the early eighteenth century, some far later, for example, those of Stornoway in the Isle of Lewis in the Outer Hebrides, which did not start any register until 1780.

While the Scottish registers may not compare favourably with the English ones regarding regularity and commencement, they are usually in some respects better and possibly very much better. Scottish registers in fact are far more variable than the English ones and they seem to have depended more on the whim of the parish clerk. Sometimes he was conscientious and gave a great deal of information: at other times he was careless and gave little or none.

Another disadvantage is that there were virtually no records of burials. In some parishes there are accounts for the hire of the mortcloth at funerals which gives you an approximate date of death. Some of the larger burial grounds too have records of their burials but these are not normally of an early date. There has been much progress in recent years in the copying of monumental inscriptions in church graveyards, but so often there was no stone or the old stones were used again on the other side for new inscriptions. In the latter case you can of course sometimes make out the old inscription.

These are the principal disadvantages, but now let us turn to the advantages which on the whole can compensate.

One of the great advantages in Scotland is the mention of the mother's maiden name. This was in accord with Scottish practice, when a woman was not regarded as losing her maiden name altogether on marriage. In all legal documents even today a woman will be referred to by both her maiden and married name, as, for instance, 'Mrs Mary Mackenzie or Gordon' for a Miss Mackenzie who had married a Mr Gordon. Thus the usual form for a baptism in a Scottish register is like this:

> Robert Johnston Son Lawful to Mr Daniel Johnston Surgeon in Cumnock and Mary McKie his Spouse was Baptized the 4th of Jany. 1754 years.
>
> (From the *Old Cumnock Parish Register*)

It will thus be appreciated that you discover the maiden name of the mother on finding the baptism of any of the children. Apart from the direct information it greatly aids identification, because in England with a common surname, such as 'Smith', you cannot be certain that a 'Jane , daughter of John and Mary Smith' was a sister of 'John, son of John and Mary Smith' even when in the same parish, but a daughter of a 'John

Smith and Mary Robertson, his spouse' in Scotland could be identified as a sister of a 'John Smith' of similarly described parentage in the same parish.

Another help in baptisms is the not-infrequent recording of witnesses, for these were naturally often relations. Sometimes the relationship is even mentioned and occasionally the information is extensive. This is an example from Ayr parish register, but it must be emphasized that this amount of information is rare.

> 1739. John Hamilton son lawl. to John Hamilton merch. at present in Jamaica and Mrs Margarit Montgomery his spouse was born on Wednesday the 24th of Octr. 1739 bapt: thursday the 25 of the sd month by Mr Hugh Hamilton Mintr. of the Gospell at Garvine uncle to the Child. Presented by Alexander Montgomery of Coylsfield uncle to the child in absence of the Parent. Witnesses Thomas Garvan prit. Provost of Ayr uncle in law to the Child, Mr Patrick Woodrow mintr. of the Gospell at Tarbolton.

The recording of a child of good social position, as the above, tends to be fuller than those of people in the lower social scale. But this is not always so. Here, for instance, from the same parish, is one of the sons of a coalheaver which has very valuable information.

> 1734. Mathew Hall son lawl. to Mathew Hall Coalheaver in Newton & Helen Hunter his spouse was born friday the 8th of Feby. 1734 bapt. at Supra [i.e. Ayr] witness James Hall grandfather to ye child & John Hall uncle to the child.

Named after her mothers mother

Sometimes in fact the information can be diminished through the higher social position of the parents. For instance a baptism from Maybole parish in Ayrshire merely records:

Margaret Hall procreate betwixt Mr and Mrs Hall spouses in Auchindrain was born the 12th of July 1774 and baptized said day at her father's house by the Ordinary Minister.

The father in this case was a small landowner and the fact that he is described as 'Mr' indicates that he was of some local standing, but as a result we lose the christian names of both parents, the maiden name of the mother and, probably because the baptism was carried out privately in the home, the names of the witnesses also.

While the English tended to name sons after earlier generations, the Scottish were even more conventional in this matter and this is a help to the genealogist. The eldest son is nearly always named after the father's father, and the eldest daughter after the mother's mother. The second son is usually named after the mother's father and the second daughter often after the father's mother. The third son is usually named after his father and the third daughter after her mother. Second christian names are seldom found until the nineteenth century, but from about 1800 we get second names creeping in and these were sometimes surnames from the mother's family.

Often the witnesses, if not relations, were influential friends and this may prove useful information. In the larger towns the list may be both long and impressive. Here is one from the Canongate parish of Edinburgh:

January 1701. John Hamilton of Bardanoch, Baillie of the Abbey of Hallyroodhouse and Catherine Arbuthnot alias Arbuckles his lady had a sone born upon monday ye 30 Oct 1700 and baptized upon fryday ye 10 of January 1701 Named Gerard after ye Surname of Elizabeth Dutchess of Hamiltoun: witnesses – Sir Archibald Cockburn of Lantourne, Sir John Johnstoun of Westerhall, John Cuninghame of Ba'ndalloch, Mr Gavin Johnstoun brother to Westerhall and several others.

Often the witnesses were influential friends

The father was only remotely related to the Duke of Hamilton, but the latter was hereditary Keeper of the Palace of Holyroodhouse, and John Hamilton of Bardannoch was his deputy. The duchess referred to is the wife of the famous James Douglas, fourth Duke of Hamilton, who was killed in 1712 in the duel in Hyde Park with Charles, Lord Mohun (the 'Lord Murdered' of Thackeray's *Henry Esmond*). He had married, as his second wife, Elizabeth, daughter and heiress of Digby, Lord Gerard.

It will be noticed here, in accord with Scottish practice, the Laird of Westerhall is referred to by his estate instead of his surname.

This same John Hamilton of Bardannoch's own baptism in the Edinburgh 'High Kirk' parish register in 1642 gives an idea of the information in a register of that period. It is usually, as previously mentioned, only in the larger towns that you find a register going back as far as that.

> Baptism 25 Januarii 1642 Johnne Hamiltoun of Murehouse [and] Anna Elphingstoun a S.[on] N.[amed] Johnne. Witn: Johnne Mr of Balmironoch, Mr Johnne Cokburne, Mr Johnne Elvis Advocat.

It is interesting to note in the above entry that the abbreviation for the Scottish title of 'Master' is the same as the ordinary 'Mr', which indicates that they were still at that period both pronounced 'Master'.

In Scotland the registers give only the proclamation of marriage, which is somewhat like the banns in England, and therefore it is not absolute proof that the marriage took place, though it normally did, of course. Sometimes the register will also state that it did so. Proclamations are usually recorded in both bride and bridegroom's parish and the information in one may be fuller than that in the other. As the record is of proclamation you do not get witnesses' names normally and this is a disadvantage compared with England after 1753. On the other hand, particularly in the larger parishes, the father of the bride is sometimes mentioned, though seldom the father of the bridegroom.

The following is an example from Edinburgh:

> *Marriage Proclamation.* 12 Decemr. 1794.
> Daniel Morison, Mercht. High Church parish and Margaret Montgomerie Hall, Tron kirk parish, Daughter of John Hall, Farmer at Ayr.

The following is an example from a small country town, Inch in Wigtownshire, and the corresponding entry in Ayr:

> *Inch Parish* Marriage Proclamations.
> August 19th 1797. Alexr. Kelly in this Parish and Catherine Hall in the Parish of Ayr gave their Names in Order for Proclamation of marriage

> *Ayr Parish* Marriage Proclamations
> Ayr. 26th August 1797. Quo Die Alexander Kelly in the parish of Inch and Katherine Hall in Ayr parish gave in their Names to be proclaimed in Order for marriage and After proclamation were married accordingly.

It will be noticed that the entry in Ayr, where the marriage was performed, states that they were married.

In certain circumstances a marriage might be authorized by the Elders without proclamation. This corresponds roughly to the English licence, but it was not used so frequently and in fact is rare and there was no loss of social status in being married by proclamation.

Such an event would appear in the register usually in the form below, from the registers of Kilbride, Isle of Bute.

> Under 'Marriage Proclamations'. 1729 July 30th Gerard Hamilton and Margaret Stewart were married without proclamation by appointment of Elders for certain honourable causes.

It will be noticed that the information in the marriage recordings is more uniform and regular than that of the baptisms. Its principal advantage over the English entry is that it often gives the name of the bride's father. On the other hand there are far more gaps in registers than in the English ones. Sometimes, though the register is not missing, there is a gap of twenty to thirty years in it, probably through the carelessness of the parish clerk in not bothering to make the entries. The old parochial registers in the General Register Office have now to be seen on microfilm.

The old registers are today well kept and carefully bound, but it is unfortunate that so few have been copied. The efforts of the Scottish Record Society have produced in print some half dozen or so, and these are about all that exist. The Church of the Latter Day Saints have microfilmed all the old parochial registers and have produced some microfiches of these and will eventually have microfiche available of all the Scottish registers, arranged in index form by counties, the names being in alphabetical order by counties. Scotland, being a comparatively sparsely populated country has only some nine hundred old parishes and their registers are certainly among the most valuable records of that historic and romantic country.

Census Returns

The above returns for 1841, 1851, 1861, 1871, 1881 and 1891 are held in the New Register House. Particular searches can be made by post on the official forms, provided the name of the person to be searched for and his or her full address at date of census can be given. There is a fee for a single search and a further fee for an extract. You may also make a general search but this must be carried out personally either by yourself or someone searching on your behalf. The fee for a general search varies according to the length of time.

Chapter Nineteen

SCOTTISH RECORDS II

In Scotland there are no county record offices, although a system of regional record offices is developing. The bulk of the public and many privately donated records are held in the Scottish Record Office, the address of which is P.O. Box 36, H.M. General Register House, Edinburgh EH 1 3YY. Some Sheriff Court records, which may include their own registers of deeds, were held locally, but since the establishment of the West Register House in Charlotte Square almost all of these have been transferred there, sorted, repaired when necessary and then had a repertory made of them and after that transferred to the Register House in Princes Street.

People tracing their ancestry in Scotland have several advantages over those doing so in England and Wales. One is the existence of the *Sasines Registers.* This vast register records the transfer of the ownership of land from one person to another. It is therefore possible to trace the owner of a parcel of land, even if it were only a small cottage or croft, from at any rate the early seventeenth century. These registers thus preserve the titles for the whole of the land in the kingdom.

The registers are in three parts, namely:

(i)The *Old General Register of Sasines,* 1617-1868 contained in 3,779 volumes. There are also minute books, which are kind of digests or abstracts and which are much the best way of searching the portions which are unindexed.

(ii) The *Particular Registers of Sasines* for the various counties, running parallel with the above General Register. For a brief period, 1599-1609, there is also what is known as the *Secretary's Register.*

(iii) The *New General Register,* which is kept in county divisions. This modern register had by 1928 reached 36,000 volumes and is increasing at the rate of about 500 folio volumes a year.

The Scottish Record Office is gradually indexing both the General Register and the various county particular registers. The county registers were being indexed alphabetically and have so far covered for varying periods as far as Lanarkshire, but not for all periods. If your ancestor lived in one of these counties you are lucky. The General Register has been indexed for the period 1700-1720.

From 1781 there are abridgements to the sasines, both general and particular and there are excellent indexes for both persons and places for these. The abridgements,

contd. on p. 100

PART OF A SCOTTISH SASINE OF 1697

PART OF A SCOTTISH SASINE OF 1697: William Edward and Marjorie Rattray his wife take seisin of property in Coupar Angus.

This sasine records that it was registered at Perth 23rd August 1697 and that in the presence of the Notar Public and other named witnesses there appeared personally on the ground of the land in question 'ane discreet man John Sanders ballie substitute of the regalitie of Coupar ballie in that pairt of Mr John Ogilivie ballie depute of the sd regalitie be the precept of Seisine underinsert speciallie constitute,' and also was present William Edward in Coupar for himself and on the behalf of his spouse Marjorie Rattray, and William held in his hand a disposition by the said John Ogilvie 'to and in favor of the said William Edward and Marjorie Rattray the Longest Liver of ym two in Lyfrent during all the dayes of yr Lyftyme And the aires Lawllie procreat or to be procreat betwixt them Which faylzeing the aires or assigneys of the sd William Edward Whatsomever in fie Heretablie and Irredeemablie Without any kynd of Reversione Whatsomever . . .'

It then goes on to describe that particular piece of land in detail, mentioning the other lands with which it was bounded. This often gives valuable information as it frequently shows who previously held the lands, sometimes mentioning any relationship which may have existed between the present and previous holder. In this case the lands are 'ALL AND HAILL that his tenement of land with houses biggings yeard and kiln and frie ishue and entrie yrto Lyand on the Eist syde of the toune of Coupar boundit with that croft called St Catherines Croft sometyme perteining to the deceast Agnis Halyburton and now to John Ramsay Lawll sone to the deceast George Ramsay of Gallway on the Eist and South the Lands somtyme to Alexander Campbell of Ballgershoe and now to the said William Edward on the West and the heighway that Leads from the toune of Coupar to New Calsay on the North Pairts . . .'

The Sasine later describes how William Edward and Marjorie Rattray or their 'certaine Actourney in their names' took 'reall actuall and Corporall possessione' of the property by delivering to them 'of earth and Stone of the ground of ye saids Lands', thus fulfilling the traditional requirements of the law.

PART. RE. SEIS. PERTH, SCOTTISH RECORD OFFICE

EDINBURGH

though greatly reduced in length from the original documents, give most, if not all, of the information a genealogist is likely to want, so that it is often quite unnecessary to consult the original document, though it is always advisable to do so in the case of important members of the family, as there is sometimes hidden away in the original some significant item.

The *Commissariot Records* in the Scottish Record Office contain the confirmation of wills, called in Scotland 'testaments testamentar,' and administration, called 'testaments dative'. The Commissariot of Edinburgh, like the P.C.C. in England, covered the whole country, and the inferior commissariots originally coincided with the Scottish dioceses. As indexes of all of them up to 1800 have been published by the Scottish Record Society it is far easier to discover the existence of a testament in Scotland than of a will or administration in England. Full details of these commissariots, including their jurisdiction and the dates for which testaments exist, will be found in A.J. Camp's *Wills and Their Whereabouts.*

Another valuable record is the *Retours of Service of Heirs,* usually referred to just as *Service of Heirs.* In Scotland when a landowner died his lands did not pass to his heir until the latter's claim had been established. This was done by a procedure under a Brief of Succession issued by Chancery. A jury, empanelled by the Sheriff of the County, had to decide that it was the true heir on the examination of proofs submitted to them. When the heir had proved his succession he had still to take sasine of the property. The relationship of the heir is always specified and sometimes you may get a string of generations revealed, if a distant relative succeeds to some property.

These services exist from 1544. The early services have been published in three folio volumes, well indexed. These cover the period from the earliest recorded services to 1699. From 1700 onwards there are decennial indexes, which give the relationships and often all the information required by the pedigree seeker. The Special Services relate to land and the General Services to other property. The latter are particularly valuable in that there is no sasine record to supplement it.

One of the most valuable records is the *Register of Deeds.* This contains all deeds which had a clause consenting to their registration for preservation and execution. Almost anything may be recorded in this great register and often it can contain information of the highest value to the genealogist. At the moment a great portion of it is unindexed, though the indexing is progressing steadily. The searching of the unindexed portion is a somewhat laborious and tedious process, but may nevertheless be well worth while.

Like the Sasine Register, there are three series. The first, in 621 volumes, covers from 1554-1657. The second series is subdivided into three which run parallel with each other chronologically. They are divided between the three offices of the three principal clerks, i.e.,

(i) 313 volumes in Dalrymple's office
(ii) 350 volumes in Durie's office
(iii) 296 volumes in Mackenzie's office

and these cover the period from 1661 to 1811.

The third series is the more modern series and consequently of less interest to the genealogist, though the early period of it is valuable to him. It runs from 1812 to the present day and by 1928 had already reached 5,259 volumes and is increasing at the rate of about 80 volumes a year.

The third series is numbered consecutively and is indexed in MS. There are also printed indexes of the earlier periods published by the Scottish Record Office. By 1983 the printed index had reached 1696 and at the Scottish Record Office are TS indexes for 1750-1754, a MS index book for 1765 to 1769, and from 1770 onwards annual MS indexes.

These are the principal public registers which are most likely to help the genealogist in Scotland. There are a number of other registers which may be helpful in particular cases. These are principally as under.

The *Court of Session.* Progress is being made with the indexing of this Court, and in particular there is a card index at the West Register House of the unextracted processes, comprehensively from about 1675 until 1912, with an incomplete index of early-seventeenth and some sixteenth-century entries.

The *Register of Hornings, Inhibitions and Adjudications.* The *Horning* has a quaint and curious origin. It was a legal process by which a creditor could get redress against a debtor. The latter, on refusing to obey an order of the court, i.e. to pay his just debts, was denounced as a rebel against the King by a messenger-of-arms blowing three blasts on a horn. After this the debtor's goods were held escheat to the Crown against the creditor's claim, and the debtor was liable to imprisonment. The register consists of 1,284 volumes, covering the period 1610-1902. As there is no index its consultation is a matter of time and patience, but there is a minute book from 1661.

Letters of Inhibition prevented a debtor from alienating or burdening his hereditable property to the disadvantage of the creditors. The *Bond of Interdiction* was a voluntary method of obtaining the same result. There are two series of these registers and a minute book covering the period of 1652 to 1868.

Scotland being a small country, the *Register of the Privy Council* often contains information about lesser people. Before the institution of the Court of Session in 1532 it had jurisdiction in civil and criminal cases. After that its functions were more limited, but covered appeals and seditious offences against the peace. The Register is printed in abbreviated form from 1545 to 1690 in thirty-seven well-indexed volumes, so that it is easy to consult and therefore worth doing, even though the genealogical content may not be great.

The *Accounts of the Lord High Treasurer* have been published in eleven volumes from 1473 to 1566 and are equally well indexed and therefore as easily consulted.

The *Registrum Secreto Sigilli,* or Register of the Privy Seal, has been published from 1488 to 1542 in two volumes. It covers such matters as pensions, tacks of Crown lands, commissions to minor officers of state or of court, presentations to benefices and so forth.

The *Registrum Magni Sigilli,* or Register of the Great Seal, includes all the grants of land by the Crown to subjects, the confirmation of charters by these subjects to their vassals, patents of nobility, commissions to the great officers of state, letters of pardon and remission, of legitimation, charters of incorporation and a few birth-briefs, or certificates of descent.

A volume edited by Dr Maitland Thomson includes all the early surviving charters and also William Robertson's *Index of Missing Charters* (published in 1798) with a number of additions. This covers charters from 1306 to 1424. From that date onwards the registers have been printed in 10 volumes continuing the series down to 1668 and the work is still continuing. The charters are in condensed form and are in Latin to 1652, afterwards in English. There is hardly a family of any note in Scotland which does not appear somewhere in this register.

Notaries' Protocol Books contain sasines of lands, contracts of marriage, bonds and obligations and other legal transactions of a varied character. They often contain deeds not found elsewhere. These are the books which were presented to a notary on admission to office in which he was bound to record all his official acts. They had, on his death, to be returned to the Lord Clerk Register, but unfortunately this did not always happen and many have turned up in private hands. As a notary was a local officer the names found in his protocol book are often those of people living in the district in which he practised. The Scottish Record Society has published a number of these books. Others are to be found in the Old Register House, where there is an index to them.

The *Lyon Office Records* are the official records of the Lyon King of Arms, Edinburgh, whose offices are in the New Register House, on the first floor.

The principal registers are the *Register of Genealogies* which begins in 1727 and continues to the present day, with a gap between 1796 and 1823. This register has not been used greatly, owing to the high fees for registering genealogies in it. Far more valuable is the other great register, the *Register of All Arms and Bearings in Scotland* which extends from 1672, the year of the Act requiring all persons claiming arms in Scotland to register them, until the present day. Because the cost of registering genealogies in the Register of Genealogies was expensive, people used often to include a great portion of their genealogy in their matriculation of arms and therefore, particularly in recent times, the Register of Arms is often most valuable. In Scotland it was necessary for younger sons to prove their right and to have their arms registered, or matriculated, with a difference to show that they were a cadet of the family. Although this was often not done, those conscientious members of the family who did so brought the information about the family up to date in these matriculations. There are also in the Lyon Office nine volumes of birth briefs, funeral entries and funeral escutcheons and these have been indexed and published by the Scottish Record Society.

Apart from the official records in the Lyon Office there is an extensive library there which contains much valuable material and the Lyon Office officials are very co-operative in allowing you to consult it. Here there are many printed and MS family histories and indexes. If there is any likelihood that the family you seek were armigerous a knowledge of Scottish heraldry is useful. A good book is *Scots Heraldry* (2nd ed. 1956) by a former Lyon King of Arms, the late Sir Thomas Innes of Learney, but the tracing of the existence of arms prior to 1903 can be done through Sir James Balfour Paul's *An Ordinary of Scottish Arms in the Lyon Register* published that year and its continuation from 1902 to 1973, as Volume 2 of the work by David Reid of Robertland and Vivien Wilson, published in Edinburgh in 1977. *The Scots Peerage,* edited by Balfour Paul, is often valuable, as it is very full and traces collaterals to a considerable extent. It is in nine volumes and has an excellent index.

The *Scots Magazine* (1739-1826) is roughly the equivalent north of the border to the *Gentleman's Magazine* in England. This magazine contains many notices of birth, marriage and death, and there is a MS index to it in the Lyon Office. A background of Scottish history is certainly a great asset. A short history, interestingly written, is *The Story of Scotland* by Janet Glover (1960) and a rather fuller one, in six volumes, is Agnes Muir Mackenzie's *History of Scotland.*

The Edinburgh City Library has a good reference library for Scottish material and also has its Edinburgh Room, where there is a great deal of material, including runs of Scottish newspapers, such as the *Edinburgh Courant* and the *Edinburgh Evening News,* covering the late eighteenth century and the nineteenth century. The National Library of Scotland, near St Giles', is the equivalent in Scotland to the British Library in London.

There is also the Scottish Genealogy Society, (Secretary, 21 Howard Place, Edinburgh) which publishes *The Scottish Genealogist*, a quarterly publication, and holds meetings in Edinburgh, usually monthly. The Society has a Library at 9 Union Street, Edinburgh, which is open to members on Wednesdays from 3.30 to 6.30 p.m.

The Scots Ancestry Research Council is another organization which might be consulted. Its headquarters is at 20 York Place, Edinburgh 1.

For ministers of the Church of Scotland and their families, there is the excellent *Fasti Ecclesiae Scoticanae* in seven volumes, with two supplement volumes. These contain many thousands of notices of all the ministers of the Presbyterian Church of Scotland and much information about their families. Further information about them and of ordinary church-goers may be obtained from the *Kirk Session Records*, which are either in the Scottish Record Office or still in the hands of the minister or session clerk. These may contain information on the arrival of a new member of the congregation, with a note as to the parish from which he or she came. Fuller details of these and other records will be found in the author's *In Search of Scottish Ancestry*.

Chapter Twenty

IRISH RECORDS

It is no use beating about the bush and trying to play down the appalling loss to Irish genealogists in the destruction in 1922 of the Four Courts in Dublin. This act of vandalism caused immense havoc and much of the history of Ireland was lost in the destruction of irreplaceable documents. All but a handful of the wills, both originals and bound copies, of the Prerogative Court of Armagh and of other diocesan courts were destroyed and all those Protestant church registers of baptism, marriage and burial which had been deposited there, numbering about a thousand. Such a blow to the Irish genealogist was staggering and many genealogists will not in consequence undertake genealogical research of families in Ireland. In general it needs to be said that, unless the parish registers of the locality happen to be among those surviving, because they were never sent to the Four Courts, or unless the family concerned owned property, it is not usually possible to trace Irish families.

This may sound depressing, but it is as well to realize the position before setting out, so that you are not disappointed later on. Having said this one can now turn more optimistically to examine what survives.

Possibly the very destruction of these valuable records has pricked the Irish conscience and determined them to collect and edit what is left, for a great deal has been done to collect what is called substitute material and the Irish Record Office in Dublin and the Northern Irish Record Office in Belfast have done valiant work in the last few decades in this direction. Then there already existed a great deal of material in print, for the Irish, like the Scots, took interest in their forbears.

It is useful, as always, to have a background knowledge of the history of the country, and to remember that Ireland is made up of composite elements, divided between Protestant and Catholic. There have been many waves of invaders and settlers even since Norman times, who incidently took with them a number of Welsh people. The settlement of Englishmen during Elizabeth I's reign, the 'Undertakers', is well known. They were granted large tracts of land on condition that they settled them with Protestant settlers. Then there came the settlement in Cromwell's time and after the Restoration the main Scottish Presbyterian settlement in Ulster. Among William III's forces which landed in Ireland and defeated James II's army at the Boyne, were some French Protestants, a number of whom remained in the country. Huguenots have settled in Ireland and so have Quakers, and of course there have been many minor waves of settlers throughout

Ireland's history, although in the nineteenth century one thinks of it as a country from which its people emigrated, mostly to Canada and the United States, rather than one to which people immigrated.

Returning to the surviving records, fortunately the civil registration of births, marriages and deaths was not destroyed, these records being in a building on the Quays, the Old Custom House. Unfortunately civil registration in Ireland did not start until 1864, which is later than both England and Wales, and Scotland, and it did not have the advantage that the later start in Scotland had of being far better than its predecessor when it did begin. The Irish civil registration gives only the same details which the English one gives and cannot emulate the Scottish registration. There was, however, a registration of Protestant marriages from 1845.

The registration is on a county basis, which is rather more convenient than the registration districts in England. However, like most civil registration, it would have been far more useful had it been started earlier. Most family researches even today are concerned with a period further back than the civil registration, even from the information they cull from family sources. However, sometimes a marriage taking place just after the commencement of the registration may be useful, especially a Protestant one, which may have taken place shortly after 1845 and will give you the father of the two parties.

In Ireland there were only two kinds of probates, that in the Diocesan Court and that in the Prerogative Court. In general, if all the property was in one diocese, it would be proved in the diocesan court. There were no archdeaconry courts, as in England and no peculiar courts, which made it much easier. You may be thinking this information is rather tantalizing as the wills do not exist, but it is useful to bear this information in mind, for, as mentioned above, there is a certain amount of substitute material available.

The most valuable of this material are the Betham extracts of wills, which are extracts from almost all the wills proved in the Prerogative Court of Armagh from 1536 to 1800. They consist of the genealogical information in the wills taken down by a former Ulster King of Arms. These are at the Public Record Office in Dublin and there is another set at the Genealogical Office, Dublin Castle, done out in pedigree form, with many annotations, sometimes inaccurate. There are also some abstracts of wills of a later period, covering wills throughout the whole island proved between 1829 and 1839, taken on behalf of the Tax Commissioners. There have been several lists of wills known to exist, published in the Reports of the P.R.O. in Dublin and in 1930 Father Clare produced a list of copies of wills known to exist and their whereabouts. The Reading Room at the Record Office in Dublin has also a card index of all wills or abstracts in their possession. The indexes of the probates and administrations since 1857, when, as in England, their registration was centralized, still exist and can be seen at the P.R.O. and though the wills themselves are absent, the indexes give useful information, such as the date of death, the address and names of the executors. An index of Prerogative wills from 1536 to 1810 was published by Sir Arthur Vicars and there have also been published indexes of a number of the diocesan wills.

There are also MS indexes to marriage licence bonds for some dozen dioceses, indexed under both the man's and the woman's name. Some of these have been printed, namely Cork, Ross, Cloyne, Dublin, Ferns, and Kildare, but the printed indexes only go up to 1800, whereas the MS ones cover that often valuable period up to 1857.

At Dublin Castle, in which is the former office of the Ulster King of Arms, now the office of the Chief Herald of Ireland, there are, beside the Betham extracts, which are fully indexed, the Prerogative Marriage Licences from 1630 to 1858 and the Ossory Consistory Licences from 1734 to 1808. There are also here the heraldic records of the former kingdom, the Funeral Certificates, 1588 to 1729, which show the parentage of all those whose funerals were attended by the King of Arms or his representative, their arms, their wife's name and the names of their children and the date and place of burial. This collection has never been indexed, but extracts from it have been published. Here also are the official Grant Books, containing the Grants of Arms to people in Ireland or of Irish extraction up to 1958. The amount of material here is very great and Mr Basil O'Connell has been indexing the documents for several years. The material is not normally available to the public, but a comprehensive report of a family will be prepared for a reasonable fee.

The Friends' Meeting House in Eustace Street contains all their carefully kept records for all parts of Ireland, dating back to the mid-seventeenth century. These records are all well indexed and in clear beautiful writing. There are also some hundreds of MS pedigrees of Quakers in Ireland. A volume of Quaker wills has been published, edited by Miss Eustace and a book on Quaker records is being compiled by Miss Goodbody.

The Church of Ireland Representative Body in St Stephen's Green, Dublin, has a list of the Protestant Church of Ireland registers surviving and in local custody. This list, made after 1922, is arranged by dioceses. There are some 600 of these registers. Searchers are, however, advised to make detailed enquiries as to their exact whereabouts, because, with the diminishing Protestant population and the continual amalgamation of the churches, it is often found that the registers are now in some neighbouring church to that in which they are shown to be in this list. Often the editor of Crockfords is a good person to consult as to the up-to-date information regarding these registers.

The Church of Ireland Representative Body also has some other useful MSS in its library. These include collections of Canon Leslie, who published the succession lists of many of the Irish dioceses and the MS collection of the Rev. H.B. Swanzy, which contains, among other matters, some hundreds of pedigrees of families in various parts of the country, but particularly from the North of Ireland.

The principal salvation for the Irish genealogists is the existence of the Register of Deeds. This is in Henrietta Street and contains transactions relating to the transference of ownership or tenure of all land in Ireland since 1708. There is nothing corresponding to it in England and it can be compared with that of the Register of Sasines in Scotland, though that registration goes back much further.

This Irish register is a vast one. Even up to 1832 there were some 800,000 deeds and since then they have swollen enormously. All the deeds have been transcribed into registers so that the original need not be referred to unless there is doubt as to accuracy in copying or you want to see an actual signature. These deeds often contain copies, complete or extracts, of wills when these relate to some land transference.

There are two great indexes to these deeds, one of names and the other of places. The indexes are completely alphabetical, unlike the calendars for the P.C.C. wills at Somerset House, except for a period from about 1790 to 1800, when they are only alphabetical as far as the initial letter and you have then the tedious work of looking through all the names beginning with that letter.

This Irish register is a vast one

Unfortunately the name index only includes the grantor, or person transferring the land, whether by sale or gift, and not the grantee (or new proprietor). However the topographical index will show you the succession of owners of any given property and you can thus trace when the ownership first came into the family. These indexes themselves are vast and occupy a whole wall of shelves in the building. There are probably some thousand volumes of the indexes alone.

These deeds are valuable in revealing, not only the ownership of land with all the relationships recorded, but also such documents as marriage settlements, articles of partnership, bonds, mortgages and so forth when they concerned land.

There is no charge made, either in the Public Record Office or the Register of Deeds, for people working on their own family history. A useful recent publication is the three volumes of abstracts of complete wills for the period 1708–85 which have been found among the deeds in this register edited by Miss P.B. Eustace.

There are a number of other libraries and institutes which have considerable genealogical material. The National Library is particularly wealthy in local newspapers and also files of sales notices of properties which went through the Incumbered Estates Court. These give the right by which former owners held land and its descent through the family.

The Trinity College Library has much valuable material, such as the lists of Chester Refugees. The Royal Irish Academy has a number of seventeenth-century inquisitions giving details of land transactions.

Since the establishment of the Republic, Belfast has had its own Record Office. There have been some steps taken to avoid overlapping, but inevitably there is material in Belfast referring to the Republic and vice versa. The Belfast office has an excellent card index covering the whole of one wall, mainly to typed parish registers, early lists of freeholders and tenants, tithe payments, extracts from deeds and law suits, hearth tax, musters and subsidy rolls. It is also compiling a series in photostat copies of Ulster parish registers and there are also there some original registers from Northern Ireland.

The Presbyterian Historical Society in Belfast has a fine collection of typed and indexed parish registers and other material on the Presbyterian elders and their families. The Linenhall Library in Belfast has the best collection of Irish directories, parish and family histories and printed works on Ulster history. There is also here a most valuable genealogical item, namely the MS transcript of all the births, marriages and deaths published in the *Belfast News Letter* from 1738 to 1800.

Irish newspapers in general can be of great use in view of the destruction of so many parish registers and other records. Dublin and a number of counties, Cork, Waterford, Limerick and Kilkenny, have newspapers which began their existence in the eighteenth century and which give the space to notices of birth, marriage and death. When they mention a marriage they usually mention also where it took place, so that often a good local paper will give the information which the lost register would have done.

You do not need to go to Ireland or employ a record searcher in Ireland to see many Irish newspapers. There is a good collection of them at the British Museum Newspaper Library at Colindale. In general, however, they do not begin before 1826, in which year an order was made that a copy of every Irish newspaper should be sent to the English government. A particularly useful paper was the *Hibernian Chronicle* and the Irish Genealogical Society in Great Britain has a card index of all births, marriages and deaths for long runs of it.

No searcher of Irish records should neglect the valuable abstracts made by W.H. Welply, from documents since destroyed. There are some twenty volumes in typescript of his work at the Society of Genealogists, one of three existing sets and the only one this side of the Irish Sea. One volume of the wills has been indexed by Mr Michael Leader who is also the author of two excellent articles on Irish records in the *Genealogists' Magazine* for September and December, 1958.

The number of printed works of interest to Irish genealogists is considerable. The edition of *Burke's Landed Gentry of Ireland*, published in 1958, brings many Irish families up-to-date, though one is sorry to see many others have disappeared from its pages. In 1976 Burke's *Irish Family Records* was published, covering the descents of prominent Irish families, the new title being thought more appropriate now so many landed families have had to sell their lands. This is a very large and detailed volume, which includes a number of families which have not previously appeared.

The series of volumes called *Memorials of the Dead in Ireland,* published by the Irish Memorials Association, contain many thousands of inscriptions from gravestones and other memorials. Many of them are indexed in the great slip index of the Society of Genealogists. It will therefore be seen that though searching in Irish records may be a disappointing and heartbreaking affair, yet there is more material available than may be first realized after appreciating the great losses of records which they have suffered.

Chapter Twenty-one

WELSH RECORDS

In general modern Welsh genealogy follows the pattern of English genealogy. The civil registration since 1837 is for England and Wales and the probates of Welsh wills since 1858 are recorded in the calendars at Somerset House. In earlier times, too, the Church of Wales recorded the baptisms, marriages and burials in its parish registers, though it must be remembered that nonconformity was strong in that principality. Earlier wills, too, were proved in the ecclesiastical courts, as in England. The four bishoprics of St Asaph, Bangor, Llandaff and St David's had their consistory and archdeaconry courts and there were a number of peculiars, mainly in Herefordshire and a certain amount of overlap in jurisdictions in the diocese of Chester and in Shropshire. These jurisdictions are explained and listed in A.J. Camp's *Wills and their Whereabouts*, referred to earlier, in the section on Wales. It should be noted that a large number of wills of Welsh people were proved in the Consistory Court of Chester, and these are now held with the other Welsh wills, all of which have now been moved to the National Library of Wales at Aberystwyth. Here they are being well cared for and indexes gradually compiled for those sections not adequately covered by existing ones. If unable to visit the library a letter to the librarian there will receive every attention.

Very few of the Welsh parish registers have been published and some of them have been lost or have been kept badly. But there are a certain number of MS copies, some held by the Society of Genealogists, and the Bishops' Transcripts are held at the National Library.

It is particularly valuable in dealing with Welsh pedigrees to have some knowledge of the Principality's customs and history. As with other Celtic races living in a mountainous country, racial feeling was strong and the habits of centuries not easily discarded. The Welsh, like the Scots, were noted for having a great love of heraldry and genealogy, and 'as long as a Welsh pedigree' is a well-known proverb. Unfortunately, as in Scotland, many of the old pedigrees, stretching far back, were recorded from memory and are not often able to be substantiated by documentary proof. Nevertheless a great many Welsh pedigrees have been recorded and it is interesting to note that up to 1804 as many as 7,773 of them had been registered at the College of Arms.

The Welsh people earlier on did not use surnames but used the Welsh 'ap' meaning 'son', like the Celtic 'Mac' or the Norman French 'Fitz'. This absence of surnames, together with a limited number of christian names in a family, makes tracing of lines somewhat difficult.

Another difficulty is that in these Welsh pedigrees dates are seldom mentioned and the family home not always given. Some of these pedigrees recorded descents of fantastic length and Guttun Owain in one case traces an Elizabethan landlord to 'Adam, son of God'!

One of the best known books on Welsh pedigrees is Lewis Dwnn's *Heraldic Visitation of Wales,* published in 1846, but there are a number of publications of value such as Richard Fenton's *A Tour in quest of genealogy,* 1807, and his *Historical Tour through Pembrokeshire,* 1811 (new edition 1903), and Sir Samuel Rush Meyrick's edited *Heraldic Visitation of Wales* mentioned above and his *History and antiquities of the county of Cardigan,* 1810.

The Welsh records in the Public Record Office are in the process of being transferred to the National Library of Wales. They are listed in the 1963 *Guide to the Public Record Office,* Volume I.

The earliest Welsh records date from 1277, after the subjection of the rising of Llewelyn ap Griffith. At this period the MS known as the Welsh Rolls begins and it is continued until the time when the Principality was incorporated with England. They contain a vast amount of personal detail. There are extracts from them in the B.M. Harleian MS 320 and also calendars of Welsh Rolls were printed by Sir Joseph Ayloff in 1774.

The Welsh language continued in use until comparatively recent times and is still used in the more rural parts, and there have been recent moves to revive its use. A knowledge of the language, if you are doing any extensive search in Welsh genealogy is naturally useful and it may be necessary for you to enlist the services of some Welsh genealogist who is familar not only with the language but also with the customs of the nation.

Welsh is still spoken in the more rural parts

The use of surnames became stabilized in Wales far later than in England, and not until about the turn of the sixteenth century. Thus in 1650 a man might be described as David Jones, and in 1550 his ancestor may have been designated 'David ap John ap Rhys'. While the earlier designation tells us that he was David the son of John, who was in turn the son of Rhys, there is no surname to link him to any family. On the other hand the man of 1650 is no easier to identify, for Jones was the Smith of Wales, the most common surname there. Next in order of prevalence come Williams, Davies, Thomas and Evans. You will notice that Smith does not even appear among the five most common names in Wales, as it does in England and Scotland and even in Ireland.

It is interesting how far back a name recorded in the Welsh language can take you. John Jones of Gelli Lyfdy, who was writing about 1604-08, mentions his 'Uncle Harri Wynn ap Tomas ap Rhys ap Howel ap Ifan Vychan ap Ifan ap Adda', thus recording on one short statement seven generations or some 250 years in space of time. Such record is certainly valuable, but it tells us nothing about the individuals, and does not help us much to identify them, for instance, as husbands. This in combination with a surname would have been far more valuable. The Russian system of names comes near to this, for in that, while each person has a surname, his second christian name indicates the name of his father. Thus Nicolas Borissovitch Youssoupoff we know at once was of the family of Youssoupoff and that his father was Boris Youssoupoff. His father would be called Boris Gregorovitch Youssoupoff, because he was the son of Gregory Youssoupoff and so on, each generation indicating the previous generation.

The publications of *Archaeologia Cambrensis* and of the *Transactions of the Honourable Society of Cymmrodorion* have contributed much to the study of Welsh genealogy. For those interested particularly in earlier Welsh genealogy there is an article by Major Francis Jones, Wales Herald Extraordinary, in the latter publication, being an address to the 1948 Session and published in the Transactions in 1949, entitled 'An Approach to Welsh Genealogy'.

Chapter Twenty-two

THE DOMINIONS, THE U.S.A. AND OTHER COUNTRIES

Possibly because the people in the dominions, formerly British colonies, were anxious to preserve their links with their mother country, the civil registration in general in them is much fuller than that of England and Wales and can be compared favourably with that of Scotland. A death certificate of Tasmania of the period following 1897 gives, for instance, the date and place of death, usual residence and length of residence in the Commonwealth; the name, surname and birthplace, sex, age, rank or profession, age at marriage and re-marriage, issue, living and dead, males and females, cause of death and name of medical attendant, name of the informant, with his or her signature, description and residence, where registered and the signature of the registrar. A marriage in Tasmania in 1843, on the other hand, gives only the date and place of marriage, names and surnames of bride and bridegroom, ages, rank, their signatures, the name of the clergyman, etc. performing the marriage, when registered and the signature of the registrar or officiating minister, and below, the names of the witnesses and the statement as to the rites and ceremonies under which the marriage was performed. A New Zealand certificate of death of the late nineteenth century gives, in the description of the deceased, the date and place of death, christian name, surname, rank, profession or occupation, sex, age, cause of death, duration of last illness, medical attendant certifying and when he last saw the deceased. Under the heading 'Parents' it gives the name and surname of both father and mother, the maiden surname of the mother and the rank or profession of the father. Under the heading 'If burial registered' the date and place of burial, name of minister officiating, or names of witnesses, and the religion of minister. Under 'Where born' it gives the place of birth and how long the deceased had been in New Zealand. If deceased was married the questions to which answers are required are: Where married, at what age married, to whom married, age of widow, if living. If issue living, then the ages of each sex. The final requirement is the signature of the informant, his or her description, residence and if entry a correction of a former entry, signatures of witnesses attesting the same. This is followed by the signature of the registrar and the date of registration.

Probably few if any dominion registrations equal or excel this New Zealand registration for detail, but those of Canada and South Africa are good.

Details of the information which is given in such registration can be ascertained from a useful government publication of the General Register Office, called *Abstracts of arrangements respecting registration of births, marriages and deaths in the United Kingdom and other countries of the British Commonwealth... and in the Irish Republic,* published in 1952. It includes lists of registers and records kept at Somerset House and elsewhere in England and Wales.

Many dominions have census returns of an earlier date than those surviving in England. The Society of Australian Genealogists has done much work in indexing early registration and census returns. This society publishes a journal and there is also the *Quarterly Journal of the Genealogical Society of Victoria,* which publishes articles particularly connected with that state. A series of such, called 'Tracing Ancestors and Constructing Family Trees' by C.E.S. Davies, beginning in an issue for December 1962, gives a good account of how to trace information in the state.

Two articles by Anthony P. Joseph in the *Genealogists' Magazine* for March and June 1981 on "Anglo-Australian Genealogy" are very informative and valuable.

Wills in the dominions and colonies naturally vary in their completeness. As in England in earlier times, they were at first under the church authorities and the civil registration of wills started approximately at the same time as it did in England and Wales, varying with each dominion and state. As early immigrants often still had some property in England, their wills may also be proved in the P.C.C. or, if in Scotland, in the appropriate commissariot.

The libraries in the headquarters of the High Commissioners in London of many of the dominions have much information about early immigrants.

American Ancestry

The number of people who emigrated to the United States particularly in the late eighteenth and nineteenth centuries, is far greater than most people imagine. On the other hand, if all those families who claimed to have gone over in the *Mayflower* had really done so, they would have required, not the accommodation of a small vessel of a few

contd. on p. 116

The number of people who emigrated to the United States ...

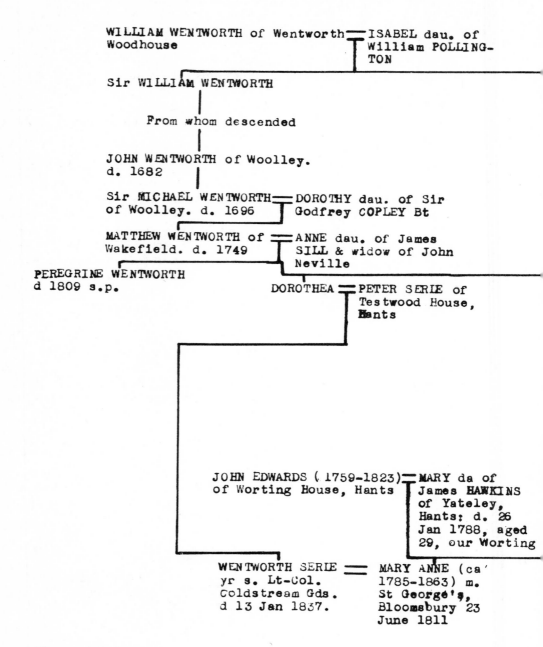

WILLIAM WENTWORTH of Wentworth━━ISABEL dau. of
Woodhouse   William POLLING-
                                      TON

Sir WILLIAM WENTWORTH

From whom descended

JOHN WENTWORTH of Woolley.
d. 1682

Sir MICHAEL WENTWORTH━━DOROTHY dau. of Sir
of Woolley. d. 1696   Godfrey COPLEY Bt

MATTHEW WENTWORTH of ━━ANNE dau. of James
Wakefield. d. 1749   SILL & widow of John
                       Neville

PEREGRINE WENTWORTH
d 1809 s.p.   DOROTHEA━━PETER SERIE of
                             Testwood House,
                             Hants

JOHN EDWARDS (1759-1823)━━MARY da of
of Worting House, Hants   James HAWKINS
                              of Yateley,
                              Hants: d. 26
                              Jan 1788, aged
                              29, our Worting

WENTWORTH SERIE ━━ MARY ANNE (ca'
yr s. Lt-Col.   1785-1863) m.
Coldstream Gds.   St George's,
d 13 Jan 1837.   Bloomsbury 23
                  June 1811

Wentworth Pedigree

This shows two branches of this family, in England and America, which still kept in touch with each other through occasional marriages.

JOHN WENTWORTH of North Elmsall

from whom descended

SAMUEL WENTWORTH of Portsmouth,
New Hampshire

JOHN WENTWORTH, Lt Governor ═══ SARAH HUNKING
of New Hampshire

```
              1770      1760
Col. MICHAEL═══MARTHA═══BENNING WENTWORTH        MARK HUNKING═══ELIZA-
WENTWORTH of   HILTON   Gov. of New Hamp-        WENTWORTH       BETH
Portsmouth,    d 1805   shire. b. 1696; d        (1709-1785)     da of
N.H. d. in N.  aged 68  1770. He m. 1st                          John
York 1795               Abigail, da of John                     RINDGE
                        Ruck.
```

```
                        THOMAS WENTWORTH═══ANNE   Sir JOHN WENTWORTH
                        of Portsmouth, N.H. TAS-  (1737-1820) last
                        d 1768              KER   royal governor of
                                                  New Hampshire.
```

```
MARTHA  ═══JOHN WENTWORTH
d. 1851    Attorney Gene-
s.p.       ral of Prince
           Edward Island
```

JOHN EDWARDS (ca. 1785-1850) ═══ MARY ANN da of T. WENTWORTH
Capt. R. Canadian Rifle Regt.   & May Ann, his wife. m. at
served in Peninsular War with   St Margaret's, Westminister
20th Lt Dragoons.   15 Aug 1820; bur Worting
                                2 Mar 1826 (She was an adopted da
                                of Martha, widow of John Wentworth
                                Attor-Gen of Pr. Edward Island)

hundred tons, but the combined resources of the *Queen Mary* and the *Queen Elizabeth*. But great numbers of people came over in later times and it is estimated that between 1770 and 1890 eleven million people crossed the Atlantic to the States from Great Britain alone. This is the estimate in *The Great Migration* by Edwin C. Guillet, published by the University of Toronto Press in 1963.

The ancestry of people who emigrated from the British Isles to the United States can vary greatly in the ease or difficulty with which it can be traced. One of the main difficulties is in discovering where in this country the immigrant came from. If that can be discovered then his ancestry in this country may be traced for a number of generations.

Had the Custom House in London not been burnt down in 1814 it might have been comparatively easy to trace an emigrant's home in England, for it was the responsibility of the local customs houses from where emigrants sailed to record certain details about them, which included their age, place of residence and trade. Unfortunately these local records were called in to London for deposit in the Custom House there in the early nineteenth century and thus were destroyed in this disastrous fire in 1814. However, it is no good crying over spilt milk and one must just make use of surviving records as much as one can.

The first task is to find out all you can about the emigrant on the United States side of the world. There are many good books on genealogy in the United States and it is not proposed to go fully into that matter in this work. But among records in the United States there may be mention of the home in Great Britain from which the migrant came and this clue can then be followed up. It is the cases where no such clue can be found that are the difficult ones. Even then, if the surname is an uncommon one it may not be so difficult. Such a book as Guppy's *Homes of Family Names* may provide the clue. Then, when the name is uncommon, it is worth while searching the P.C.C. wills for the period before and after the ancestor emigrated, as someone of the name may have proved his will in the P.C.C. and may in it mention relations in the United States. His will in any case should give his description and will no doubt reveal where he came from, or at any rate, the county. Then Boyd's Marriage Index at the Society of Genealogists and the Index of Apprenticeships there will probably reveal people of the name and indicate the locality from which they came. It depends of course on the date when the emigrant left the British Isles. Naturally it is easier to trace more recent emigrants. Those who migrated in Stuart times are already on the fringe of the time before which it is seldom possible to trace any but the more exceptional families.

It is necessary to be thinking about the historical background all the time. There is no doubt that many of those who in the time of Charles I refused to pay the forced loans emigrated to America in search of a freer life. Information about some of these may be gleaned from the Domestic State Papers in the P.R.O.

From early times until the fifth year of the reign of Charles I, the King in his own name granted licences to people to 'pass beyond the seas'. After that year the power to grant such licences was delegated to officials. Unfortunately very few of the records listing these licences have survived. Of them, those of emigrants to America have been published in Hotten's *Original List of Emigrants*. Some of these licences have also been published in *The Genealogist*. *The Dictionary of Scottish Emigrants to the U.S.A.*, 1972, ed. by Donald Whyte, is also valuable.

In the case of a common name where no clue can be discovered as to the place of origin in this country, the only thing to do is to make abstracts of all wills, both in the P.C.C. and in local courts, of people of the name for some ten or so years before and after the time when the person emigrated; in the hope that some mention may be made of the relation in the United States. It is useful to remember that during the Commonwealth period in England all the wills were registered centrally, the local courts being abolished; so that the wills of this period are an indication of the county from which people of a particular name came.

Where the surname is common, an unusual christian name may prove very valuable. This has been mentioned generally in the first chapter. The christian name pattern should be carefully examined for the generations which are known on the American side of the Atlantic, for it is likely that immigrants may have been more anxious to perpetuate christian names of ancestors in Great Britain than those were who remained in their mother country. That same tendency is also noticed in those who emigrated to the British Dominions and in both cases an unusual christian name can sometimes be as useful as a rare surname.

Other Foreign Ancestry

People sometimes come across an ancestor who is a foreigner and, regarding it as a dead end, do not pursue the matter further. There is no need for them to feel that way and it may be quite possible, and will certainly be interesting, to trace the ancestor for some generations in his own country. It will of course vary according to the country concerned, for some countries have much better records than others. But on the whole, where the records still survive, they are usually better and fuller, at any rate as far as European countries are concerned, than those of England and Wales.

If the ancestor is a fairly recent one, say of the nineteenth or late eighteenth century, the best way is to write to the Consul General of the country concerned in London (his address can be found in *Whitaker's Almanack*), giving him the details and asking him to tell you to whom you should write. He will then give you further information on the matter. There have been a number of articles on sources for genealogy in various countries in the *Genealogists' Magazine* in recent years. These are listed in the Bibliography at the end of this work. A number of countries also have genealogical societies and these may be able to help you.

The three extracts given below, one a baptism of 1841 from the then newly formed country of Belgium, the others, a marriage and a burial certificate from the Grand Duchy of Brunswick in 1829 and 1857 respectively, will give some idea of the amount of information which can be expected in some Europeans states.

Eglise Evangélique. Consistoriale Française et Allemande de Liège. Baptême.
[translation] On the 29th August 1841, at the time when the English service is celebrated in the temple, was baptized by Dr Etough, English priest, ANNA ELIZA legitimate daughter of Freelove HAMMOND, Barrister, and of Lucy *Tyeth*, his wife, living at the Château de Bomal near Marche (Luxembourg Belge,) where the child was born the 5th April 1840.
The Godfather and Godmother were: William Hammond Esq. Doctor of Medicine, living at Whitstone in Middlesex, (England) and Anna Eliza Green, living in London.

ÉGLISE ÉVANGÉLIQUE

Consistoriale

Française et Allemande

DE LIÉGE .

Baptême

L'An milhuitcent quarante un le vingt-neuf Août, à l'époque
où le service anglais se célébrait dans le temple, a été baptisée
par le Docteur Etough, prédicateur anglais: *Anna Elisa*
fille légitime de Freelowe *Hammond* Eqr, Avocat, et de
Lucy Fyeth son épouse, domiciliés au Château de Bomal près
Marche (Luxembourg belge), où l'enfant est née le cinq
Avril milhuitcent quarante. ————
Furent Parrain et Marraine: William *Hammond* Eqr, Docteur
en Médecine, demeurant à Whitstone dans le Middlesex (Angleterre)
et Anna Elisa Green, demeurant à Londres. ————

—— *Pour Extrait Conforme au Registre*
—— *le 20 février 1843.* ——

Boissard
Pasteur Président.

Baptism of 1841 of Liège in the then newly-formed country of Belgium.
(From the Author's Collection)

The other translated extracts are from a church register of Brunswick at a time when it was an independent state under the rule of the Grand Duke of Brunswick.

EXTRACT from the REGISTER of PROCLAMATIONS and MARRIAGES, of SAINT CATHERINE in BRUNSWICK

On the 4th October 1829, here in the HOUSE of SAINT CATHERINE, were married, Mr *Michael Charles Edwards,* 2nd Lieutenant in Great Britain and Lieutenant in the Service of the Grand Duke of Brunswick, son of Mr John Edwards formerly landowner in the county of Hampshire in England, and of his wife, Mrs Massey Maria, née Hawkins, their lawful son, and *Johanne Dorothea Henriette Heineking,* spinster, daughter of the late burgher and master tailor, Johann Heinrich Christian Heineking and of his surviving widow Dorothea Christiane Elizabeth, née Krämer, their lawful daughter.

EXTRACT from the REGISTER of Those Buried in SAINT CATHERINE in Brunswick.

In the year 1857, on the evening of the 26th June at 5 o'clock, Lieutenant *Michael Charles Edwards,* formerly in the Service of the Grand Duke of Brunswick, born the 30th September 1795, died of a stroke and was buried on the 30th June.

The Germans, with their love of detail, tended to be full and informative in their records of birth, marriage and burial, and the Dutch records are very good also. But the civil registration in Spain must surely be the fullest in Europe or of any country in the world.

This civil registration unfortunately was only established in 1870. Before that time people were dependent on the church registration, which was, however, very good.

The details given in the civil registration include the following information.

Birth Certificates: christian name, surname, age, place of birth, residence and profession of the person who presents the child to the Registrar and his or her relationship to the child.

Hour, date and month and year and place of birth of the child. Sex. Christian name of the child.

Christian names, surnames, places of birth, residence and profession of the parents and maternal and paternal grandparents if known and nationality if they were foreign.

Legitimacy or illegitimacy of the child if known. In the latter case the type of illegitimacy is shown except in the case of children known as 'naturales', which is a legal term for children born of unmarried parents where the paternity is admitted.

Marriage Certificates: details of the registers in which the births of both parties were recorded and the date of the entries.

Christian names and surnames, places of birth, marital state, profession and residence of the parents and of the paternal and maternal grandparents if they are known.

Legitimacy or illegitimacy of both bride and bridegroom in the latter case mentioning the type of illegitimacy unless they are 'naturales' or abandoned children.

In the cases where one of the parties cannot be present and the marriage is by proxy, details of the document by which the absent party gives authority to the proxy and the christian name, surname, age, place of birth, residence and profession of the proxy.

Dates of the publication of banns or specification of marriage in *articulo mortis* or dispensation of banns with mention of the authority concerning the same.

Statement that there is no impediment to the marriage.

Permission of parents if either party is under age.

Names of any 'natural' children who are made legitimate by the marriage.

Christian names and surnames of any previous husbands or wives of either party who are dead, with dates and places of death and registers in which the deaths were recorded.

Mention of the reading of the bride and bridegroom of the articles of the laws of marriage which they should know.

Declaration of mutual acceptance by both parties and declaration by the Church that they have been united.

Death Certificate: day, hour and place of death.

Christian name and surname, age, place of birth, profession and residence of the dead person and of his wife or her husband if the deceased were married.

Christian names and surname, residence and profession of the parents of the dead person, if known, and mention whether they are still living.

Cause of death.

Whether the deceased has left a will, and if so, the date and place and name of the lawyer who drew it up.

The cemetery in which the dead person is to be buried.

Chapter Twenty-three

VARIOUS OTHER SOURCES

Not every apprentice had to sleep under the table and not all of them were unfairly beaten or starved. Many of them in fact were kindly treated by their masters and quite a number of them married a daughter of their master. This last fact is, of course, of particular importance to genealogists. There is the story of how John Osborne, apprenticed to Sir William Howitt, saved his master's daughter when she fell from a window of their house on London Bridge, and later married her and founded the line of wealthy merchants who later became politically important and dukes of Leeds. Not all apprentices saved their master's daughters in such dramatic circumstances and founded ducal houses. But apprenticeship affected the lives of these young boys in several ways. They often moved to a new locality and afterwards stayed there.

Apprenticeship is one of the earliest forms of learning a trade or skill. The young boys were bound by indentures signed by the parents and the master to whom they were apprenticed for a term of years, usually five or seven. Apprentices lived under strict discipline and the penalties for disobeying a master or for running away were severe. Indentures of the seventeenth century enacted that 'by and dureinge all which said terme the said John Smith his said Master will and faithfully shall serve, his secrets shall keep, his Lawful Commandments every where shall gladly doe. He shall not wast the goods of his said Master nor lend them unlawfully to any person. He shall not comitt fornicacon nor contract Matrimony within the saide terme. He shall not play at any unlawful games; Taverns nor Alehouses he shall not haunt neither shall he absent himselfe by day nor by night but as a true and faithfull Servant shall behave himselfe towards his said Master as well in wordes as in deeds dureinge the said Terme'. Altogether he had to be a pretty good and well-behaved young man and if his master came across him one night 'haunting' one of his favourite alehouses, there was trouble in the wind.

These indentures were held by the master and the parents and were not registered centrally, though the City Livery Companies of London and some provincial cities and boroughs, such as Nottingham, have surviving registers of apprentices going back a long way, as also have a number of parishes of the apprentices bound by the parish. But in 1710 a tax was put on apprenticeship indentures, and this, fortunately for the genealogist, meant a central registration of all apprentices. The original registers are now in the P.R.O. and one of the most valuable collections at the Society of Genealogists is the Apprentices Index, which is a typescript index of information from the registers,

Taverns nor Alehouses he shall not haunt

covering all England and Wales between the years 1710 and 1774. For each entry is given the name of the apprentice, followed by the name of his father (or mother, if she was a widow), the name of the master, the trade to which he was apprenticed and the amount paid. Often the place of residence of the father and of the master is mentioned. The information in the years after 1760 is not so full and unfortunately often leaves out the parent's name. However, this is an extremely valuable index, as the number of boys apprenticed during that period is great and it is covering one of the difficult periods in genealogical research. Among its other uses, it often indicates the movement of a family from one locality to another.

There are, however, two classes of apprentices which are not found in this index, because they were exempt from the stamp duty. One is the parish apprentice, the poor boy or girl, perhaps an orphan, who was apprenticed by the overseers of the parish to learn a trade. The other is the apprentice paying less than a shilling fee for his indenture, in other words a nominal amount. These were often boys apprenticed to a relation, who took the boy on for a nominal amount out of kindness. It is unfortunate genealogically that this particular category should be missing.

The City of London is unique in many ways. One of these was the system of livery companies. Until the end of the eighteenth century you could not practise a trade within the city boundaries unless you were a freeman of the city. There were three ways in which you could get such freedom, namely, by patrimony, by servitude or by redemption. To become a freeman by patrimony you had to be the son of a freeman who was such at the time of your birth. Obtaining your freedom by servitude meant serving an apprenticeship in one of the livery companies. On completion of such apprenticeship you were admitted a freeman of the company and this qualified you for the freedom of the city.

After some years of service in your trade you might be admitted to the livery of the company to which you belonged and you were then known as a 'liveryman'. Obtaining your freedom by redemption meant being admitted by paying a sum of money for the privilege, but in this case you were not a member of a livery company and had none of the privileges attached to it.

Members of the livery companies were described as 'citizen and grocer', or 'citizen and draper' and so forth, according to the company to which they belonged. In earliest times this meant that they were actually occupied in the trade indicated, but even in Jacobean times it was becoming customary for people to enter some livery company merely for the honour and privilege and these people might be earning their living in quite a different way. Thus you might find a member of the Glovers Company earning his living as a butcher or as an attorney. Early on, of course, fathers put their sons' names forward for apprenticeship in their own company, just to keep the family link and there are several families which can show a long period of unbroken family connection with a particular livery company. Today sometimes sons are apprenticed to members of the company, their father's friends, a mere nominal apprenticeship, though the indentures must still be signed and properly executed. One of the conditions of such, as we have already seen, is that the apprentice shall not marry during his apprenticeship and if he should do so the young man, perhaps a recent graduate from one of the universities, must write seeking his master's forgiveness for doing so. This is, of course, readily given and usually a dinner party is thrown in to celebrate the occasion.

If it is known that an ancestor was a member of a particular city livery company, then the records of that company may give valuable information about his parentage and other details of his career. You should write to the clerk of the company concerned, whose address can be found in *Whitaker's Almanack*. But if you do not know that he belonged to any company but know that he was a freeman of the city (and he probably was if he was practising a trade there), then you should apply to the City Chamberlain, in whose office are kept the registers of freemen. For a small fee he will have them searched for you for a period of five years and then, if an entry is found, further details will be supplied for a small additional fee. The City Chamberlain's office is in Gresham Street, near the Guildhall.

The matriculation registers of the universities have already been mentioned. Another large and growing class of record is that of the registers of public and other schools. Some of these go back a long way and are well produced. An example of an excellent school register is that of Westminster. Eton, strange to say, has a poor one. The best of these registers give useful information about the parentage and also about the subsequent career of the pupil. This source is not confined to public schools. There are many lesser-known schools, such as Bury St Edmunds Grammar School, which have had excellent registers published. Apart from published registers, if it is known that a boy went to a certain school, enquiry there may produce much information from MS sources there and if the school is contemplating publishing a register sometime it may be glad of any additional information you can give them of individuals who were there.

Sometimes in a will a reference may be found to some insurance company policy, or an old policy may be found among family papers. This can lead to useful information. In early times when someone wanted to take out a life insurance policy, the companies did not have medical examinations, but relied on information about other members of the family. Thus old proposal forms often contained replies to questions as to the names of parents, brothers and sisters, their ages if still living or if dead, their age at death. This might have to be supported by documentary evidence or may have been checked against such evidence. Unfortunately many of the old insurance companies have destroyed their earlier records or sent them for pulping during the drive for paper in the last war. Some, however, have kept them, or at any rate their early registers. The latter, though not nearly so valuable as the proposal forms, will tell you the date at which a policy was taken out and will give the address of the person then and possibly other information.

Other possible sources of information about people are the records of banks. Many private banks, which flourished particularly in the eighteenth and early nineteenth centuries, have now disappeared, but this is usually through being taken over by one of the bigger banks and it is not too difficult to trace what has happened to a particular bank. Their records may be carefully preserved, and these may give valuable clues as to their clients, their movements and perhaps their financial position. Sons frequently went to the same bank as their fathers, often being introduced when twenty-one, with a present of five pounds to start them off. Present-day information from banking accounts, is of course, confidential, but banks would probably be willing to reveal information in their books of, perhaps, a hundred and fifty years ago.

Another interesting and little realized source of information is contained in the tontine ledgers and papers at the P.R.O. A tontine is a form of annuity in which each subscriber invests money and the interest from it is shared by the subscribers during their lifetime, or by the subscriber's nominee during his or her lifetime. As the nominees die the share drawn by the surviving nominees increases, until eventually one nominee is drawing the total interest. The British government organized three main series of life annuities and tontines on this basis during the eighteenth century. The first series were the three life annuities of 1745, 1746 and 1757. The second series were the three further life annuities of 1766, 1778 and 1779 and the tontine of 1789. The third series were the three Irish tontines of 1774, 1775 and 1777. These records belong to the National Debt Office records and are designated NDO 1, NDO 2 and NDO 3 respectively. The information in the annuity records is not as useful genealogically as that in the tontine. The latter give, among other details, the following information: Name of the subscriber, his address, name of nominee (usually a young child), the names of his parents, the age of the nominee, the date when the nominee died or was buried, the names of the executors, administrators and assigns, and the volume and folio where the will or assignment may be found, the names of attorneys and the reference for the powers of attorney. When it is remembered that the number of subscribers, mainly middle class, for the English tontine of 1789 was 8,349, the extent of this source can be estimated. Francis Leeson's Guide to the *Records of British State Tontines and Life Annuities of the 17th and 18th centuries* (Pinhorn Handbook No 3, 1968) gives detailed information on these valuable records in the Public Record Office.

You will notice in Appendix A, one of the questions in the suggested questionnaire for sending to members of the family inquiries about any old receipt books which may survive in the family. This enquiry may sound more culinary than genealogical, but the information old receipt books can reveal is sometimes quite surprising. In the days before cooking had achieved its commercial glorification, receipts were handed down as valued knowledge in families, and the special receipts were frequently named after their

An excellent Pudding . Mrs Lloyds receipt

3/4 lb of flour 3/4 lb of Suet 3/4 lb of figs 3/4 lb of currants
2 oz of citron 6 eggs leaving out the whites of 3 a wine glass
of Brandy and to be boiled 6 hours.

Mrs Thomas of Dicketts receipt for furniture paste
1 ounce of White Wax 1 do of Yellow 1 Do of White Soap
1 Pint of Water to be boiled till reduced to half a pint.

Mrs Tyeths Sponge Cake

The weight of Six eggs in Sugar, the weight of four in flour,
the yolks of them well beaten and mix'd with the Sugar —
and the whites beaten to a froth, and added after all.

Baked in a Slack Oven.

Cushions.

2 lbs of Moist Sugar 1/2 pint of water 6 drops of Lemon.

to be boiled till it will not stick to a bit of pipe diped in cold water
to be cooled on a marble slab greased with butter.

Mrs Costers plain Cake

4 1/2 of flour 1/2 butter one lb will do 3 lbs of fruit half a pint of yeast
set with raw Milk and baked 1 hour and half a little nutmeg may

Entries in the receipt book of the early 19th century in the author's possession.

exponents, who were often members of the family, or else close friends. An old receipt book of the early nineteenth century which I am fortunate enough to have, reveals, for instance, the wholesome ingredients of 'Mrs Tyeth's plain cake', 'An Excellent Pudding' in accordance with Mrs Lloyd's receipt, 'Mrs Thomas of Dickett's receipt for furniture paste', 'Mrs Coster's plain Cake'. Mrs Coster was my great-grandmother, and Mrs Tyeth her mother, while Mrs Lloyd was the former's elder sister. Mrs Thomas of Dickett's was a friend, in fact nearly all the people who had conferred their name on some priceless receipt were relations or friends. It will be thus appreciated that among all these culinary plums there were many genealogical clues.

A Clue to French Ancestry

On one occasion, when giving a talk to the Birmingham and Midland Society for Genealogy and Heraldry, after mentioning the genealogical clues which might be contained in old family recipe books, one of the members told me that her family had always folded their pastry in a particular way and other people had remarked on how unusual was this way of doing it. It was only when she went to France and was staying with a French family that she noticed that they folded their pastry in the same way as her own family did. The member asked me whether I thought this was an indication that the family had French ancestry somewhere further back. I replied that I considered that it was quite likely. This was the kind of way of doing something which would have been carried on in the family for generations. Of course earlier members of that family might have been staying in France and noticed that French people folded their pastry this way, but it would have been less likely they would have adopted this way themselves if they were already doing it in the English way. A marriage with a French woman further back in the family pedigree would be more likely to have introduced this culinary custom. She would have passed it on to her daughters and daughters-in-law and in this way it could quite well have come down in the family for some generations.

Continuation of House Names

Another interesting clue is the house name. Even from ancient Greek and Roman times the custom of passing on the name of the family home to later homes held by the later generations existed.

This custom was certainly prevalent in England, and if you discover a family of the same name living in a house with an unusual and similar name to your own family home, this may be a clue that should be followed up. I myself have come across many instances of this custom. A branch of the Croker family in Ireland had an estate named Ballynaguarde, which was reowned for its great beauty. When one of the Crokers was dying he was visited by his minister, who tried to comfort him by saying to him, "You are going to a place which is even more beautiful than Ballynaguarde". The dying Croker roused himself to say, "I doubt it".

A descendant of this Croker, Crofton Croker, a colonel in the Royal Army Service Corps, who served in World Wars I and II, named his house at Barton-on-Sea, Hampshire, "Ballynaguarde". Another Croker, Henry Croker, a major in the army, who was born in 1758, married Harriet, only daughter and heir of Arthur Dillon of Quartertown, Co. Cork, and in this way Quartertown came into the family. His descendant, Engineer-Captain George Fitzgerald Croker, who served in World Wars I

IDENTIFICATION BY SIGNATURE

1. James Irons' signature of 4 November 1685.

2. James Irons' signature of 7 March 1691.

(Reproduced with the approval of the Keeper of the Records of Scotland)
[Scottish Record Office, ref. Register of Deeds 1686 DUR LXV 5 and 1694 MACK LXXIV 1081]

and II, retired and named his house in the Avenue, Fareham, Hants., "Quartertown". Furthermore Brigadier William Pennefather Croker, a brother of Engineer-Captain Croker, who also served in both World Wars, named his house "Lynham" at Barton-on-Sea, New Milton, Hampshire, because this Irish Croker family was a branch of the Crokers (or Crockers) of Lynham, Devon.

Another instance was of a family called Conry which went out to South Africa in the nineteenth century and was settled at a farm called Spestos. A descendant returned to live in England at Bow in Devon and named his house "Spestos Grange", and his grandson, a Brigadier in the Indian Army, John de Lisle Conry, when he retired, built a house at Yelverton in Devon which he named Spestos. John Harris of the Inland Revenue Service was born in the parish of Coldridge, Devon, in a district called Woodhayes and in consequence named his house at Ivybridge, Devon, "Woodhayes". Even a name like "Ivybank" can be passed on. Daniel Morison, Controller of Customs in Glasgow, lived in his retirement at Ivybank, Rothesay, Isle of Bute. His third son Kenneth Lockwood Morison, named his house at Formby, Lancs., "Ivybank".

Identification by Signature

In the eighteenth century, when education was not so widespread as today, even the upper classes had sometimes only a scanty schooling. Some country squires were educated and cultured men, but others, like the bluff and irascible Squire Western in Fielding's *Tom Jones*, had little use for learning and some of these were quite pleased that they could write their own name and sign documents, as they were occasionally required to do.

Sometimes signatures on documents are the only means of identifying people. The two signatures of James Irons in the accompanying illustration identify the two signatures as having been made by the same person. The upper one is signed on 4 November 1685 and the lower one on 7 March 1691. I am sure it will be agreed that this distinctive signature is of the same person. In the first document he is described as "James Irons in Bridgend of Lentrathen" and in the second one as "James Irons in Coupir Grange". One knows that in 1685 he was living in Lentrathen but in 1691 he had moved to Coupar Grange. This was useful information in the pattern of the life of the family, for James Irons' having moved to Coupar Grange near Coupar Angus indicated how his daughter Margaret came to meet George Edward, a merchant of Coupar Angus, and later to marry him.

Chapter Twenty-four

PLACES OF SEARCH

I. The Society of Genealogists

The library at the Society of Genealogists at 37 Harrington Gardens, London, S.W. 7, near Gloucester Road Underground Station, is unique in having the best collection of printed books and MSS on genealogy in the British Isles. As far as the printed books are concerned, it is probably true that most of them are in such national libraries as the British Library, the Bodleian Library and Cambridge University Library, but in all these libraries it is necessary to apply for each book and then wait for its delivery, which can take as long as half an hour or more. At the Society you have the inestimable advantage of finding these books all on open access shelves. So often in genealogy you only want to look at a book for a matter of seconds, to glimpse in the index or at the chapter headings to see if it is at all likely to have information you want.

The library has arrangements for allowing occasional searchers to use it on payment of a half-day or full-day fee, but if you are likely to use it more than a few times it more than pays you to join the Society, for in addition to being able to use the library whenever you want to, you have other advantages, such as being able to get the magazine at the members' rate and being kept in touch with developments in genealogy by attending the annual general meeting and lectures. You are also allowed to borrow certain books from the library, where there are duplicates for loan.

The library is arranged in a series of rooms, named after former presidents of the society, and some indication as to the contents of these may be the best way of giving you an idea of the material available.

The Mountbatten Room on the ground floor is the Members' Room, where you can obtain tea and coffee from machines. In this room are books and MSS bound records recently added to the library.

The Farrer Room, on the ground floor, facing you as you come into the hall, contains the catalogue card indexes, the index of family histories, of which the society has probably the best collection in England, including many privately printed which are not in the national libraries and many in pamphlet form. Then there is the index of parish register transcripts, and other material relating to, and arranged under, counties. At the east end of this room are shelves containing books on religious denominations, clergy lists, and also a number of runs of genealogical magazines, such as *Miscellanea Genealogica et Heraldica, the Ancestor,* and the *Genealogist.* There is naturally also here a complete set of the Society's own periodical, *The Genealogists' Magazine,* which, with its indexes, is invaluable for searching out a wealth of information which has been contributed to it over the years. There are also the various genealogists' guides, such as the invaluable *Genealogist's Guide* (1903 repr. 1967) by G.W. Marshall, its sequel *A Genealogical Guide* (1953) by J.B. Whitmore, and a further sequel by Geoffrey B. Barrow, *The Genealogist's Guide* (1977); also the more recent American publication by Smith and Gardner in three volumes *Genealogical Research in Great Britain*. Then there are the Society's own two publications, which are complementary to one another, *A Catalogue of Parish Register Copies in the Society of Genealogists* and the *National Index of Parish Register Copies* which contains those registers of which copies are known to exist outside the Society of Genealogists, and also all the volumes so far published in the National Index of Parish Registers.

Here also are a fine set of Army Lists, going back to the mid-eighteenth century, though unfortunately there are a number of gaps; and a good set of the Navy Lists covering the same periods; a collection of regimental histories; collective naval biographies, such as Marshall's *Royal Naval Biography,* to the names in the 12 volumes of which there is a useful MS index, and O'Byrne's *Naval Biographical Dictionary.*

The remainder of the room is in general given over to books, arranged by counties from Hampshire to Yorkshire and also sections for Scotland, Ireland and Wales. (The earlier counties from Bedfordshire to Gloucestershire are in the Raglan Room on the first floor.)

Also in Room Farrer on the ground floor are the printed Phillimore's *Marriages* and the Trinity House Petitions dating from 1700 to 1854. There are also here the published matriculation registers of Oxford, Cambridge and other universities, and school registers. Works on Wales, Scotland and Ireland and places abroad are in other rooms. On the Farrer shelves, besides printed books there are MS copies of parish registers and of monumental inscriptions (referred to as M.I.'s). The larger county histories, such as the folio volumes of Bigland's *Gloucestershire,* which are too large to arrange with their counties, are at the east end of the room.

Upstairs on the first floor are two rooms, Raglan and Tweeddale. Raglan, the south room, contains books on London, including a good collection of directories going back to the mid-eighteenth century. In this room also are two TS collections which are among the most valuable the Society possesses. One is Boyd's Marriage Index, which is a very large TS index of marriages from many parishes. Many are arranged by counties, though unfortunately many counties have not been covered. For those that have been the index is of great assistance, for it includes many of the printed and MS copies of registers up to the time the index was made (1925-1955). They are arranged in twenty-five-year groups, from the earliest times up to 1837. There are also a great many miscellaneous volumes, which contain various parishes and in some cases marriage licences and extracts from such publications as the *Gentleman's Magazine.*

The second great collection in this room is the *Apprentices Index*, to which reference has already been made in Chapter 23. It covers the period 1710 to 1774 and the preface to Volume I gives details of the abbreviations and the system followed.

There are here also records of the City Livery Companies and of admissions to the Inns of Court. Raglan also contains sections on Wills and Marriage Licences.

The Tweeddale Room is devoted to the MS collections. Individual pedigrees and information on families are arranged in boxes in alphabetical order on the shelves. These may produce for you, if you are lucky, a ready-made pedigree of the family you are seeking. There are also boxes in the Tweeddale Room Annexe containing information about localities and these too should be consulted for background information about the places where your ancestors lived, which is often so valuable.

In 1981 the Society obtained the use of three further rooms on the second floor. The Document Collection by Places, the Macleod Collection (rich in Scottish material) and the county periodicals are now here.

In 1977 the Society acquired the Index to some 25 million extracts, mainly of baptisms, and also a considerable number of marriages in the British Isles 1538-1875 compiled by the Genealogical Society of Utah and known as the *Computer File Index*. These are recorded on microfiche, arranged in counties and can be read on the viewers in the Tweeddale Annexe on the first floor landing.

The bookcases on the large first floor landing contain various editions of *Burke's Peerage* and *Landed Gentry, Walford's County Families, the G.E.C. Complete Peerage* and also the Society's books on heraldry, including the Crouch Collection of bookplates.

The Basement

Here are located Room Stamp and a number of other rooms.

The Stamp Room mainly houses the many family histories. Reference has already been made to Thomson's index of printed family histories. Many of these are here, together with a number of others, some mimeographed from typewriting or in MS. There is in the society an annotated copy of Thomson's index, which has additions of family histories published since the last edition of the work. In this room are also a number of important MS collections. In a cupboard on the east wall are the Williams MSS, which relate particularly to Welsh families, and the Smith MSS, containing extensions of many visitation pedigrees and also rich in families connected with the West Indies. The great slip index contains the index to this collection. There are also down here a number of *Royal Calendars* and similar publications, which, rather like an early form of *Whitaker's Almanack,* contain lists of officials and of officers in the Army, Navy and civilian life.

In another of the rooms is the *Great Card Index.* This has been built up through the industry of members of the society over the years. Though now not added to, it contains some three million slips of a miscellaneous kind, sorted under surnames and sub-divided into christian names and possibly then by periods. In general it contains extracts from parish registers, indexes to collections like the Smith MS collection, to marriage licences, chancery proceedings and so forth. As it is easy to consult it is always worth while doing so, as it is surprising what clues it may unexpectedly produce.

There are a number of very useful smaller collections. There is, for instance, the slip index collection of the late J.R.M. Glencross, which is particularly rich in material on Devon and Cornwall. There is a slip index made by the late C.W. Winstanley of wills proved in the P.C.C. from 1720 to 1725, a most useful period. Mr Winstanley's splendid personal achievement is now being followed by the society and through the efforts of a number of hard-working volunteers there is now an index in exact alphabetical order of the P.C.C. wills from 1750 to 1800 which will be searched by the staff for a small fee.

The *Fawcett Index*, a card index, is much concerned with clergy and also with Durham and the north of England.

Outside in the passage are runs of the *Gentleman's Magazine,* the *London Magazine* and the *Scots Magazine* and the small room at the end of this passage contains a microfilm reader and also a small section of law and medical directories and lists.

At the end of the south passage, opposite the room containing the Great Card Index, is a small room with sections on the U.S.A., Australia, Canada, New Zealand, South Africa and India, with a small section on the West Indies, Channel Islands and some foreign countries. This section of the library is, however, a small one and there is probably more material to be found, for instance, in the library at Australia House and in similar Commonwealth libraries in London.

Apart from the more direct advantages of belonging to the society one must not overlook such facilities as the members' room, where there are copies of genealogical and allied subject periodicals from all over the world and where at four o'clock on most days you can get a cup of tea and cake or biscuit. There is nothing like such refreshment after an arduous and perhaps frustrating search, especially when one meets other enthusiasts who will sympathize with you, probably help you and surely stimulate you in your efforts. Here you may meet many members with years of experience whose combined wisdom and knowledge is quite extraordinary and who, like Private Willis in *Iolanthe*, 'think of things that would astonish you'.

whose combined wisdom and knowledge is quite extraordinary

Chapter Twenty-five

PLACES OF SEARCH

II The Public Record Office

The Public Record Office was established in Chancery Lane in 1851 to house all the National Records of England and Wales, which before that were scattered in a number of depositories, such as the Tower of London, the Admiralty, War Office and Somerset House.

The present Public Record Office is divided into three depositories. There is the original building in Chancery Lane, where now the legal records are kept and also the Prerogative Court of Canterbury wills, their inventories, when they survive, and the administrations, all prior to 1858. After that date wills and administrations are held at Somerset House. Then there is the Census Room in the Land Registry Building in Portugal Street not far from Chancery Lane, and the third and most recent addition is the Record Office in Ruskin Avenue, Kew, Richmond, Surrey, to which the nearest station on the District Railway is Kew Gardens. Here are kept the State Papers and Departmental Records, such as of the Admiralty, Ministry of Agriculture, Colonial Office, Foreign Office, Home Office, India Office, Office of Land Revenue Records and Enrolments, Paymaster General's Office, Board of Trade, Treasury and War Office. Detailed information about the contents of the various offices is contained in the *Guide to the Contents of the Public Record Office*, published in three volumes. The first two volumes, published in 1963, are a revision and extension to 1960 of the guide by the late M.S. Guiseppi, and volume three covers documents transferred 1960-1966 and was published in 1968.

Many records of particular value to genealogists are here. One tends to be overwhelmed with the quantity of these records, but a particularly useful and helpful book is *Tracing your Ancestors in the Public Record Office*, by Jane Cox and Timothy Padfield, 1981. This explains clearly the various groups of records of value to those seeking their family history and gives the Public Record Office reference to them.

Many Public Libraries have the Lists and Indexes which give more detailed information of certain sections in the Public Record Office, and the useful pamphlets on certain sections and subjects issued by the P.R.O. have been mentioned in this book in chapters dealing with specific aspects. In general, government departments hand over their records to this depository after a hundred years, but in some cases they do so earlier. Therefore records of a hundred years ago and backwards are available to searchers. It is, of course necessary to obtain a permit to search here, but that is not a difficult matter if you can show you are engaged in original research, which genealogical work usually is.

When in doubt how to proceed with your search it is advisable to get guidance from one of the officials at the Record Office, who are very helpful. You cannot, of course, expect them to do more than indicate the useful sources, as they have their time taken up in many directions. The Record Office staff will, however, answer by post a small inquiry not entailing a great deal of research and this is useful for someone living at a distance from London. If the subject entails a longer search, they will send you a list of searchers who work there on such matters. Many of these are experts, but genealogy is such a specialized study that it is often better to find out the name of one who has had experience particularly in genealogical work, or to employ someone you know to be a reputable genealogist.

The officials at the Record Office who are very helpful

Among the great sources here for genealogists are the census returns of 1841, 1851 and 1861, now in the Public Record Office Census Annexe in Portugal Street (south of Lincoln's Inn Fields). These are available to be seen on microfilm. Some of the towns are indexed by streets so that you can find in which volume the person you seek will be. With villages and smaller towns there is usually no index, which entails searching through the whole population, but this is not such an overwhelming task as it sounds. The details you will get out of these census returns have already been explained in Chapter 4. The beginning of each enumerator's book indicates the area covered and this will often mention the particular street or square for which you are searching. It is always advisable to consult a good map of the area to see where the different parts of the town or village lie.

The Admiralty and War Office records are at Kew. On the shelves there will be found the lists of these records. There are some useful MS lists, such as the lists of returns of army officers' services for 1828 and 1829. There is also a most useful calendar of extracted information of parentage from the baptismal certificates in the Lieutenants' Passing Certificates for the Royal Navy. This has been more fully mentioned in the chapter on naval ancestry.

Chancery proceedings can reveal considerable information about families. Some further information about them will be found in Chapter 29.

Home Office records may reveal details of naturalization (but see also publications of Denization and Naturalization of Aliens in England, 1509-1800 by the Huguenot Society) and, for people who have served in the Home Office, there may be records of service, which give useful information about the individual.

The Army records come under War Office Records at Kew. There is there an almost complete set of Army Lists and it is a convenient place to consult them. There is also a very useful card index to officers' marriages. Some of the officials in this room are specialists in military records and can be very helpful to you with their suggestions. It was through one of them, while the records were still in Chancery Lane, that I was first introduced to the Commander-in-Chief's Memoranda papers, which proved so valuable a source to me about officers' first commissions and promotion.

Chapter Twenty-six

PLACES OF SEARCH

III. The British Museum and other Libraries

The Library partly in the British Museum, now known as the British Library, in that part still in the museum is one of the most fascinating places in the world. The number and variety of characters who use and have used it is so great and so interesting that it is a study in itself. One sees every nationality under the sun, young men carrying their books in carpenters' bags, affecting the *ouvrier* style, men in skull caps who appear to spend much time sleeping, tall gaunt impressive statesmanlike men and small insignificant quiet scared creatures who may be among the most brilliant of the population. Apart from one's purpose in going there it is an experience in itself.

Here again it is necessary to satisfy the authorities that you are engaged in research which cannot be carried out easily elsewhere and you will then be provided with a ticket which you must show to get past the guard at the doorway.

You will quickly find that a large section of the round room is devoted to genealogical works, because a large number of people who use the library are engaged in such work. Until you begin to work in this field you do not realize how many other people are interested in it.

On the shelves in the Reading Room you will find such sets as the *Gentleman's Magazine, Scots Magazine, London Magazine* and so forth, and this is one of the best places to consult them, as even the Society of Genealogists has not, for instance, a complete set of the *Gentleman's Magazine* and in the museum library they are well bound and easily get-at-able. You will find also on the shelves volumes of the *Victoria County Histories* and other county histories, such series as the *Rolls Series*, and the publications of the various learned societies. In the centre is the catalogue, which, as already mentioned, should be consulted to see if any family history or pedigree of the family exists already. Also it may reveal details of any member of the family who may have written a book or pamphlet at some time or other. Around these centre shelves also will be found the decennial indexes to the Scottish Service of Heirs, mentioned in the chapters on Scottish records.

Other books must be applied for, and take from half an hour to an hour to come to your seat. The library has also good collections of early newspapers, such as the *Burney Collection* (see Chapter 10), which are in this building, as also is a complete set of *The Times*. But other newspapers are out at the Newspaper Library at Colindale.

The MS Department of the British Museum is also in this building and is very large. It is necessary to get a separate ticket to use it, but this can be done quite easily. Apart from many heraldic and family papers, diaries and so forth, there are such original MSS as the returns made for O'Byrne's *Naval Biographical Dictionary*, which as mentioned in Chapter 13 often contain far more information than the published dictionary itself.

The map room here is another asset. Here you can track down the map of your district nearest to the date you want and apart from the enormous collection of maps made by individuals throughout history, there are the complete sets of the earliest Ordnance Survey maps, the six inch and the twenty-five inch to the mile scales being especially valuable. There are also tithe redemption maps, which give much detail of an earlier period.

The Department of Prints and Drawings may also have useful genealogical material. There is, for instance, the Franks Collection of Bookplates. Of these there are indexes published which you can see in most large reference libraries. Similarly the index to engraved portraits may sometimes be useful if you have an ancestor sufficiently prominent to have been painted by some well-known portrait painter, which may also have been engraved.

Guildhall Library

Probably the library of next greatest importance to the genealogist in London is that of the Corporation of London, the Guildhall Library. This great and efficiently run library has probably most of the books a genealogist will normally require and it has one great advantage over the British Library and that is that any book you apply for will be brought to you within a matter of minutes, so that it cuts out those half-hours of waiting at the British Library. On the other hand, a disadvantage is that there are far fewer books on open access here. The resources of the library are, however, freely available to the public without any formality such as obtaining a ticket and persons to recommend you. It is not, of course, a lending library.

The library was established to provide material to illustrate the development and history of London and naturally it is very rich in London material, and because London is the capital of England and the centre of its trade, all the main source books of English history are also here. There is an extensive commercial library and other fields are also covered selectively, so that here you have all the material of a general kind you would expect to find in a large reference library, besides the particular and extensive special fields. There are, however, some fields excluded, such as modern fiction, poetry and drama, but this is not likely to perturb the genealogist.

The London collection, the most extensive anywhere, comprises printed books, manuscripts, prints, drawings and maps. Although the emphasis is on the city itself, the county area is also covered to a considerable extent, and to a lesser extent the suburbs outside the GLC boundaries.

The manuscript collection includes many of the original parish registers of the city churches, which have been deposited here and are therefore easily consulted. The Harleian Society has published a great many of these city parish registers, but there are many more here which are so far unpublished and of which no MS copies exist. There are also here the wills and administrations of the Archdeaconry of London and the Bishop of London's Commissary Court up to 1858. There are many deposited MSS of the city guilds and the wards. Among these records of great use to genealogists are the registers of the Society of Apothecaries. As has been explained in the chapter including the records of doctors, many medical men got their qualification by becoming a Licentiate of the Society of Apothecaries.

It should be noted that the City of London's municipal archives, that is the record of their day-to-day activities, are not kept here, but in the Corporation's Record Office nearby.

The Guildhall Library has the best collection of London directories anywhere and it also has a very fine collection of directories of towns and other counties.

University of London Library

The library of the University of London, which is housed in the tower of the Senate House in Bloomsbury, has a large section specializing in bibliography. It also has one of the best biographical libraries, including all the corrections and additions to the *Dictionary of National Biography* which have been contributed to the *Bulletin of the Institute of Historical Research* in the special section of it devoted to such corrections and additions. These are kept in alphabetical order and can therefore easily be consulted. There are here a good collection of collective biographies, such as Boase's *Modern English Biography* which is less often come across in reference libraries.

The public libraries of the various London boroughs combine to cover the publication of all books, each library being allotted a section of the Dewey Classification and undertaking to purchase all books published in that section. In this way it is made certain that some public library in London has a copy of any book published.

Royal Borough of Kensington Library

The library which covers the section of the Dewey Classification dealing with genealogy and heraldry, namely Class 929, is the Kensington Borough Library. It had already specialized to a great extent in this field and in the new large reference library in its building off Kensington High Street you will find a very comprehensive collection of books on the subject. There are, for instance, on the open shelves all the editions of Burke's *Landed Gentry*, including the 1847-52 second edition, with the useful index of names. There are also good runs of *Burke's Peerage* and of genealogical publications of the past and present.

Other Specialist Libraries

The library of the College of Arms, with its extensive collection of genealogical and heraldic books and MSS will be dealt with in the chapter on *Genealogy and Heraldry*. The library is not, however, open to the public.

Various libraries specializing in particular aspects of genealogy, such as the Minet Library with its Huguenot collection, have been mentioned under the chapter dealing with such records.

While the majority of specialized libraries tend to be in London, there are some in the provinces which have good genealogical collections. Manchester Public Library specializes in published family histories and its published catalogue of this section is well worth consulting. Queen's College, Oxford, has a fine collection of genealogical MSS given to the college by Sir Joseph Williamson, but the collection relates almost entirely to seventeenth and earlier centuries. Gonville and Caius College, Cambridge, has also a good genealogical collection of MSS. A number of depositories and other places where genealogical MSS may be found are mentioned in Richard Sims' *Manual for the Genealogist, Topographer, Antiquary and Legal Professor*, but, as this useful book was published in 1856 much of the information in it is out-of-date, not in the detailed information given but in the places where the sources and records are to be found. For north country genealogical records an important depository is the Borthwick Institute, York.

The Institute came into existence in 1939 through the desire of Archbishop Temple for the provision of some means by which the York Diocesan archives might be made accessible for scholars and students. After the 1939-1945 war the fifteenth-century guild-hall known as St Anthony's Hall became available and was gratefully accepted by the City Civic Trust for transformation into a record repository. The Pilgrim Trust generously assisted financially with the cost of the conversion of the building.

Later the Institute benefited greatly under the will of William Borthwick of Bridlington and in consequence was given the name of the Borthwick Institute of Historical Research. It was opened in 1953 and since 1963 has become part of the University of York.

Its main object is to encourage and further research into ecclesiastical institutions within the Northern Province of York. Their records are also of interest to researchers in local, economic, social and family history.

The collection is mainly of the archives of the archdiocese of York, covering the mediaeval five archdeaconries of York, East Riding, Cleveland, Richmond and Nottingham.

The huge archdeaconry of Richmond, covering large tracts of Lancashire, Cumberland and Westmorland was in 1541 transferred to the newly-created diocese of Chester, and the archdeaconry of Nottingham in 1837 became part of the diocese of Lincoln.

There are several millions of documents at the Institute. A large proportion of these are of interest to genealogical researchers. They comprise about 75% of the parish records in the archdeaconry of York.

More details of these records will be found in the *Guide to Archive Collections in the Borthwick Institute of Historical Research*, published by the Institute in 1974 and obtainable from it. There are two particularly interesting registers of baptisms. The late-eighteenth century baptismal registers of Tadcaster give the names, profession and residence of both grandparents, and those of Bilton in Ainsty between 1570 and 1606 give the names of godparents. How fortunate are family history researchers who find ancestors in either of these parishes in the appropriate periods!

The great collection of *Bishop's Transcripts* of the York diocese is particularly valuable in covering gaps in the parish registers. There are over 10,000 documents covering 800 parishes and chapelries in the diocese. They survive from 1600, though the earliest transcripts are few. From 1660 they continue, with gaps, until the mid-nineteenth century. Much time in recent years has been spent in cleaning and restoring these documents and listing them.

The marriage bonds and allegations of *Marriage Licences* survive from 1660. William Paver, Registrar of Births and Deaths at York during the nineteenth century, used some of these early registers for two MS volumes now in the British Museum (Add. MSS 29667-8) and his notes of other licences between 1567 and 1714 have been published in the *Yorkshire Archaeological Journal* and in three volumes of the Yorkshire Archaeological Society Records Series.

The *Probate Records* at the Institute are considerable. The Exchequer and Prerogative courts alone are contained in some 3,000 boxes. The wills are arranged chronologically, in rural deanery bundles. These wills and administrations date from 1427, though the survival of those before 1591 are scanty. From 1660 onwards the series is generally complete, and from 1688 inventories are generally included, though these, as so often, become less detailed or absent after the middle of the eighteenth century, and are seldom found in the nineteenth century.

Apart from original wills and administrations there are probate registers from 1389 to 1859 which contain the registered copies from both the Exchequer and Prerogative courts.

Fuller details of the holdings of the Borthwick Institute are given in an article by Dr David M. Smith, Acting Director of the Borthwick Institute, in the *Genealogists' Magazine* for March 1975, Vol. 18, No. 1, pp 7–13.

Details of the holdings at the Institute will also be found in Anthony J. Camp's *Wills and their Whereabouts*, 1974.

County Record Offices

The setting up of county record offices throughout the country has greatly assisted in preserving many genealogical records. The earliest county to have a record office was Bedfordshire, where one was opened in Bedford in 1914. Since then, and particularly since the 1939–45 war, many have been established so that today most counties have record offices and many boroughs today have their archives department which is recognized by the Master of the Rolls as an official depository for records. This not only makes the public far more record-conscious and willing to deposit records which they may have, but also, in the case particularly of the county record offices, has resulted in many parish registers being deposited in them on varying terms, very often with completely free access for consultation. Under the Parochial Records Measure of 1 January 1979 the deposit of the older parish registers, with few exceptions, is obligatory in the Diocesan Record Offices. Many of the county record offices have the additional role as Diocesan Record Office, which means they hold the records formerly kept in the Diocesan Registry and such records as the bishop's transcripts. They are also becoming more and more the depository for the wills prior to 1858 of the consistory, commissary and archdeaconry courts. This is, of course, an advantageous position, for all these records are now being well looked after and in the hands of trained archivists who appreciate the value and have an interest in the records. It has in fact led to a considerable opening-up of these records and eventually, it is hoped, will lead to a far better indexing and calendaring of them.

You can easily find out the existence and address of the county record office or of any local depositories by enquiring at your local public library.

National Register of Archives

Another body which has done valuable work since it was set up in 1945 and which is closely linked with these county record offices, is the National Register of Archives, which has its headquarters at Quality House in Chancery Lane, not far from the Public Record Office with which it works in close collaboration. In the same building is the Manorial Documents Register (see chapter 29). Most districts have local committees of the National Register of Archives. The main object of the register is to list the existence and whereabouts of all archives which may be of value nationally. This includes private collections of deeds belonging to great or small estates, records of charitable institutions, public bodies such as boroughs, local treasury, educational, police and fire services, in fact the records of any body or individual which may be of interest and value. These include diaries, journals, family photographs, especially if they are identified, marriage settlements and so forth. One of the great services which these bodies have performed is in the saving from destruction of so many of these records, which individuals may have thought to be just so much old junk and had no idea that they might be of interest to anyone.

Chapter Twenty-seven

GENEALOGY AND HERALDRY

In theory heraldry should be the greatest assistance to genealogy but in practice, owing to its abuse, the assistance it can give is limited and may often be misleading.

The law of the right to the use of armorial bearings is quite clear in the British Isles. In England, Wales and Northern Ireland the granting and registration of armorial bearings is under the jurisdiction of the Earl Marshal, assisted by the College of Arms, acting on behalf of the Sovereign under charters granted to him and them.

Unlike a British peerage, which descends ordinarily only to one representative, usually the eldest male descendant of the original person to whom the peerage was granted, arms are different in that they descend to all sons and to their sons in perpetuity, and to daughters who may also, if they are heiresses or co-heiresses in heraldry, transmit the right to quarter those arms to their children, provided the husband is entitled to bear arms. But to have a right to arms in England and Wales you must be able to prove you are descended in the male line from someone to whom arms have been granted or to whom the right to bear arms has been recognized at one of the visitations made by the kings of arms or heralds during the sixteenth and seventeenth centuries, or have obtained a grant of arms yourself.

In theory only the eldest and his eldest son in perpetuity bear the undifferenced arms. Younger sons should bear difference marks, such as a crescent for the second son, a fleur-de-lys for the sixth and a cross moline for the eighth son. These should be carried on, so that a sixth son of a second son would bear a fleur-de-lys upon a crescent. But you can see how impractical such a scheme becomes when it has gone, say, four generations, when the difference marks have become far too small to recognize. Had these difference marks been placed next to each other instead of on top of each other, rather like a row of medals along the top of the shield, then it would have been easy to see that someone was a fourth son of a second son of an eldest son of an eighth son and so forth. This would have been of the greatest value genealogically. But no such simple plan was adopted. The heralds said the cadency marks must be on top of each other. Consequently cadency marks are seldom used and are today regarded as optional by the College of Arms. Another reason why they may not have been used is that it would have required a very exact knowledge of your descent and many people could not be bothered to find out. Heraldry came to be abused even in the eighteenth century, people adopting arms to which they had no right because they did not want to admit they were not entitled to any

People adopting arms to which they had no right

arms at all. This snobbery reached its height during Victorian times. Stationers used to advertise that they would let people know the arms to which they were entitled if they would send them their name and county. Some people may even have thought they really were entitled to the arms conferred upon them by these unworthy stationers. Others were quite content to salve their consciences by not enquiring too deeply into the matter. Thus, if you find your grandfather used a certain crest (which is an integral part of armorial bearings and not something which can exist alone), this should enable you to identify him with the family to which he belonged, but if it was used spuriously, then it will only mislead and disappoint you. It is always worth while investigating any crest or shield of arms you may come across which is reputed to be your family arms, but refer the matter to the College of Arms, who will not charge much merely to indicate to whom this crest or these arms belong. But be prepared to find you have no connection with the family in question and you will not be disappointed. If, on the other hand, the arms are genuinely borne, then you will be led to much information about the family straight away and it will have been well worth your while investigating the matter. Remember, however, that the number of people genuinely armigerous is very few in relation to the population. Fox-Davies' *Armorial Families* is a useful work, as the editor tried to include only persons genuinely armigerous. The few exceptions are shown in italics, to indicate that their right to the arms shown had not been produced. The first edition of the work was published in 1895 and the last in 1929.

In Scotland the law of arms is somewhat different from that in England and Wales. The authority which acts on behalf of the crown is the Lyon King of Arms. He has the advantage over his English colleagues in being himself a judge and the enforcement of the proper use of arms in consequence is far stronger in Scotland. In general the same right exists to arms, namely that you descend from someone to whom arms have been granted, but there were no visitations in Scotland. In 1672 an Act was passed requiring all persons entitled to arms to register them in the Register of All Arms and Bearings in Scotland and even today, if you can prove that your ancestors in the male line used arms, it is possible to register that right to yourself without getting a grant. This is done by what is called 'matriculation' which merely means registering, in the same way as you register, or 'matriculate' in a university. In Scotland, as in England, only the eldest son is entitled to use the undifferenced arms. A younger son has the right to matriculate his arms, that is, to register them, when the Lord Lyon will give him some difference to signify that he is a cadet and not the eldest son. This requirement has kept the use of arms much purer in Scotland. Unfortunately few younger sons today trouble to register or matriculate their arms. Nevertheless even those who do so help to keep the system regularized and today the registers of matriculation are not only wonderful examples of heraldic art but contain a great deal of genealogical information. For in matriculating your arms the Lyon Court encourages you to record as much of your genealogy as you can, so that there will be on record, not only your male line but your female lines also, as far as you know them and can substantiate the descents with reasonable proofs. Some account of the records of the Lyon Office has been given in Chapter 19.

The situation in Ireland differs also, owing to the destruction of so many of their records. Before the establishment of the Republic of Ireland the armorial authority in Ireland was the Ulster King of Arms. He had the right to issue to you a Confirmation of Arms if you could reasonably show that certain arms had been used by your family for three or more generations. This sounds a loose arrangement and it was so, compared with the requirements of other parts of the kingdom. But it was felt that Irishmen should not be debarred from their inheritance of arms through the destruction of their records. Today Northern Ireland is still controlled by Ulster King of Arms, whose office is now amalgamated with Norroy, so that he is known as Norroy and Ulster King of Arms. Arms for the combined office were granted in 1981.

The Republic of Ireland has taken over the records at Dublin Castle and has established a Chief Herald of Ireland, who is responsible for all matters of heraldry in the Republic. He and his office are very helpful and will send you extracts from their records for reasonable fees.

Heraldry is a large subject and it is not possible in this short chapter to deal more than very briefly with it. A number of books on the subject are mentioned in the bibliography for those who may be interested in further reading.

In Scotland, as mentioned in the chapter on Scottish Records, the Lyon Office library is open to people for consultation on application and payment of a small fee. No such facility exists in England. The College of Arms collection belongs to the College and is normally only consulted through an officer of arms. One can understand the college being careful of its unique collection and not wishing it to be handled by the general public, who are not always too careful in handling precious records. But it does seem a pity that it is not more accessible to suitable people, perhaps on similar lines to documents in the Public Record Office. Some steps towards the opening up of their records has developed in recent years. One is the founding of the Friends of the College of Arms. Another is the publication of Sir Anthony Wagner's *Records and Collections of the College of Arms,* which gives a good idea of the records which exist there. The recent volume of the *Survey of London*, covering the college, deals very fully with it and its collection.

In Ireland also a number of recent publications have given some indication of the contents of the records at Dublin Castle under the Chief Herald of Ireland. Information has also been published on the heraldic and other records held by the Northern Ireland Record Office in Belfast.

There has been an increasing interest in heraldry in recent years. The foundation of the Heraldry Society in 1947 by John P. Brooke-Little, the present Norroy and Ulster King of Arms, has given members of it the opportunity to meet at lectures and congresses others interested in this subject and listen to talks by experts on the various aspects of heraldry.

A number of books have been published recently on the subject. Those of the late C.W. Scott-Giles, *The Romance of Heraldry, Shakespeare's Heraldry* and the *Civic Heraldry of England and Wales* have been among these. Brooke-Little himself has edited new editions of previous well-known books on the subject, such as Fox-Davies's *Complete Guide to Heraldry* and Boutell's *Heraldry,* besides his own books, such as his *Kings and Queens of England* and *An Heraldic Alphabet* and various articles. Lt-Colonel Rodney Dennys, Somerset Herald, produced in 1976 *The Heraldic Imagination* and in his last book, *Heraldry and the Heralds*, he discusses the various activities and duties of the heralds and their place in the modern world. The book is informative, charmingly written and with many amusing anecdotes. The book *Heraldry,* by Ottfried Neubecker and Brooke-Little jointly, with its illustrations in full colour, covers the subject in its widest aspects. *Heraldry: Customs, Rules and Styles* by Carl-Alexander von Volborth, devoted mainly to European heraldry, is attractively illustrated in its bold and richly colourful designs.

A recent book on the royal families of Europe, *Lines of Succession,* by Jiri Louda and Michael Maclagan should prove interesting and popular. Jiri Louda has provided the family trees while Michael Maclagan, the Richmond Herald, has written the text, giving the historical background to the royal family trees. It contains 150 genealogical tables which feature some 2,000 heraldic illustrations in full colour.

Chapter Twenty-eight

GENEALOGY AND BIOGRAPHY

Genealogy and biography have in common that they are both concerned with people. The biographer is writing about some one person who is either of some importance or of some notoriety and in whom many people are interested. The genealogist is tracing a line of people whose descent is mainly of interest to the family to whom they belong. In recent times the descent of quite ordinary people has become of interest to a number of other people, because such descents bring interesting information to other fields of study, such as demography, statistics, genetics and social and local history. This is particularly the case when the bare pedigree has been clothed with family information, such as the occupation or trade of the members and to what extent they were influenced by their father in their choice of it.

Biographers are of course interested in any morsel of information they can discover about their subject. The biographer's dream no doubt is to discover new and unpublished information about some great person which can be revealed to the public with much excitement and widespread acclaim. Perhaps he might discover, he thinks, in some old lumber room an old faded bunch of letters written by Dryden or Pope, or some further diary by Samuel Pepys! But such hopes must usually remain just dreams. More often the biographer is led to write about someone because he has a special interest in him or her and perhaps because he can write, he feels, about him from some new angle. Many figures who in the past were not of particular interest may, through the mellowing influences of time and because interesting letters and diaries have survived, giving a vivid picture of their lives and times, have become of sufficient interest to justify a book about them. This is perhaps why old scrap books have in recent years become increasingly valuable and have been sold at well-known auctions for high prices.

It is just here where the genealogist may be of value to the biographer, for the genealogist, in his searching among the minutiae of unimportant people, may come across something which reflects on some greater person, or something which throws light on some great historical event, showing it up in quite a different light to that generally accepted.

Biographers in general know little of genealogical methods and this is one way in which a genealogist can help a biography. Occasionally the "shy shade" of a biographer may be seen in the Public Record Office in Chancery Lane, searching amidst the P.C.C. wills there for a will of his subject or of a close relation to him. But probably few do even this and fewer still pursue the search for a will into the minor courts, the bishops' and archdeacons' courts or in fact have any idea where to search for them.

Some biographers realize the value of the genealogist's expertise and employ his help. A typical example of how help can be given was that which Hugh Peskett told me about. His help was enlisted by Professor R.H. Cause who was engaged on a biography of Alfred Marshall, the economist. Hugh Peskett was able to discover that the economist's grandfather was William Marshall, partner in the Newton Abbot and Totnes Bank which failed when Alfred Marshall was a child. This fact may have been significant in having triggered off Alfred's interest in economics.

Biography can of course be a great help to the genealogist and a number of collective biographies are mentioned in Chapter 9 on Some Printed Sources and in Chapter 10 on Periodicals and Newspapers. You may think there is not much chance of your having an ancestor included in such a work as the *Dictionary of National Biography*. However, even a collateral ancestor may have crept into it and it is surprising how much information about the parentage of biographees is included and nearly always there is mention of any collateral relations who are also mentioned in the Dictionary. However, there are a great many biographical dictionaries devoted to people in various occupations or walks of life which are far less exclusive than the D.N.B., as will be seen by consulting Phyllis Riches' *Bibliography of Universal Collective Biographies*, published in 1934, a very useful book.

If you should have any foreign ancestors of distinction, nearly all the European countries have their dictionaries of national biography, a number of them based on our D.N.B. It is interesting also how many of the dominions of Great Britain have been bringing out their own dictionaries of national biography. Canada has an ambitious plan for a 20-volume dictionary, covering both French and English Canadians. The first volume, from 1000 to 1700, was published in 1966, volume 2 (1701-1740) in 1969, Volume 3 (1741–1770) in 1974, Volume 9 (1861–1870) in 1976 and Volume 10 (1871–1880) in 1972. The volumes are not being published in chronological order, but as they are completed.

New Zealand has a modest two-volume dictionary edited by G.H. Schofield published in 1940. Australia recently embarked on its *Australian Dictionary of Biography,* which is being done in chronological sections. Two volumes covering the first period, 1788-1850, have been completed as have the four volumes of the 1851-1890 period and one of the contemplated six volumes of the 1891-1939 period.

Of the former dominions and colonies, India has its *Dictionary of National Biography,* the first volume of which has been published, covering names from A to D. South Africa has also embarked on a Dictionary, and published three volumes, all self-contained, with a cumulative index in Volume III.

The United States of America has produced her *Dictionary of American Biography*, based closely on the British D.N.B., in 20 volumes, and two supplementary volumes.

The reprinting of Boase's *Modern English Biography* in three volumes with its supplementary three volumes was particularly welcome, as these 30,000 biographies cover a useful period before *Who's Who* was first published and include many people not in the D.N.B. or *Times* obituaries. Boase can give delightful reflections on the characters of some of his subjects. The entry on Henry Whitlock Torrens states that he was at Charterhouse and Christ Church, Oxford, and was rusticated with two eldest sons of the first Duke of Wellington for painting the doors of Christ Church red!

To discover if an individual biography has already been produced in case you have a distinguished member in your family whose biography you feel is worthy of being written, you can check in the British Museum Library printed catalogue or in the new catalogue which is replacing it and is now in process of being printed, to see if there is any reference under the name of the person, as there are always cross-references from the names of biographees to the author of the biography.

John Leyland (d. 1552) earned the gratitude of biographical collectors in gathering together a great deal of biographical data of his time. Anthony Hall (1679-1727) published a transcript, unfortunately not particularly accurate, from Leyland's work in his *Scriptoribus Britannicus Commentarii,* consisting of 593 short biographies, published in 1709.

Donald A. Stauffer in this century published two useful books, jointly by Princeton University and the Oxford University Press, *English Biography before 1700* (1930) and *The Art of Biography in 18th century England* (1941). Each of these works lists all the biographies discovered by the author written during the periods and these are entered under the author and under the biographee, and there is also a valuable list of the most important books used in the study of this period.

The *British National Bibliography* also lists annually under the classification number 920 all biographies written during the year it covers. Also the new edition of A.J. Walford's *Guide to Reference Material,* Vol. 2 (1975) lists recent biographical dictionaries and other biographical works.

The great amount of MS biographical material in the Society of Genealogists repays a visit by biographers. Many do so, especially American biographers who are increasingly writing British biographies. The Society would probably benefit in developing its biographical sources and in drawing greater attention to them. There are, for instance, periods of indexes to the obituary notices in *The Times* which are not greatly used. But it is in the MS collection of the Society that the biographer may make his most useful finds. It is unfortunate that there is no comprehensive catalogue of the contents of these MS collections. That is something which still awaits doing. The task is a large one and, as in so many matters, would require finances which are not at present available. Even so, the rough alphabetical arrangement in boxes under the families' names is useful, as is the similar arrangement to topographical information.

Probably one of the best libraries specializing in biography in London is that of the University of London in the Senate House. Details of its specialized holdings are given on p. 138.

County Record Offices can also help a biographer with information about someone belonging to the county in question. Apart from their collection of MS archives, they have often a useful collection of printed books covering the county, and it is convenient to have such a collection all together and easily consulted. For further details see p. 140.

That most ephemeral vehicle of information about people, the newspaper, has the disadvantage that it is very difficult to discover where to find the bits about some person in whom one is interested, as so few newspapers are indexed. For that reason *The Times*, which has been indexed since its inception in 1785, is probably used more than any other newspaper by biographers and others seeking information about people. Nevertheless there are sometimes indexes for at least some periods of local newspapers. The Reference library of Bath Public Library has an index to the *Bath Chronicle* over quite an extensive period of the eighteenth and early nineteenth centuries. As Bath is a great centre of fashion, the *Bath Chronicle* gives not only information about national events and London life, but also about Bath society; who has lately arrived and departed. These indexes also include notices of births, marriages and deaths there.

There is also a splendid slip index in the Exeter City Library made by the late Professor Burnet Morris from 1914 onwards, which contains references to West Country people from a great number of sources. The professor, who was a barrister, was a life member of the Society of Genealogists. He was born in 1859 and died in 1952. There is an article by myself on this index in the *Genealogists' Magazine* of June 1962. This index contains over a million slips.

Since Ireland lost so many of its official records, wills and parish registers in particular, in the destruction of the Four Courts in 1922, the newspaper, with its notices of births, marriages and deaths, has become particularly important. The *Belfast News Letter* has been indexed for these notices for quite an extensive period from 1738 to at least the first quarter of the nineteenth century. This indexing of newspapers and references to people mentioned in them is valuable to both biographers and genealogists.

Chapter Twenty-nine

MANORIAL, CHANCERY AND OTHER LEGAL RECORDS

It has already been emphasized that the chances of getting your pedigree back further than the seventeenth century are remote. If you are fortunate and the parish registers of the parish in which your ancestors lived go back to the time of their institution in 1538, then you may reach back to that date. You may even get further if the wills of your ancestors survive, the earliest of which in the P.C.C. is 1383.

Another possible but even more fugitive source is the manor court roll. These rolls are often still in private hands and, apart from the difficulty in tracing who owns them, the chances of their surviving at all are not great. Nevertheless many such manor court rolls do survive and those known to do so are registered with the Historical MSS Commission, Manorial Documents Register, Quality House, Quality Court, Chancery Lane, London, W.C.2. There is legislation today guarding against their destruction or sale overseas.

Should such rolls survive, then you may learn much of your earlier ancestors and may succeed in tracing them, even though they were only humble people, for perhaps two hundred years prior to the start of the parish registers, that is, back into the fourteenth century. In the manor court rolls were recorded all copyholders' deeds such as marriage settlements or mortgages of an estate. Furthermore, the jury which assembled at the death of a tenant of the Lord of the Manor recorded after their investigations of what estate the tenant died possessed, the name and relationship of his heir and what fine and heriot was due to the Lord. Such 'presentments', as they were called, often included extracts from the deceased's will and other deeds.

John West's *Village Records* (Phillimore, 1982) gives good information on manorial records, with facsimiles and transcriptions of documents.

Apart from these possibilities, one is only able to trace further back than the mid-sixteenth century people of distinction and rank, or those who owned land.

There are a great many records which may have bearing on the pedigrees of such landowners. Many of these are fully described in Richard Sims' *Manual for the genealogist, topographer, antiquary and legal professor,* but it must be remembered that this volume was published in 1856, before the opening of the P.R.O. and therefore much of the information regarding the locality of deeds and records is out-of-date. Moreover, since Sim's day, a great deal has been done to open up records to the public, many deeds and calendars have been issued and much work indexed and copied. Sims is very valuable in giving you an idea of the contents of various records and the two volumes of the *Guide to the Public Record Office* (1963, 1968) will indicate which of them are now there and give recent information about them. Particularly helpful is *Tracing Your Ancestors in the Public Record Office* by Jane Cox and Timothy Padfield (1981), previously mentioned.

In this work I can only indicate briefly some of the more important genealogical sources among these early records.

Chancery proceedings are of high importance in this aspect. It is often said that few land-owning families have gone through history without some dispute resulting in a Chancery case. Such a case, if discovered, may reveal a host of information about relationships, and the papers of the case may include chart pedigrees (among the Master's papers), certificates of baptism, abstracts of deeds and wills and other documents from the family muniment room.

Some dispute resulting in a Chancery Case

The proceedings in Chancery are by bill of complaint, which is in the form of a petition to the Lord Chancellor, Lord Keeper or to the Lords Commissioners of the Great Seal. The bill is followed by the answer and the evidence is given by means of affidavits, depositions and other proceedings. Thus the whole story is told on paper and you can read today all the evidence which was considered at the time by the court.

One of the difficulties in making use of Chancery proceedings is the discovery of their existence. Apart from some very early proceedings, there are no printed calendars and the MS calendars in the P.R.O. are divided between the six clerks in Chancery (or 'Prothonotaries' as they were called), whose calendars run concurrently. It is thus necessary to search each year in six different places. Apart from this it is very difficult to identify a particular case, for the calendar or index merely says 'Smith v. Jones', or whatever the names are. This may not be so bad if you are searching a rare name, where you would be interested in any case concerning someone of the name. But where the name is common, as Smith or Jones, as mentioned above, then the process of searching can be one of length and weariness. Such a search could only be undertaken where a very great deal depended on the result. But, if fortunate, you may discover the existence of a Chancery suit through other sources. Sometimes there is mention of a Chancery suit in a will and when you know there was definitely a suit and have some idea of the date, then it is not too long a task to track it down even though dealing with a common name and you have to search through a number of 'wrong numbers'. Another possible clue is the mention on the back of a deed that it was produced in some Chancery suit. Solicitors had the habit of making such notes and sometimes gave the actual reference of the case. A particularly good exposition of Chancery proceedings is in R.F.E. Garrett's *Chancery and Other Proceedings,* published originally in the *Genealogists' Magazine* as an article in September and December 1965 and later as a booklet by Malcolm Pinhorn. This is strongly recommended. A further article by Mark H. Hughes in the same magazine in September 1975 refers to the great value of Mr Garrett's articles and the value of the Bernau Index, a microfilm of which was acquired by the Society of Genealogists not long after Mr Garrett's articles appeared. The Bernau Index is extensive and refers mainly to Chancery proceedings in the eighteenth century and how to track them down. This is particularly valuable in a century which in many ways is a difficult one in which to trace Chancery proceedings. As the writer points out, even for this period the Bernau index only lists two of the six clerks' divisions, namely Whittington-Sewell and Purcas-Winter. As for the other four clerks there is "no key save the rather useless calendars". Another article in June 1979 by P.W. Coldham, "Genealogical Resources in Chancery Records", based on a lecture, gives further information on the kind of genealogical information you may find in a Chancery proceeding, if lucky even a five-generation pedigree. At the end of this article is a valuable list of the various indexes and aids to Chancery Bills and Answers, Affidavits, Town Depositions, Country Depositions, Decrees and Orders and Reports and Certificates.

My own article in the *Genealogists' Magazine* of March 1969 "Should Fanny have been sent to France" may give readers some idea of the variety of information which may be discovered in Chancery proceedings.

The number of manorial records which have survived are coming to the notice of the Manorial Register more and more every year.

Early transfer of land can sometimes be traced by the discovery of a deed of Bargain and Sale, which is by indenture, enrolled in one of the courts of Westminster, or else in the county where the lands were. It is unfortunate that the provision of the statute enacting such procedure was evaded through the use of the 'Lease and Release' method devised by lawyers for conveying land, for if the method of 'Bargain and Sale' had been continued there would have been an almost universal record of the conveyance of freehold land throughout our history, rather like the Sasines Registers in Scotland.

The records of Bargain and Sale belong mostly to early periods, though the procedure was not abolished officially until the nineteenth century. They are enrolled on the Close Rolls and the grantors are indexed in books called 'Indentures', while the grantees are covered by the Close Roll index. These records are, of course, at the P.R.O. in Chancery Lane. Some early conveyances were also by charter.

Many of the deeds relating to Lease and Release, which were not, unfortunately, registered centrally, but merely held by the two parties, are finding their way into the various county record offices and gradually some record of land holding is being built up by these offices.

A FINE OF 1193

A FINE OF 1193: The Latin original, with many words contracted, reads in extended form:-
Haec est Finalis Concordia facta in Curia Domini Regis apud Westmonasterium a die Pasche in tres septimanas anno Regnon. Ricardi Regis Angliae et Franciae quarto . . .' 'This is the final agreement made in the Court of our Lord the King at Westminster in the third week from the day of Easter in the fourth year of the reign of Richard King of England and France'.

The fine, after recounting the names of the persons before whom the proceedings took place, show that John Waleys, clerk, William Snapedon and Nicholas Fortescue were the plaintiffs and John Boold and Margaret his wife the deforciants in a suit concerning five messuages and the quarter part of an acre of land in Sutton Prior and Sutton Vautor, near Plymouth, Devon. In the outcome the former paid John Boold and his wife ten silver marks.

These fines were in three parts, each being separated by cutting the parchment with a wavy line, as can be seen in the illustrations. The end part, known as the foot of fine, was registered and kept in Chancery and from the 7th year of King Richard I until this form of land transfer ceased in 1834 during King William IV's reign the series is almost unbroken. They are now kept in the Public Record Office. The illustration shows that part shown in the diagram as "other part". The foot of the fine would be retained by Chancery but this fine is too early for its foot to be in the P.R.O.

If there was any dispute about the matter later the two parties had to bring their respective parts of the deed together and show that the wavy lines fitted. This was an ingenious and simple way of warding against fraud. Genealogically these fines help in tracing the descent of land and often establish relationships at an early period.

FROM THE AUTHOR'S MS COLLECTION

'Feet of Fines' are another valuable record of land transfer and genealogically are of first class importance, because the vendor joined with his wife and children or other heirs in order to avoid or overcome entail or dower. The foot of the fine was enrolled in the court, the other two pieces being held by the two parties. The records of these feet of fines are almost perfect from the 7th year of King Richard I until 1834 and they form a rich record of a proportion of the land ownership in the country. It will be noticed that the illustration of part of a fine in this volume is one of the 4th year of King Richard I, and thus earlier than the continuous feet of fines in the P.R.O.

The Court of the Exchequer had also an equity side, the pleadings in which can be of value, particularly the depositions of the court, which may often reveal relationships. The calendar of these is in the 38th and following reports of the Deputy Keeper.

Lay Subsidy Rolls and Hearth Tax Returns are also useful as indicating the existence, locality and to a certain extent the status of people. Inquisitions Post Mortem, which were held on the tenants-in-chief, are found only for the larger landowners but in those cases are most valuable. They reveal the heir of the property concerned and his relationship to the previous owner. Indexes for them have been published for a number of years and some counties have printed or typescript abstracts of them. They survive from the time of Henry VIII until the end of Charles I's reign in 1649.

The Recusant Rolls are useful in giving the names and residence of people who were found guilty of non-conformity, either as Roman Catholics or Protestant dissenters. These are in the P.R.O., but there is a useful return of all recusants who were convicted, giving their quality and place of abode, in August 1677, in the British Museum MSS Department (Add MS. 20,739). The Protestation Oath Rolls of 1641-2 are kept in the Record Office of the House of Lords. These are lists of people holding office who affirmed their loyalty to the crown, and another similar roll is the Association Oath Roll signed in 1696 when William III was on the throne. The latter is in the P.R.O.

As location is such an important feature in genealogy it is often useful to note in cases where an ancestor was a tenant of some landowner, as perhaps revealed by manor court rolls, whether the same landowner had property in other parts of the country. Sometimes tenants, who were often also employees, moved to some other estate of their employer and landlord, because he was able to offer them employment there of a better nature or interest. You may therefore find, when a line seems to disappear, that it continues back on some other estate of the same landlord.

Chapter Thirty

DEVELOPMENT OF FAMILY HISTORY

In recent years much emphasis has been made by genealogists in developing family history rather than the discovery of a mere pedigree. Even those family histories which have been written have sometimes, with honourable exceptions, been a recording of facts about the family which has not made for interesting reading.

A number of writers on the subject have made the point that a family history which has emphasized the historical background, giving some information, for instance, as to how the events of the time may have influenced the movements and occupations of the ancestors concerned, and how, in dealing with a trade or occupation in which a forbear was concerned, a description of the kind of work necessitated by the time in which the person lived, can add greatly to the interest of such a family history.

As a result of this developing interest, family history societies have been growing considerably in England, particularly in recent years.

In 1974 the Federation of Family History Societies was formed to co-ordinate the activities of these societies and most, if not all, of such societies formed since the Federation was founded have become members of it, together with a number of societies which have an interest in family history. The latter include the Society of Genealogists in London, the Heraldry Society, the Institute of Heraldic and Genealogical Studies, Devon and Cornwall Record Society, the Scottish Genealogy Society and a number from the Commonwealth (nine from Australia) and the U.S.A.

There is now (March 1982) a family history society covering every county in England (a few being two counties together, as Somerset and Dorset) and some counties have two such societies namely Cheshire and North Cheshire, Kent and North-West Kent, Central, North and West Middlesex societies, East and West Surrey, East Yorkshire and York societies. There are also societies covering a particular place and its neighbourhood, such as the Folkestone Society.

Of the English societies, there are seven with a membership of over a thousand, namely The Birmingham and Midland Society for Genealogy and Heraldry (3,400), the Cornwall Society (1,291), The Devon Society (1,620), Essex (1,020) The Society for Lincolnshire History and Archaeology (Family History Section) (1,020), Northumberland and Durham (1,172) and Sussex (1,020).

The Federation publishes quarterly *Family History News and Digest*, and a number of special publications from time to time, such as *Marriage Indexes, Aids for Genealogists* and

Census Returns (1841-1871) on Microfilm. Those wishing to join or to obtain any of the Federation's publications will find the name and address of the secretary among the "Useful Addresses" in Appendix C.

Family history societies serve several useful purposes. In the first place members are able to discuss their problems with each other at meetings. Most societies have regular meetings at which they may have a speaker on some subject connected with family history. Then these societies do good work in transcribing or at any rate encouraging the transcription of parish registers, in recording monumental inscriptions in church graveyards, which each year are becoming more weather-worn and consequently more difficult to read, in discovering and sorting out other records of genealogical value and perhaps persuading their owners to hand them over to the county record office of their county, and perhaps also in helping to index archdeaconry, consistory, and commissary wills and administrations and also those of any peculiars which may exist in the district, which may be in the diocesan registry, quite probably now incorporated in the county record office. In all these ways family history societies are doing good work and their general contribution to the preservation of records throughout their county is of inestimable value to scholars and local historians, economists and sociologists throughout the country.

In Scotland and Wales, with their more sparsely populated areas, the development of family history societies has been more difficult on a county basis and has tended to be growing in the greater populated areas around the larger towns. Scotland has its Scottish Genealogy Society based in Edinburgh, which has recently increased its membership and now has library premises with limited opening times. While genealogical records are particularly centred in Edinburgh at the Scottish Record Office in Princes Street and the West Register House in Charlotte Square, societies have nevertheless been established in recent years in Glasgow, Aberdeen, Inverness, North-East Scotland and Tayside areas, and it is likely these will increase in number.

In Wales there is a South Wales Society and the possibility of another starting up elsewhere, while the National Library of Wales at Aberystwyth has been increasing its holdings of family history material and indexing and making more available such material as it comes in.

In Northern Ireland there is the Ulster Genealogical and Historic Guild centred in Belfast. The Republic of Ireland is covered by the Irish Genealogical Research Society in London. All these societies are members of the Federation.

One-Name Societies

Another development in Family History is that of societies formed for people particularly interested in a surname which they may be searching. The idea of co-ordinating the work of people searching for a particular surname has been current for some years in the United States and is rapidly developing here. By uniting with other people searching one surname it is, of course, a benefit to all the members. Certain members can undertake certain parts of the necessary work. One could, for instance, concentrate on wills and administrations of the name up to 1700, another on them from 1700 to 1800. Others could extract all of the surname in parishes in certain areas. Others could extract those of the name in census returns, and so forth.

It is important that every name (and its variants) should be extracted, with the necessary details, as agreed by the group. This information must then be made available to other members. For this reason some journal or newsletter issued at intervals is necessary and meetings of the society must be held from time to time to talk about tasks and projects. Naturally these one-name societies are more suited to an unusual surname than to one which is widely in use.

In September 1979 the Guild of One-Name Studies was formed in Great Britain. The address of the secretary is given in Appendix C of this book. The guild is a member of the Federation of Family History Societies. It issues an information sheet giving full details of the five categories within the guild, namely: Constituted Societies (U.K.); Family Groups (U.K.); One-Name Researchers (U.K.); Overseas Groups; Preliminary One-Name Studies (U.K.). The Guild from time to time publishes a *Register of One-Name Studies*, which can be obtained from the Federation of Family History Societies or from the Guild of One-Name Studies.

In the first edition of this book I had a chapter, as now, on "Writing it up" in which I tried to show the way in which a bald factual account of a family can be made so much more interesting by building up around it some of the historical background and by giving reasons which may have enticed people to take up their occupations and details of those occupations at the time when they lived and also the way in which the conditions of the time in which they lived could affect the lives of the people, for instance the movement of working class people from the country into the towns during the period of the Industrial Revolution.

By infusing some of the atmosphere of the time into your family history, you can bring it to life and consequently make it engaging and entertaining to read and also more valuable in the account of the times which it gives. I hope I have succeeded in showing how in this way your family history can be stimulated.

The trend in recently published books on tracing your ancestry has been towards family history rather than pure genealogy or mere tracing of the line without any attempt to describe the type of lives people lived. Stella Colwell's *Family History Book* (1980) is a good example of this. On page 80 of it, under the heading of "Writing the Family History", she says "The danger in writing a family history is that it can become little more than a list of names; always bear in mind the need for the story you are telling to be an interesting one", and she goes on to expand this ideal throughout her book, illustrating it with three particular families and the kind of way you can interlace its record with the events of the time. All this is emphasized with excellent illustrations, by a calendar of dates which relate the period to the events which were current, and the very good bibliography.

Donald Steel's *Discovering your Family History* is another good example of this emphasis. Donald has constantly stressed the family history side of genealogical work. His earlier work with Lawrence Taylor, *Family History in Schools* (1973), put forward the idea of teaching history through boys' and girls' own family story, a method which has been adopted with success by a number of schools. His more recent book, published by the BBC in 1980, in conjunction with the BBC television series "Family History", which traced the Gordon Honeycombe family, naturally emphasizes this idea of family history. For instance, Gordon Honeycombe's great-great-grandfather William Honeycombe, who was born in Liskeard in 1786, became a millwright and then a sawyer in the dockyard at Plymouth Dock (later Devonport). Donald gives an excellent description of the work of a sawyer in the dockyard there in the early nineteenth century. The term "top sawyer" did not refer to his senior rank, but to his position in sawing the wood, when he stood on top and held the upper handle of the saw and did not have to shield his eyes against the sawdust which the "bottom sawyer" needed to do. But the top sawyer was the senior man and in charge of the sawing of the great tree trunks from which were made the planks of wood which formed the decks and sides of the great wooden walls of England. The description of the sawyer's work and conditions is well illustrated with near-contemporary illustrations.

The first 102 pages of this book show how the Honeycombe saga evolved stage by stage from the basic sources, with each generation set against the influences which affected their lives. The last 60-odd pages of the book under the heading "Reference Section" themselves form an excellent guide to the general tracing of a family history, with instances from the Honeycombe family's generation stories used as examples. The last ten pages of the book are a splendid bibliography, giving examples not only of basic sources but also sources of background information under a great variety of headings, including, of course, a considerable section on "Historical Background" and also sources for "Pictures" with which to illustrate the family story.

Chapter Thirty-one

FOUNDLINGS

The naming of foundlings, or 'dropt children' as they were often called in earlier times, was always subject to a certain extent to the whim of chance, though there is a certain pattern in their names. Very occasionally there was a note pinned to the child by the mother begging the finders to call the child by a particular christian name, but there was seldom any indication of his parentage or surname. Only rarely was there some family possession, perhaps a locket round the infant's neck, which later led to his or her identification. Almost always the surname and frequently the christian name had to be decided upon by someone having no idea of the child's origin. This may have been the parson or the parish clerk or possibly the person accepting the care of the child.

The names given were in many cases connected with the place where the child was found and, as this was often on the steps or in the porch of a church, the surname 'Church' was frequently given. A variation on this was that given in 1750 to a foundling of St Andrew's parish, Plymouth, named 'Eliz. Churchstile', probably because she was left at the churchstile. Another, in the register of St Ann's, Blackfriars, London in December 1806, was baptized, for the reason apparent in a note in the register, 'Thomas Bridge (a child dropt on the bridge)'. Less original is 'Eliz. Found', baptized in 1772 in the above mentioned Plymouth parish.

These children were often given the christian name of the saint to whom the parish in which they were found was dedicated, but sometimes the saint's name was used as a surname. This is constantly so in London parishes. In St Martin's, Ludgate, a number of foundlings in the eighteenth century were given the surname 'Martin', like 'Moses Martin (a Foundling)' baptized there in 1736. A variation from this is 'John Lud, a Foundling' baptized in February 1744. The favourite name bestowed in the parish of St Ann's Blackfriars, seems to have been 'Fryer'. There is, for instance, the baptism in 1742 of 'Jane Fryer, a Foundling'; in 1744 of 'Mary Fryer, a foundling', and in 1782 of 'Ann Friar, a child dropt'. In the adjacent parish of St Andrew by the Wardrobe there is in 1737 a foundling baptized called 'Andrew Wardrobe' and in the nearby parish of St Bride's there are a number called 'Bride's', like 'Tobias Bride's', baptized in 1737. No doubt the apostrophe was dropped later and descendants were just 'Brides'.

Perhaps one of the strangest names registered is that in the previously mentioned parish of St Andrew, Plymouth, in 1725 of 'Moses Noplace, a Child found in a Basket at a place called No Place in this parish'. There is still in the city a 'No Place Inn' at the top of

Eldad Hill, near Wyndham Square, which indicates the locality of this strangely-named part of the parish. The christian name 'Moses', the name of the first mentioned foundling in the Bible, was for that reason sometimes given to foundlings, especially when, as in this case, the child was found in a basket. An ingenious name through the transposition of the name of the parish, is that of a child found in Coupar Angus, Scotland, who was christened 'Angus Cooper'.

The way in which these children were named may have seemed arbitary and haphazard, but this method of naming from locality was, after all, only following one of the sources of surnames when they first came into existence. Earl Attlee's ancestors were so called because they lived 'at the lee' and people of the name of 'Attwood' came from ancestors who lived 'at the wood'. Many persons called 'Scotland' or 'Ireland' are so because an ancestor crossed the Border or the Irish Sea and became known in England as 'Ian of Scotland' or 'Patrick of Ireland'.

Hospitals for the care of abandoned children came into existence in Europe in early times. There were such places in Trèves, Milan and Montpellier in the seventh and eighth centuries. One was opened in Venice in the fourteenth century and in Paris and Lyons in the seventeenth century.

In England that founded in 1799 by Captain Thomas Coram in London was probably the most famous. Outside it there used to hang a basket suspended by a rope, into which mothers in desperation would place their offspring. From time to time the basket would be pulled up to take in for care whatever tragic harvest the tides of everyday life had brought ashore. This was not unlike a convent in Spain which had a round turntable of stone, upon which a mother would place the child and then ring a bell, when the stone would be turned, carrying the child within through an aperture in the wall.

Many abandoned children must have owed their lives and care to the bounty of this good-hearted Captain Coram, whom the memorial tablet in the chapel of the hospital aptly describes in its eighteenth-century style as 'a man eminent in that most eminent virtue, the Love of Mankind'. With the development of the welfare services and the modern practice of finding private homes for foundlings with foster mothers, the need for special foundling homes is disappearing, but it is good to know that Captain Coram's name continues in remembrance in the organisation which has now evolved, known as the 'Thomas Coram Foundation for Children'.

To the researcher in family history the discovery of a foundling ancestor must be a major disappointment. Even the baptism of a base born forbear will indicate at any rate the mother's name. But nearly always the foundling leaves the genealogist with a line beyond which it is not possible to penetrate. The social historian, on the other hand, may find much interest in the upbringing and character development of these children left without the normal ties of relationship or natural parental affection. They have often grown up with an unusual independence, sometimes with a great affection for their friends and fellow men, which has led them to do great good in the world, which they have learnt to face with a cool courage often lacking in the over-indulged child of a small family.

Chapter Thirty-two

WRITING IT UP

Do not put off for too long writing up or at least producing a pedigree of the results of your labour. Some people postpone doing this until, as they say, they have collected all the material. The result often is that they never do put their results on paper, because there never will be a time when you have collected *all* the material. It may be difficult to decide at which particular point you should write up what you have collected. Certainly when you have, for instance, got back to the eighteenth century you might consider putting your results into some form which will record your work and make it available to others who may be interested, particularly, of course, future generations. How often genealogists sigh and say 'If only grandad had put down even on a small piece of paper some of what he knew about the family!' Make sure future generations do not say that of you!

Another advantage in getting out an account of the family fairly soon is that you will stimulate interest in other members of it and may get some of them sending in corrections, uncles writing indignant epistles declaring 'Great-uncle Joe was never in the 43rd — it was the 57th of course' or that 'Jeremiah never had a son called Geoffrey — he was actually christened "George", though always known as "Smug".'

In Chapter 2 I have made some suggestions on the best way of recording pedigrees in chart form and the methods by which it can best be reproduced. This chart pedigree is one of the simplest ways of recording information about the family and even if you decide, as I hope you will, to write up your family in some narrative form, you will need a chart pedigree or perhaps several chart pedigrees to illustrate it. There is no doubt the chart pedigree shows the family ancestry in a clear and simple way, but you are limited in the amount of information you can get on it for each member. Often pedigrees in historical works or biographies, perhaps produced by people far from expert in such matters, are deplorably lacking in detail and sometimes in clarity. On the other hand, if they are overburdened with detail the thread of the line is lost. Examples of chart pedigrees with a great deal of detail but still not overburdened are Crisp's *Visitations,* which are a kind of modern nineteenth-century equivalent of the Herald's visitations of earlier times.

Turning to narrative pedigree, perhaps the simplest kind is that which forms notes to a chart pedigree. This can be quite effective and is merely done by having note marks, either numbers or letters, preferably in brackets to show they are nothing to do with the information, against the person; and against these note marks, on as many separate sheets as they may require, you can give as full details as you like on the person in question. This keeps the chart pedigree from becoming unwieldy and at the same time gives fuller information on individuals for those who want them. By this method you can often keep a chart pedigree of twelve or more generations on a single sheet, for it is only necessary to give brief details, enough to identify the person.

A clear and concise method of narrative pedigree is that used in such publications as *Burke's Peerage* and *Burke's Landed Gentry*. If you study the way in which the generations are recorded in these publications it will guide you for your own, should you decide to use this method. Such a form of pedigree can easily be duplicated from typewriting, in fact the Supplement to the 1952 edition of *Burke's Landed Gentry* is reproduced from a form of typewriting probably by one of the litho processes. This used no doubt a form of Varityper, which is a glorified typewriter in which you can get italic as well as roman type and other variations.

You will notice that in this kind of recorded pedigree it is necessary to continue the pedigree down one line, which is done by using the words 'of whom presently' against the person through whom you have decided to continue the line. This is often the eldest line, but need not necessarily be so. In the past with the landed families it was usually through the eldest son that the lands descended, and in the case of a peerage this also descended through the eldest son. But through whatever line you decide to take your pedigree, you must exhaust all the descendants of the other members of the family as you come to them. In the case of a pedigree which starts far back, this sometimes means continuing on for many generations, each one indented further and further into the page until you are approaching or even exceeding the halfway division. For this reason you cannot give too much detail for each person, or otherwise it may go on for several pages and get confusing. Some of the pedigrees of older families in the *Peerage* or *Landed Gentry* are very extensive and yet still keep their clarity. An example of an old peerage with many younger branches is that of the Earl of Huntingdon and a family in the *Landed Gentry* well extended is that of Giffard. A study of these and other such pedigrees will soon instruct you on how the matter is handled.

An important concern in this type of recording is the numerical notation beside each member of the family, which helps to show to which generation he or she belongs. Some people use a mixture of roman and arabic figures, both upper and lower case, in perhaps this order: I, I, (I), (i). One slight disadvantage of the roman figures is that they take up varying space, i.e. I, II, III, IV and so on. But this need not be of great consequence, so long as the indentation is kept even, regardless of the number of spaces which the roman figures take up. Other people prefer to use arabic figures throughout, which, under 10, remain single-spaced. In either case after the first runs of generations are exhausted, they have to be continued with additional symbols and these are best in the form 1a, 2a, 3a, and then the children of those so marked will be 1b, 2b, 3b and so on, the figure always indicating the position in the family, with separate runs for sons and daughters. Thus a male 1b will be the eldest son of perhaps 1a or perhaps 2a. This may sound somewhat complicated, but an examination of pedigrees in this form will soon make the method clear. An example of such a pedigree is given in Appendix B.

But possibly you may want to try something a little more ambitious in the way of a family history. Various methods of doing this are outlined in Sir James Balfour Paul's introduction to Margaret Stuart's *Scottish Family History.* It is a great mistake to imagine that only the histories of famous families make interesting reading. All family histories are to a certain extent the history of the times through which they lived and the history of a family which never rose to prominence or held high position can make nevertheless an interesting contribution to social history. Unfortunately this is not true of many of those produced, but this is because of the way in which they are written rather than because the subject matter is uninteresting. Some are merely a schedule of dry facts which, although valuable to the immediate family, could be so much more attractively presented. Others, which try to relieve the monotony of such dull recitation, often tend towards the facetious, possibly impelled with a desire for modesty which is really a false modesty. This is irritating to the reader and worse than a mere factual account.

One of the interests in a family saga is in the recording of the reasons which enticed people to take up their occupations. This was often because their father or uncle was in that trade or job, but at other times it was a reflection of some national event. For instance, the movement of working class people from the country into the towns during the Industrial Revolution period affected a very large number of families. There was also the magnet of London and many families had adventurous members who moved into the capital during the period from about 1775 to 1825, some considerably raising their financial and social status in doing so.

If you decide to write up your family history in the more ambitious narrative style, then do try to infuse into its pages some of the atmosphere of the times through which it passed. Let us take the following account of an imaginary family as an example.

John Smith, cloth-worker of Trowbridge, Wiltshire, married on the 15th July 1776 at Bradford-on-Avon, Wiltshire, Mary Roberts, daughter of William Roberts, woolworker there.

They had an only son, James Smith, baptized at Trowbridge 20th May 1778 and married at Bideford, Devon, on 17th June 1797 Anne Hodge. He served in the Peninsular War as a corporal in the 29th Foot and was present at the battles of Rolica and Vimiero in August 1808 and at Albuera on the 11th May 1811. He died at Bideford, aged seventy-three in September 1851 and was buried in the parish church there on the 16th of that month. His wife Anne died there in May 1820. They had issue four children, namely . . . etc.

This is a factual account which has value, but this sort of style can get very monotonous when carried on for many pages. Let us take these same facts and re-write them to include some historical background.

John Smith was a cloth-worker in Trowbridge, working in an industry for which that Wiltshire town was famous in the eighteenth century. In 1776, on the 15th July, only eleven days after the historic Declaration of Independence by the American colonists, the news of which when it reached this country was to cause a shudder of presentiment to pass through the minds of thinking Englishmen, this young cloth-worker married in the picturesque fourteenth-century church of nearby Bradford-on-Avon Mary Roberts, whose father William was employed in the wool trade for which that town had long been renowned.

James, their only son, was baptized at Trowbridge on the 20th May 1778. He grew up during the French wars and as a young man enlisted in the 29th Foot or

Worcestershire Regiment. Promoted to corporal he found himself stationed with his regiment in the pleasant North Devon market town and seaport of Bideford. It is not surprising therefore that he found a bride among the Bideford girls and this nineteen-year-old, fair-haired, blue-eyed Corporal of Foot on the 17th June 1797 was married in the parish church of that town on the hillside of the Torridge river to Anne Hodge of the same parish.

This fair-haired, blue-eyed Corporal of foot

However he was not long able to enjoy married life at home, for, a rebellion having broken out in Ireland, his regiment within nine months of his marriage was sent over there, embarking from the little port of Appledore at the mouth of the Torridge.

From Ireland the regiment was later sent to Spain and there Corporal Smith saw fighting in August 1808 at the battles of Rolica and Vimiero, at the former of which his colonel, Lt-Colonel the Honble. G.A.F. Lake, was killed and the regiment suffered considerable casualties. At Vimiero they were more fortunate, only losing a corporal and two privates.

Later, in 1811, he was in action again at Albuera, and there the regiment suffered severely, there being five officers, a sergeant, a corporal and a drummer and seventy-four privates killed, and the sergeant-major, three sergeants, two corporals and forty-seven privates later died of their wounds.

But John Smith survived to return to Bideford and lived long enough to receive in 1849 the much delayed Peninsular General Service Medal with clasps for the three battles in which he had participated. Anne, his wife, predeceased him by some thirty-one years, dying in May 1820. John himself was buried in the grounds of Bideford parish church on 16th September 1851, age seventy-three.

They had four children . . . etc.

This expanded account, expanded through adding some details of the background of the times, has, I think, infused some colour into what Pooh Bah in *The Mikado* called 'an otherwise bald and unconvincing narrative'. It has required some further research. A short history of Wiltshire gave the background to the towns of Trowbridge and Bradford-on-Avon and a history of the Worcestershire Regiment produced the information that the regiment was stationed in Bideford in 1797 and gave some account of its future history. The description books of the regiment at the P.R.O. would show Corporal Smith as having had blue eyes and fair hair on his enlistment. An historical chronicle, such as Steinberg's *Historical Tables* or Margaret A. Rolleston's *English History Note Book* will guide you to the comtemporary events.

Whatever methods you decide upon by which to record your researches, when you have finally accomplished the task you will be able to sit back with the happy feelings of one who has, like Longfellow's village blacksmith, 'something attempted, something done' and like him 'earned a night's repose'. You may even experience some of the feelings of that great historian Edward Gibbon who, after years of toil and labour on his *Decline and Fall of the Roman Empire* on at last completing it, felt that he was parting 'with an old and agreeable companion'. At any rate, in the tracing of your family you have met with many new companions who have, in the course of time, and as you have more and more unravelled the course of their lives, become in fact 'old and agreeable'.

Letters of past members of the family

APPENDIX A

Suggested Questionnaire for sending out to the family. The general queries may apply to most families, but the more detailed enquiries will, of course, vary greatly in different cases. Plenty of room should be left after each question for the replies.

General Questions
Do you know of the existence of any of the following, relating to earlier members of the family:

Family Bible, giving dates of baptism, marriage, burial etc.
Family pedigree or written account or notes of the family.
Any copies of wills, any diaries, note books, birthday books, old receipt books, account books, tontine or stock and share certificates, old deeds relating to property, estate maps, bank books, life assurance policies, apprenticeship indentures, family samplers, funeral cards or bookplates.

Baptism, marriage, death or burial certificates.

Deeds concerning the freehold, leasehold or receipts for upkeep of graves.

Letters of past members, particularly from those abroad.

The name of the family lawyer, and any marriage settlements.

Old family portraits, miniatures, or photographs.

Medals and decorations, certificates of service in the Army, Navy or East India Company. Any family traditions of service in these forces, any particular regiments with which they have been connected.

Any family traditions of any sort whatsoever, e.g. that they came from such and such a place or county, or from abroad, that they were engaged in a particular trade or occupation.

Specific Question
The earliest known member of the family is JOHN SMITH, who married at St Clement Danes, London, in August 1831, MARY ROBINSON. John Smith died 15 January 1876, aged 69, so was born about 1806-07. Have you any information as to where he was born, who his father and mother were and where they were married, or any other information?

APPENDIX B

Example of a Tabular Pedigree suitable for reproducing from typewriting and using only arabic figures.

STEVENS OF PLYMOUTH

ROBERT STEVENS, married at St Andrew's Plymouth, 21 Feb. 1757, Mary, dau, of Nathaniel Smith, and had issue,

1. JOHN, of whom presently.
2. ROBERT, b. 18 June, bapt. St Andrew's 2 July 1765.
3. JAMES, bapt. St Andrew's 10 Nov. 1771

1. JOAN, bapt. St Andrew's 26 Aug. 1758.
2. MARY, b. 25 May, bapt. St Andrew's 4 July, 1760.
3. WINIFRED, b. 27 July, 1767.
4. JENNY, b. 3 Mar., bapt. St Andrew's 26 Mar. 1769.

The eldest son,
JOHN STEVENS, merchant and shipowner of Plymouth, b. 19 Sept., bapt. Charles Church, Plymouth, 27 Oct. 1762, d. at Plymouth 3 Feb. 1831, bur. at Plympton St Mary's, mar. at St Andrew's, Plymouth, 2 Aug. 1790, Sarah (d. in Plymouth 26 Feb 1845, aged 75) dau. of John Lee of Modbury, Devon, and had issue,

1. JOHN, bapt. Charles Church, Plymouth, 20 Jan., d. 11 Nov. 1793, bur. at Plympton St Mary's.
2. ROBERT, bapt. Charles Church, Plymouth, 21 Sept. 1794, d. 11 Mar. 1795, bur. Plympton St Mary's.
3. JOHN LEE, of whom presently.
4. JAMES, shipping agent, bapt. Charles Church, Plymouth, 14 February 1798, d. unm. 13 June 1869.
5. THOMAS, shipowner and coal merchant, Mayor of Plymouth 1854-5, b. 23 Nov. 1799, bapt. Charles Church, Plymouth, 3 Jan. 1800, d. Plymouth 8 Dec. 1869, mar. 20 Mar. 1821, Mary Maddick (b. 10 Feb. 1802, d. 28 Sep. 1876) dau. of George Sanders,

of Brixham, Devon, and by her had issue,

(1) JOHN HOOPER JARMOND, b. 13 Jan. 1823, drowned at sea, 1843.

(2) THOMAS JONES, shipowner and coal merchant, b. 24 July, 1824, d. 19 Aug. 1901, mar. 20 Mar. 1846 his 1st cousin Mary Maddick Sanders (b. 23 Aug. 1823, d. 22 Mar. 1904) and by her had issue.

    1a. JOHN, shipping agent of Plymouth, b. 21 June 1847, d. 21 Dec. 1885, mar. 17 Sep. 1877 Eliza Huxham (d. 9 June 1887) and by her had issue.

        1b. GEORGE HERBERT.

        2b. ARTHUR VIVIAN.

        1b. KATE WINEFRED.

    2a. THOMAS SAMUEL, master mariner, later in business in London, b. 10 Apr. 1849, d. 5 Sep. 1909, mar. 24 June 1874, Jessie Turner (d. 1924), 2nd dau. of Frederick Herron, of Plymouth, and by her had issue.

        1b. FRANK HERRON, solicitor, b. 1875.

        1b. BARBARA PEARL.

    3a. MACKWOOD, clerk in Holy Orders, sometimes rector of Addington, nr. Winslow, Bucks, b. 3 Apr. 1853, d. 20 May 1920, mar. 1st, 19 June 1878, Alice Margaret Griffinhoofe (d. 9 Aug. 1881) and 2nd, 18 June 1895, Mary Christina Badcock (b. 17 Dec. 1853, d. 16 Nov. 1932), leaving no issue by either marriage.

    4a. CHARLES, major in the Indian Staff Corps, b. 20 May 1857, mar. Mary Ann Englebach, and d.s.p. 13 Feb. 1932.

    5a. PERCY, b. 19 Jan. 1859, d. unm. 1940.

    1a. MARY, b. 13 Aug. 1850, d. 7 Mar. 1852.

    2a. SALLY, b. 26 Aug. 1851, living in Sep. 1901.

    3a. IDA, b. 23 Aug. 1854, d. 2 Jan. 1925.

    4a. ANGELINA, a member of the Clewer Sisterhood, Berks, b. 19 Jan. 1856, d. at Folkestone, Kent, 28 May 1901

(3) SANDERS, shipowner and coal merchant, b. Plymouth 13 Jan. 1826, d. Teignmouth, 18 Mar. 1910, bur. Plymouth Cemetery, mar. Plymouth, 14 June 1851, Emma Ruth (b. in Plymouth 7 Jan. 1832, d. 17 Oct. 1889), dau. of James Marshall, builder, of Plymouth, and had issue.

    1a. MARSHALL, a founder and first manager of the Manchester Ship Canal. M.P. for Eccles, Manchester, 1918-22, b. Plymouth 18 Apr. 1852, d. there 12 Aug. 1936, mar. 1873, Louisa Blamey (d. Torquay 8 Jan. 1932), dau. of Philip Blamey of Cusgarve and St Blazey, Cornwall, and by her had issue.

        1b. DOUGLAS FAIRWEATHER, b. 1874, d. young.

        2b. BLAMEY, M.Sc. Manch., mining engineer, b. Plymouth, 26 May 1875, d. Mexico, 1939, mar. in Brookline, Mass. U.S.A., 19 Feb. 1906, Phoebe Margaret (d. 5 Feb. 1948). dau. of Samuel Walter Reynolds, of Pinkneyville, Illinois, U.S.A., and had issue,

            1c. REYNOLDS, b. Seattle, Washington, U.S.A., 19 June 1908, d. Manchester, 30 Oct. 1927.

            2c. GORDON, b. Mexico City, 23 Oct. 1913, mar. Derby, 22 Mar. 1943, Edna, dau. of Leonard Roberts, and has issue.

                1d. ROBERT BLAMEY, b. 1 May 1946.

                2d. DAVID MICHAEL, b. 25 Sept. 1949.

1c. LOUISA ELIZABETH, B.Sc. Manch., b. Penticton, Canada, mar. 22 July 1948, Alejandro Manuel Raimúndez, B.B.C. European Service.

2c. VICTORIA, b. Brooklyn, New York, mar. Mexico City, 2 Nov. 1936, George Hinton, mining engineer, and has issue 1 s. and 2 daus.

APPENDIX C

SOME USEFUL ADDRESSES

ENGLAND and WALES

Army Museum Ogilvy Trust
Ministry of Defence (Army)
85 Whitehall
London SW1A 2NP

Army Records Centre
Bourne Avenue
Hayes, Middx UB3 IRS

Association of Genealogists and
Record Agents
Hon. Secretary
80 Pollard Road
London N20 0UD

Baptists Historical Society
Baptist Union Library
4 Southampton Row
London WC1B 4AB

British Library, Reference Division
Great Russell Street
London WC1B 3DG

British Red Cross Society
The Secretary
9 Grosvenor Crescent
London SW1X 7EI

Canterbury Cathedral Archives and
Library
The Precincts
Canterbury CT1 2EG

Catholic Central Library
47 Francis Street
London SW1P 1DN

Catholic Record Society
c/o Miss R. Rendel
114 Mount Street
London W1Y 6AH

Chaplain of the Fleet
Ministry of Defence
Lacon House
Theobalds Road
London WC1X 8RY

Church of Jesus Christ
of Latter Day Saints
Hyde Park Chapel
64 Exhibition Road
London SW7 2PA

Civil Service Department
Alencon Link
Basingstoke
Hants RG21 1JB

College of Arms
Queen Victoria Street
London EC4V 4BT

Corporation of London Record Office
Guildhall, London EC2P 2EJ

Federation of Family History Societies
General Secretary
96 Beaumont Street
Milehouse
Plymouth PL2 3AQ

General Register Office (CA Section)
Tichfield, Fareham, Hants PO15 5RU

General Register Office
Office of Population
Censuses and Surveys
St Catherine's House
10 Kingsway
London WC2B 6JP

General Registry
Finch Road
Douglas
Isle of Man

Greater London Record Office
County Hall
London SE1 7PB

Guildhall Library
Aldermanbury
London EC2P 2EJ

Historical Manuscripts Commission
Quality House, Quality Court
Chancery Lane, London WC2A 1HF

Home Office
Lunar House
40 Wellesley Road
Croydon CR9 2BY

The Hon. Society of
Cymmrodorion
118 Newgate Street
London EC1A 7AE

Huguenot Library
University College
London WC1E 6BT

Huguenot Society
Miss I. Scouloudi, Hon.
Secretary
67 Victoria Rd
London W8 5RH

House of Lords Record Office
Westminster, London SW1

Imperial War Museum
(1914-18 War)
Lambeth Road
London SE1 6HZ

The Archivist
International Red Cross
British Red Cross Training Centre
Barnet Hill
Wonersh, Guildford
Surrey GU1 3PJ

India Office Library and Records
Foreign and Commonwealth Office
Orbit House
197 Blackfriars Road
London SE1 8NG

Irish Genealogical Society
of Great Britain
The Secretary
The Challoner Club
59-61 Pont St
London SW1 0BD

Jewish Museum
Woburn House
Upper Woburn Place
London WC1H 0ED

John Rylands University Library
Oxford Road
Manchester M13 9PP

Lambeth Palace Library
London SE1 7JU

Land Registry
Lincoln's Inn Fields
London WC2A 3PH

Manx Museum Library
Kingswood Grove
Douglas
Isle of Man

National Army Museum
Royal Hospital Road
London SW3 4HT

National Library of Wales
Aberystwyth SY23 3BU

National Maritime Museum
Greenwich
London SE10 9NF

Naval Personnel Records
(Recent records)
Room 2007 OS9 (a)
Ministry of Defence
Empress State Building
London SW6 1TR

Presbyterian Historical Society
of England
86 Tavistock Place
London WC1H 9RR

Principal Registry of the
Family Division (previously
Principal Probate Registry)
Somerset House
Strand, London WC2R 1LA

Registrar General of Shipping
and Seamen
Llantrisant Road
Llandaff
Cardiff CF5 2YS

RAF Personnel Management Centre
Eastern Avenue
Barnwood
Gloucester GL4 7AN

Royal Artillery Record and
Manning Office
Imphal Barracks
York YO1 4HD

Royal Courts of Justice
Strand, London WC2A 2LL

Royal Marines Drafting and
Record Office
HMS Centurion
Grange Road
Portsmouth PO13 9XA

Salvation Army
(Investigating Officer for
tracing persons)
110-112 Middlesex Street
London E1 7HY

Society of Friends Library
Friends House, Euston Road
London NW1 2BJ

Society of Genealogists
37 Harrington Gardens
London SW7 4JX

Southampton City Record Office
Civic Centre
Southampton SO9 4XL

Spanish and Portuguese Synagogue
9 Lauderdale Road
Maida Vale
London W9 1LT

United Synagogue, Offices
of the
Alder House, Woburn House
Upper Woburn Place
London WC1H 0ED

Dr William's Library
14 Gordon Square
London WC1H 0AG
(Nonconformity generally)

The Weiner Library
4 Devonshire Street
London W1N 2BH

SCOTLAND

National Library of Scotland
George IV Bridge
Edinburgh 1

Registrar General of Scotland
New Register House
Princes Street
Edinburgh EH1 3YT

Scots Ancestry Research Society
3 Albany Street
Edinburgh EH1 3PY

Scottish Genealogy Society
Miss Joan P.S. Ferguson
Honorary Secretary
21 Howard Place
Edinburgh EH3 5JY

Scottish Record Office
PO Box 36
HM General Register House
Edinburgh EH1 3YY

Scottish Tartans Society
Davidson House, Drummond Street
Comrie, Crieff
Perthshire

Court of the Lord Lyon
King of Arms
New Register House
Princes Street
Edinburgh EH1 3TY

NORTHERN IRELAND

Presbyterian Historical Society
of Northern Ireland
Church House
Fisherwick Place
Belfast BT1 6DU

Registrar General of Northern Ireland
Fermanagh House
Ormeau Avenue
Belfast BT2 8HX

Public Record Office of
Northern Ireland
66 Balmoral Aveue
Belfast BT9 6NY

General Register Office
Oxford House
49-55 Chichester Street
Belfast BT1 4HL

REPUBLIC OF IRELAND

Registrar General of Ireland
General Register Office
Custom House, Dublin 1

Public Record Office
Four Courts, Dublin 7

National Library of Ireland
Kildare Street, Dublin 2

Register of Deeds
Henrietta Street
Dublin

CHANNEL ISLANDS

The Registrar General
States Office
Royal Square, Jersey

Societe Jersiaise
The Library
The Museum
9 Pier Road
Jersey

The Registrar General,
The Greffe, St Peter Port
Guernsey

AUSTRALIA

Society of Australian Genealogists
Richmond Villa
120 Kent Street
Observatory Hill
Sydney NSW 2000

CANADA

British Columbia Genealogical Society
The Library
Langham College
100W 49th Avenue
Vancouver V5Y 2Z6
Canada

Maritime History Group
Memorial University of
Newfoundland
St John's
Newfoundland
Canada

Public Archives of Canada
395 Wellington Street
Ottawa
Ontario K1A ON3
Canada

SOUTH AFRICA

Genealogical Society of South Africa
40 Haylett Street
Strand, Cape Town, South Africa

U.S.A.

British Information Service
845 Third Avenue
New York, NY 10022
U.S.A.

Genealogical Society of Utah
50 East North Temple
Salt Lake City
Utah 84150, U.S.A.

National Archives and Record Service
United States of America
General Services Administration
Washington DC 20408

BIBLIOGRAPHY

Bibliography of the principal books and articles mentioned in each chapter and a number of others. Place of publication is only mentioned when outside the United Kingdom.

Chapter 1 Discovering what is already known

ANDERSON, M.,*Genealogy and Surnames: with some heraldic and biographical notices.* 1865
BARDSLEY, Charles Wareing, *English Surnames,* 1st edn repr. with new intro by L.G. Pine, 1969
BARROW, Geoffrey B., *The Genealogist's Guide*, 1977
BERNAU, Charles Allan, *? County* [the first part of an index of surnames with the county of origin, compiled from the Chancery Depositions in the P.R.O.], 1932
BROOKES, Reuben Solomon *and* BROOKES, Blanche, *A Guide to Jewish Names,* 1967
CAMP, Anthony John, *Tracing your Ancestors,* new rev. edn, 1970
COX, Jane, *and* PADFIELD, Timothy, *Tracing your Ancestors in the Public Record Office,* 1981.
GARDNER, David E., *and* SMITH, Frank, *Genealogical Research in England and Wales,* 3 vols [in progress] U.S.A., 1956-64
GUPPY, Henry Brougham, *Homes of Family Names in Great Britain,* 1890
GUMBLEY, Walter, *Unusual baptismal names,* 1956
HARCUP, Sara E. (compiler) *Historical, Archaeological and Kindred Societies in the British Isles,* 1965
HASSALL, William Owen, *Index of persons in Oxfordshire deeds acquired by the Bodleian Library 1878-1963* (Oxford Record Soc. publication vol. 44), 1966
HIGGS, Audrey H. *and* WRIGHT, Donald, *West Midland Genealogy: a survey of the local genealogical material available in the public libraries of Herefordshire, Shropshire, Staffordshire, Warwickshire and Worcestershire,* 1966
HITCHING, K. & K., *References to English Surnames in 1601: an index giving about 19,650 references to surnames contained in the printed registers of 778 English parishes,* 1910. [Similar work for 1602, (1911)]
HUGHES, James Pennethorne, *How you got your name: the origin and meaning of surnames,* rev. ed., 1961
HUGHES, James Pennethorne, *Is thy name Wart? the origin of some curious and other surnames,* 1965

JOHNSTON, G.D., 'Legal Terms and Phrases' *Amateur Historian* III, 249 (Winter 1957-8)

KAMINKOW, Marion J., *A New Bibliography of British Genealogy with notes,* U.S.A., 1965. [This valuable genealogical aid largely replaces H.G. Harrison's *Select Bibliography of English Genealogy,* 1937]

LEA, J. Henry, *Genealogical research in England, Scotland and Ireland,* 1906 [still useful for its succinct lists]

LOYD, Lewis Christopher, *The origins of some Anglo-Norman families;*ed. by Charles Travis Clay and David C. Douglas, 1951

MCKINLEY, Richard Alexander, *Norfolk Surnames in the 16th Century,* 1969 [Dept. of Local History, University of Leicester, *Occasional Paper,* 2nd ser. no. 2]

MAIDBURY, Lawrence, 'Family History in Surnames', *Amateur Historian,* II, 114 (Feb-March 1955)

MANCHESTER PUBLIC LIBRARIES, *Reference Library – Subject Catalogue, Section 929 Genealogy,* 3 parts, 1956-8, [includes good collection of individual family histories]

MANDER, Meda, *Tracing your Ancestors,* 1976 [re-issued as a paperback *How to trace your Ancestors* by Mayflower Books in 1977]

MATTHEWS, Constance Mary, *English Surnames,* 1966

MULLINS, Edward Lindsay C., *Texts and Calendars: an analytical guide to serial publications,* 1958 [Very useful in that it lists publications of official, national and local English and Welsh societies. Indexed]

PHILLIMORE'S *Directory for Genealogists and Local Historians,* 1963 [gives addresses of county record offices and national and local organizations, for England only]

PHILLIMORE, William P.W. *and* FRY, Edward A., *Index to Changes of Name . . . 1760-1901,* 1905

PINE, Leslie Gilbert, *The Story of Surnames,* 1965

REANEY, Percy Hide, *The Origins of English Surnames,* 1967

REDMONDS, G., *Yorkshire: The West Riding,* 1973. (English Surnames series, vol. 1)

RYE, Walter, *Records and Record Searching: a guide to the genealogist and topographer,* 2nd ed., 1897

STEEL, Donald John, 'The Descent of Christian Names', *Genealogists' Magazine* XIV, 34 (June 1962)

THOMSON, Theodore Radford, *A Catalogue of British Family Histories,* 2nd ed., 1935

UNETT, John. *Making a Pedigree,* 2nd edn 1971. [Good on Chancery Proceedings, Manorial and other Medieval sources]

WAGNER, Sir Anthony, *English Genealogy*, 2nd edn enlarged 1972 [Considerable and valuable material has been added on the rise of families in social status]

WALFORD, Albert John *and* PAYNE, L.M., *Guide to Reference Material,* 1959. Supplement, 1963, by Walford, Payne and C.A. Toase. [Sections on biography (920) and Genealogy and Heraldry (929) valuable]

WHITE, Geoffrey H., 'Companions of the Conqueror', *Genealogists' Magazine* IX, 417 (Sept, 1944)

WHITE, Geoffrey H., 'Notes on Anglo-Norman Genealogy', *Genealogists' Magazine* IX, 463 (March 1945)

WHITE, George Pawley, *A handbook of Cornish Surnames,* 1972

WHITMORE, John Beach, *A Genealogical Guide: an index to British pedigrees in continuation of Marshall's Genealogist's Guide, 1903,* 1953

WITHYCOMBE, Elizabeth Gidley, *The Oxford Dictionary of English Christian Names,* 3rd ed., 1973

Chapter 2. Keeping Your Records

GREENWOOD, Herbert William, *Document Photography,* 3rd ed., 1947
HOLMSTROM, John Edwin, *How to take, keep and use notes,* 1947

Chapter 3. The Civil Registration

GENERAL REGISTER OFFICE, *Abstract of Arrangements respecting Registration of Births, Marriages and Deaths in the U.K. and other countries of the British Commonwealth . . . and in the Irish Republic,* 1952 [includes lists and registers kept at Somerset House and elsewhere in England and Wales]
MAIDBURY, Lawrence, 'The General Register of Births, Deaths and Marriages', *Amateur Historian* III, 108 (Spring 1957)
SMITH, George Tulloch Bisset, *Vital Registration,* 2nd ed., 1907 [a manual of the law and practice concerning the registration of births, deaths and marriages . . . etc]

Chapter 4. Census Returns

BERESFORD, Maurice, 'The Unprinted Census Returns of 1841, 1851, 1861, for England and Wales', *Amateur Historian,* V, 260 (Summer 1963)
HECTOR, Leonard Charles, 'The Census Returns of 1841 and 1851', *Amateur Historian,* I, 174 (June-July 1953)

Chapter 5. Parish Registers

BRADBROOK, William, *The Parish Register,* 1910
CAMP, Anthony John, *A Key to Boyd's Marriage Index,* 2nd ed., rev. and enlarged, 1963
CATALOGUE *of Parish Register Copies in the Possession of the Society of Genealogists.* Rev. enlarged ed., 1963
CHURCH OF JESUS CHRIST OF LATTER DAY SAINTS *Parish and Vital records listings* LDS Church, July 1977. Available from Mr J.F. Packe, 65 Severn Rd, Ipswich, Suffolk IP3 0PU, or from Deseret Enterprises Ltd, Manchester Distribution Centre, 18 Hammond Avenue, White Hill Industrial Estate, Stockport, Cheshire. Lists all registers covered by the CFI at date of publication and essential for making best use of the CFI
COX, John Charles, *The Parish Registers of England,* 1910
CRISP, Frederick A., (ed.), *List of Parish Registers and Other Genealogical Works edited by F.A. Crisp,* 1908. [Contains indexes to most of his publications]
GREATER LONDON RECORD OFFICE, *A Survey of the Parish Registers of the Diocese of Southwark, Inner London Area,* 2nd ed (rev)
GUILDHALL LIBRARY, *Parish Registers: a handlist. Pt. I Registers of Church of England Parishes within the City of London,* 1963
GUILDHALL LIBRARY, *Parish Registers: a handlist. Pt. II.* containing 1. Registers of C. of E. Parishes outside the City of London 2. Non-parochial Registers and Registers of foreign denominations 3. Burial Ground Records, 1964

LE HARDY, William, 'How to Read 16th and 17th Century Handwriting', *Amateur Historian,* I, 146 (Apr-May 1953)

LEWIS'S *Topographical Dictionary of England.* [Various editions published 1831-49 – separate atlas with 1835 and 1842 editions]

LOCAL POPULATION STUDIES, Original *Parish Registers in Record Offices and Libraries,* Derbyshire 1974, with Supplements 1976 and 1978

THE NATIONAL INDEX OF PARISH REGISTERS

A multi-volume series on parish records planned to cover the whole of the British Isles. The available volumes are:

Vol. 1   General Sources before 1837 (1981 reprint)
Vol. 2   Nonconformist Sources (1981 reprint)
Vol. 3   Roman Catholic and Jewish Genealogy (1974)
Vol. 4   Kent, Surrey and Sussex (1981)
Vol. 5   South West Midlands (1981 reprint)
Vol. 11, pt 1 Northumberland and Durham (1980)
Vol. 12   Sources for Scottish Genealogy and Family History (1981 reprint)

OWEN, Dorothy May, *The Records of the Established Church in England, excluding parochial records.* (British Records Assoc. Archives and the User No. 1) 1970

Register of English Monumental Inscriptions, 2 vols, 1911-14

RIDGE, Alan D., 'All at Sea: observations on the Stepney Baptism Registers', *Archives,* VI, No. 32 (Oct. 1964)

SOCIETY OF GENEALOGISTS, London, *List of Parishes in Boyd's Marriage Index*, New edn. ed by Robert W. Massey, 1976

TUPLING, George Henry, 'Searching the Parish Records-the Parish Registers', *Amateur Historian,* I, 198 (Aug-Sept. 1953)

WILLIS, Arthur James, *Winchester Settlement Papers 1667-1842, 1967* [useful to genealogists and to social historians in tracing population movements]

WRIGLEY, Edward Anthony, 'Parish Registers and Population History, I and II', *Amateur Historian,* VI, Nos 5 & 6 (Autumn 1964, Winter 1964-5)

Chapter 6 Non-Parochial Registers

BAKER, Frank, 'Methodist Archives', *Amateur Historian,* III 143 (Summer 1957)

BESSE, Joseph, 'Collection of the Sufferings' [Quakers], MS at Friends House, London, 2 vols. 1753

CATHOLIC RECORD SOCIETY, Publications Vol 1—, 1905—

CONGREGATIONAL HISTORICAL SOCIETY, Transactions, 1901—[prints early records and bibliographies]

GREEN, Alan, 'The Archives of Congregationalism', *Amateur Historian* III, 208 (Autumn 1957)

JONES, Robert Tudur, *Congregationalism in England, 1662-1962,* 1962

MORTIMER, R.S., 'The Archives of the Society of Friends', *Amateur Historian,* III, 55 (Winter 1956-7)

NEWMAN, Josiah, *The Quaker Records,* 1908 [Vol II of *Some Special Studies in Genealogy,* ed. by Charles A. Bernau]

PAYNE, John Orlebar, ed., *Records of the English Catholics of 1715: compiled wholly from original documents,* 1970, [facsimile reproduction of 1st edn, 1889]

QUAKERS. *Journal of the Friends' Historical Society,* 1903-date.
REGISTRAR GENERAL, *List of Non-Parochial Registers and Records in the custody of the Registrar General of Births, Death and Marriages,* 1841 [over 6,000 vols listed. Quaker records separately listed at back of vol. Does not include Roman Catholic nor Jewish Synagogues. Many records of Welsh Nonconformist chapels were not deposited. The records here listed have now been moved to the Public Record Office]
SHAW, Thomas, 'Genealogy in Methodist Repositories', *Genealogists' Magazine* XI, 179 (March 1952)
STEEL, Donald John, ed., *Sources for Nonconformist Genealogy and Family History,* 1973. (Nat. Index of Parish Registers vol. 2.)
STEEL, Donald John, ed., *Sources for Roman Catholic Genealogy and Family History,* 1974 (Nat. Index of Parish Registers vol. 3)
TURNER, Joseph Horsfall (ed.), *The Nonconformist Register of Baptisms, Marriages and Deaths, compiled by the Reverends O. Heywood and Dickenson, 1644-1702, 1702-1752,* 1881 [generally known as The Northowram or Coley Register]
WELCH, Charles Edwin, 'Nonconformist Registers' *Journal of the Society of Archivists* II, No. 9 (April 1964)
WELCH, Charles Edwin, 'Archives and Manuscripts in Nonconformist Libraries', *Archives,* VI, No. 32 (Oct. 1964)

Chapter 7, Wills and Administrations

BRINKWORTH, Edwin Robert, 'Records of the Church Courts' *Amateur Historian,* II, 50 (Oct.-Nov. 1954)
CAMP, Anthony John, *Wills and their Whereabouts,* rev. edn, 1974. [Full and good Introduction. The definitive book on wills]
COLE, E.J.J., 'Hereford Probate Records: abstracts of wills of Radnorshire testators 1540-1592' [to be continued], *Transactions of the Radnorshire Society,* XXIV-XXXIV, 1954-64
FRANCE, Reginald Sharpe, 'Short Guides to Records, 10, Wills'. *History,* L, 168 (Feb. 1965)
GARDINER, E.M. 'East Sussex Inventories', *Sussex Notes and Queries* XV, 124 (1939)
GIBSON, J.S.W., *Wills and Where to Find Them,* 1974
MARSHALL, George William, *A Handbook to the Ancient Courts of Probate and Depositories of Wills,* 1895
RYCRAFT, Ann, *Sixteenth and Seventeenth Century Wills, Inventories and other Probate Documents,* Univ. of York, Borthwick Institute of Historical Research (Borthwick Wallets 4), 1973
WALNE, Peter, *English Wills: probate records in England and Wales, with a brief note on Scottish and Irish wills,* U.S.A., 1964.
WHITELOCK, Dorothy, *Anglo-Saxon Wills, with translations and notes,* 1930
WILLIS, Arthur James, ed. *Wills, Administrations and Inventories with the Winchester Diocesan Records,* 1968 [a nominal index of stray probate records left behind in the diocesan registry when a separate probate registry was set up]
Wills, Commissary Court, London (London Division), Guildhall Library, London ed. by Marc Fitch (British Record Society series No. 82 and Hist. MSS. Com. joint publication JP 12), vol. 1 *1374-1488,* 1969: vol. 2, *1489-1570,* 1973

Chapter 8. Marriage Licences

COLLINS, Lydia, *Marriage Licences: abstracts and indexes in the library of the Society of Genealogists,* Society of Genealogist, 1981

GIBSON, Jeremy S.W., compiler, *Marriage Licences, Bonds and Allegations, a guide to their location and indexes.*

Probably the best concentrated collection of printed and MS marriage licences is at the Society of Genealogists. Many marriage licences have been published by the Harleian and other societies (see Mullins, E.L.C. *Texts and Calendars).* Marriage licences are also included in the *National Index of Parish Registers*

Chapter 9. Some Printed Sources

ADAMS, Charles Kingsley, 'Portraiture Problems and Genealogy', *Genealogists' Magazine,* XIV, 382 (Sept. 1964)

ADAMS, John, *Index Villaris, or an exact register of all the cities, market towns, parishes, villages and private seats, etc. in England and Wales,* 3rd ed. 1700

Angliae Notitia, or the present state of England, 1669-1755

ASLIB Directory: a guide to sources of information in Great Britain and Ireland, 2 vols, 1957

BATEMAN, John, *The Great Landowners of Great Britain and Ireland* 4th ed. rev. *etc.* [Lists all owners of 3,000 acres and above] 1878

BOASE, Frederick, *Modern English Biography,* 6 vols, 1892-1921, reprinted 1965

BRAMWELL, B.S., 'Frequency of Cousin Marriages', *Genealogists' Magazine,* VIII, 305 (June 1939)

BRIDGER, Charles, *Index to Printed Pedigrees contained in County and Local Histories, the Heralds' Visitations, etc.,* 1867 [valuable as a bibliog. to the great county histories of the 18th and 19th centuries]

British National Bibliography, 1951-date [gives published family histories for each year under the classification No. 929]

BURCHALL, Michael John *and* WARREN, Judy, eds. National Genealogical Directory, The Editors 4/33 Sussex Square, Brighton 1979 [lists 20,000 families being researched by some 1,700 family historians]

BURKE, *Sir* John Bernard, *The Book of the Orders of Knighthood . . . of all nations . . . with lists of knights and companions of each British order,* 1858

BURKE, John, *A Genealogical and Heraldic Dictionary of the Peerages of England, Ireland and Scotland, extinct, dormant and in abeyance . . .* [ed. by Sir J.B. Burke] *. . .* 3rd ed., 1846

BURKE, *Sir* John Bernard, *A Genealogical History of the Dormant, Abeyant, Forfeited and Extinct Peerages of the British Empire,* 1883

BURKE, John, *and* BURKE, *Sir* John Bernard, *A Genealogical and Heraldic History of the Extinct and Dormant Baronetcies of England,* 2nd ed., 1841

BURKE, John, *and* BURKE, *Sir* John Bernard, *The Knightage of Great Britain and Ireland,* 1841

BURKE, John, *The Landed Gentry of Great Britain,* 1st ed. [as *History of the Commoners*] 4 vols, 1837-8: 18th ed., 3 vol, 1963-72 [The 2nd-9th editions included Ireland, since then *The Landed Gentry of Ireland* has been published separately in 1899, 1904, 1912 and 1958. The 15th ed. (1937) had an Irish Supplement]

BURKE, John *and* BURKE, *Sir* John Bernard, *The Royal Families of England, Scotland and Wales, with their descendants, sovereigns and subjects,* 2 vols., 1847

Burke's Guide to the Royal Family, 1973

BURKE, *Sir* John Bernard, *Royal Descents and Pedigrees of Founders' Kin,* 2 pts., 1858

BURKE'S, *Genealogical and Heraldic History of the Peerage, Baronetage and Knightage,* 103rd ed., 1963 [1st ed. 1826; the early editions did not include the Knightage]

BURKETT, Jack (ed.), *Special Library and Information Services in the United Kingdom,* 1961

BURTCHAELL, George Dames, *The Knights of England . . . incorporating a complete list of knights bachelor dubbed in Ireland,* 2 vols, 1906

CHALLEN, William Harold, 'The Records of the City of London', *Genealogists' Magazine* VI, 503 (Sept. 1934)

COKAYNE, George Edward *and others* (editors), *The Complete Peerage,* 2nd ed. rev. and much enlarged, 15 vols. 1910-1964

COLLINS, Arthur, *The Peerage of England,* 1812 ed. 9 vols, ed. by Sir Egerton Brydges, 1812

'County Biographical Dictionaries, 1890-1937', *Bulletin of Inst. of Historical Research* XXXIV, 55, 1961 [a good list of local collected biographies]

Court Register, a monthly record of births, marriages and deaths asociated with the aristocracy, etc, 21 Nos. 1861-5

DEBRETT, John, *Debrett's Peerage of England, Scotland and Ireland* 1803-1849 and 1864 to date [usually jointly with *Debrett's Baronetage]*

DEBRETT, John *The Baronetage of England,* 1808-1840 [later editions from 1864 onwards usually jointly with *Debrett's Peerage*]

DELANY, John *and* TOBIN, James Edward, *Dictionary of Catholic Biography,* 1962

Dictionary of National Biography. [The main work in 22 vols to 1901, with supplements (3 vols), then Supplements to 1970. Additions and corrections to this work in the *Bulletin of the Institute of Historical Research 1923-1963* have been published by G.K. Hall, Boston, Mass., 1966]

DRYSDALE, Alexander Hutton, *History of the Presbyterians in England, their rise, decline and revival,* 1889

DUKES, G.R., 'Social Life in Worcestershire during the Eighteenth Century', *Transactions of the Worcestershire Archaeological Society,* N.S. XXX (1953)

English Local History Handlist, 2nd ed., 1952

EMMISON, Frederick George, *Archives and Local History,* new edn, 1974

EMMISON, Frederick George, *How to read local archives, 1550-1700* (Helps for Students of History No. 82, Historical Assoc.), 3rd edn, 1971

FANE, A.G.C., *Complete Index to Family Names appearing in Burke's Royal Families,* priv. Pr. 1932

FOSTER, Joseph, *The Royal Lineage of our Noble and Gentle Families together with their paternal ancestry,* 3 vols, 1887-91

GATFIELD, George, *Guide to Printed Books and MSS relating to English and Foreign Heraldry and Genealogy,* 1892. [Not yet completely superseded as it contains many references to MSS in the British Museum etc.]

GIBSON, Strickland, *Abstracts from the Wills . . . of Binders, Printers and Stationers of Oxford, 1493-1638,* 1907

GILSON, Julius P., *A Student's Guide to the MSS of the British Museum,* 1920 [*Helps for Students of History No. 31*]

GLASS, David Victor (ed.), *Social Mobility in Britain,* 1954

GODBER, Joyce, 'Bedfordshire County Records', *Genealogists' Magazine,* XI, 269, 304 (Dec. 1952, March 1953)

Government Publications Sectional List No. 24: Record Publications. [This pamphlet, revised every few years, lists all official publications of calendars, indexes etc. in the P.R.O. and Scottish Record Office]

Guide to Reference Material, 2nd edn, ed. by A.J. Walford, Vol. 2, 1968 ['Genealogy-Heraldry' p. 370]

HABAKKUK, Hrothgar John, 'The English Land Market in the Eighteenth Century' in *Britain and the Netherlands,* ed. J.S. Bromley and E.H. Kossmann, 1960

HABAKKUK, Hrothgar John, 'English Landownership 1680-1740', *Economic History Review,* 2nd ser. X (1940)

HARRIS, Ronald Walter, *England in the Eighteenth Century, 1689-1793,* 1963

HASKELL, Daniel Carl, *A Check List of Cumulative Indexes to Individual Periodicals in the New York Public Library,* 1942

HASSALL, William Owen, 'Local History Sources in the Bodleian Library', *Amateur Historian,* II 130 (Apr.-May, 1955)

HOLLINGSWORTH, T.H., *The Demography of the British Peerage,* 1965 [Supplement to *Population Studies,* XVIII, No 2.]

HOUSTON, Jane, ed., *Index of Cases in the Records of the Court of Arches at Lambeth Palace Library, 1660-1913* (British Record Society, Index Library, vol. 85) 1972

HOWARD, Joseph Jackson, *and* CRISP, Frederick Arthur, *Visitation of England and Wales,* 21 vols + 14 vols notes, 1893-1921. [also *Visitation of Ireland,* 1897 —]

HUGHES, Edward, *North Country Life in the 18th Century: the North-East, 1700-1750,* 1952

HUMPHRIES, Arthur Lee, *A Handbook to County Bibliography; being a bibliography of bibliographies relating to the counties and towns of Great Britain and Ireland,* 1917

HYAMSON, Albert Montefiore, *A Dictionary of Universal Biography,* 2nd ed., 1951

Index of Obituary Notices for the years 1880-1882, 3 pts, [An Index Society publication]

JONES, Philip E., ed., *The Fire Court; calendar to the judgements and decrees of the Court of Judicature appointed to determine differences between landlords and tenants as to re-building after the Great Fire,* vol. 1, 1966 [contains much genealogical information and exceptionally well indexed]

KELLAWAY, William, 'Record Publications of Societies', *Archives,* VII, 46 (1965)

Kelly's *Handbook of the Upper Ten Thousand* for 1878 (1879) 1879, 2 vols. [continued as Kelly's Handbook to the Titled, Landed and Official Classes, 1880-1977]

LASLETT, Peter, *The World we have Lost,* 1965 [useful sociological and statistical information on births, marriages and deaths in the past]

'Local County and Regional Historical etc. Societies in England', *Amateur Historian,* I, 213 (Aug-Sept. 1953)

London Inhabitants within the Walls (London City Records Office), 1966

MARTIN, Geoffrey Haward *and* MCINTYRE, Sylvia, *A Bibliography of British and Irish Municipal History,* vol. 1. General Works (Leicester Univ. Press) 1972. [Contains guides to libraries and records, with sections for Wales, Scotland and Ireland–*in progress.*]

Men and Women of the Time, 15th ed., 1899

Micro Methods Ltd, *Catalogue: Section D. Genealogy and Heraldry*

MOULE, Thomas, *The English Counties Delineated,* illus. by a complete set of county maps, 2 vols, 1837

NATIONAL PORTRAIT GALLERY, *Catalogue, 1856-1947,* 1949, *Supplement 1948-53,* 1954
O'DONOGHUE, F.M., *and* HAKE, H.M., *Engraved British Portraits preserved in the Dept. of Prints and Drawings in the British Museum,* 6 vols., 1908-25
ORMEROD, George, *Index to the Pedigree[s] in Burke's 'Commoners' . . . prepared . . . in 1840,* 1907
PINE, Leslie Gilbert, *The New Extinct Peerage, 1884-1971,* 1972
POLL BOOKS
[The British Museum General Catalogue gives lists under each county]
PUGH, Ralph Bernard, *How to Write a Parish History,* 6th ed. (based on the work by J.C.Cox), 1954
Return of Owners of Land of one acre upwards . . . showing names of such owners arranged alphabetically, addresses, extents, etc., 1871 [arranged by counties]
REANEY, Percy Hide, *The Origin of English Surnames*, 1980 [originally publ. 1967]
RICHES (afterw. SUTTON) Phyllis M., *An Analytical Bibliography of Universal Collected Biography,* 1934
RIDGE, Cecil Harold, 'How Many Ancestors have we?', *Amateur Historian,* I, 18 (Aug.-Sept. 1952)
ROBERTS, Arthur Dennis, *Introduction to Reference Books,* 3rd ed., 1956
ROUND, John Horace, *Family Origins and other studies,* 1930
ROYAL COMMISSION ON HISTORICAL MSS, *Index to Persons in Publications issued from 1870 to 1911,* 2 vols., 1935
ROYAL HISTORICAL SOCIETY, *Guide to Directories (excluding London) published before 1856,* 1950
ROYAL KALENDAR, *or Correct Annual Register for England, Scotland, Ireland,* 1767-1893 [The title varies—see *Bulletin of the Institute of Historical Research,* XV, 24, XVII, 130, XIX, 9]
RYE, Walter, *Norfolk Families* [with an index of names by Charles Nowell] 2 pts [1911-13]
RYLANDS, John Paul, *Disclaimers at the Heralds' Visitations,* 1888
SHAW, William Arthur, *The Knights of England: a complete record from the earliest time to the present day etc,* 2 vols., 1906
SOMERVILLE, Robert, *Handlist of Record Publications,* 1951 [a classified and abbreviated list of publications of over sixty English publishing societies]
SPUFFORD, Peter *and* CAMP, Anthony John, jt. editors, *The Genealogists' Handbook*, 5th edn, 1969
SQUIBB, George Drewry, *Visitation Pedigrees and the Genealogist,* 1964
STEER, Francis William, ed., *Arundel Castle Archives,* vol. 1, (W. Sussex Co. Council), 1968
STEER, Francis, *Farm and Cottage Inventories of Mid-Essex*, 1969
TATE, William Edward, *The Parish Chest: a study of the records of parochial administration in England,* 2nd ed., rev. and enlarged 1951
THOMAS, Arthur Hermann, 'Genealogical Material in the Guildhall Records', *Genealogists' Magazine,* II, 45 (June 1926)
THOMPSON, Alexander Hamilton, *Parish History and Records,* 1926 [Historical Assoc. Pamphlet No. 66]
THOMPSON, Francis Michael Longstreth, *English Landed Society in the Nineteenth Century,* 1963
TURBERVILLE, Arthur Stanley, *English Men and Manners in the 18th Century: an illus. narrative,* 2nd ed., 1929

WAGNER, *Sir* Anthony Richard, *Genealogy and the Common Man*, 1961 [Society of Genealogists Jubilee Lecture]

WALFORD, Edward, *etc., Walford's County Families of the United Kingdom*, 1860-1920 [From 1870 or 1871 onwards issued annually]

WARD, Thomas Humphrey (ed.), *Men of the Reign*, 1885 [mainly extracted but re-written from the 11 editions of *Men of the Time*. The 12th ed. (1887) ed. by T.H. Ward, cont. as *Men and Women of the time* 13th ed. (1891) to 15th ed. (1899)]

WARD, William Reginald, *The English Land Tax in the Eighteenth Century*, 1953 [Oxford Historical Series]

Who was Who, 5 vols. 1897-1959, (1920-63)

WILLIS, Arthur James *and* M. TATCHELL, *Genealogy for Beginners*, 4th edn., 1979

WOOD, W.R., *The Administration of the Window and Assessed Taxes, 1696-1798*, 1963 [Repr. from the *English Historical Review*, LXVII, No, 265 (Oct. 1952)]

WOODMAN, A. Vere, 'Buckinghamshire Records', *Buckinghamshire Record Society*, XI, 371 (Sept. 1953)

Chapter 10. Periodicals and Newspapers.

Amateur Historian, 1952-1967 [cont. as *The Local Historian]*

Blackmansbury, a journal of notes and queries, ed. by M. Pinhorn, 1964 *etc.*

BRITISH RECORDS ASSOCIATION, *Handlist of Record Publications*, 1951

BRITISH RECORDS ASSOCIATION, *List of Record Repositories in Great Britain*, 1964

British Union Catalogue of Periodicals, 4 vols, 1955-8 [a record of periodicals of the world from the 17th to present centuries in British libraries]

Supplement to 1960, 1962

CRANFIELD, Geoffrey Alan, *A Handlist of English Provincial Newspapers and Periodicals 1700-1760*, 1952 [Cambridge Bibliog, Soc. monograph 2]

European Magazine and London Review, 1782-1826

FARRAR, Robert Henry, *Index to the Biographical and Obituary Notices in the Gentleman's Magazine, 1731-1780*, 1891

FEDERATION OF FAMILY HISTORY SOCIETIES, *Family History News and Digest*, 1977 — *Register of One-Name Studies*

FOSTER, Joseph, *Marriages [of the Nobility and Gentry] 1650-1880* [The marriages from the *Historical Register* and *Gentleman's Magazine*, 1727-1867 (ed. by Miss Ada C. Gardner) and from other sources, including *The Times* 1865-80, but nothing was published beyond the name 'Alexander']

FRY, Edward Alexander, *An Index to the Marriages in the Gentleman's Magazine 1731-1768*, 1922 [Originally issued as a Supplement to *The Genealogist*, N.S. Vols 34-38]

Gentleman's Magazine, 1731-1868

Historical Register, 1716-1738 [like the *Gentleman's Magazine* contains lists of births, marriages and deaths]

INSTITUTE OF HERALDIC AND GENEALOGICAL STUDIES, *Family History*, ed. C.R. Humphery-Smith, bi-monthly, 1962 etc.

London Magazine, or Gentleman's Monthly Intelligencer, 1732-1785

MELLOR, George R., 'History from Newspapers', *Amateur Historian*, 11, 97 (Feb.-March 1955)

MILFORD, Robert Theodore *and* SUTHERLAND, Donald Martell, *A Catalogue of English Newspapers and Periodicals in the Bodleian Library 1622-1800,* 1936

Monthly Magazine and British Register, 1796-1843

MUSGRAVE, *Sir* William, *Bart, Obituary prior to 1800, as far as relates to England, Scotland and Ireland* . . . ed. by Sir G.J. Armytage, 1899

NICHOLSON, Cregoe Donaldson Percy, *The Genealogical Value of the Early English Newspapers,* 1934

READ, Donald, 'North of England Newspapers (c. 1700-c. 1900) and their Value to Historians', *Proceedings of the Leeds Philosophical Society,* VIII (1957)

TOWNSEND, James, *News of a County Town,* 1914 [Abingdon in Berkshire, drawn from *Jackson's Oxford Journal,* 1753-1835]

Chapter 11. Records of Clergymen

BAPTIST HISTORICAL SOCIETY, *Transactions,* 7 vols, 1908-20 [continued as *The Baptist Quarterly*]

BIRT, Henry Norbert, *Obit Book of the English Benedictines from 1600-1912,* rev., enlarged and cont. by Dom Henry Norbert Birt, 1913

Clerical Guide, or Ecclesiastical Directory, containing a complete register of the prelates and other dignitaries of the Church; a list of all the benefices in England and Wales etc., 1817-1836

CROCKFORD'S *Clerical Directory, a biographical and statistical Book of Reference for facts relating to the clergy and the Church,* 1858-date

DELANY, John Joseph *and* TOBIN, James Edward, *Dictionary of Catholic Biography,* 1962

FOSTER, Joseph (ed.), *Index Ecclesiasticus, or Alphabetical List of all Ecclesiastical Dignitaries in England and Wales since the Reformation,* 1890 [vol. for 1800-1840 only: no more published]

GILLOW, Joseph, *A Literary and Biographical History or Bibliographical Dictionary of English Catholics, from the breach with Rome in 1534 to the present time,* 5 vols, 1885-1902

GUMBLEY, Walter, *Obituary Notices of the English Dominicans from 1555 to 1952,* 1955

HART, Arthur Tindal, *The Eighteenth-Century Parson (ca. 1639-1830),* 1955

KIRK, John, *Biographies of English Catholics in the 18th Century,* ed. by J.H. Pollen and E. Burton, 1909 [needs to be used with caution]

MCLACHLAN, Herbert, *The Unitarian Movement in the Religious Life of England* 1934

PAYNE, John O, *Records of the English Catholics of 1715 etc.* 1889 [consists of some 400 abstracts of wills]

WADDINGTON, John, *Congregational History, 1700-1800: in relation to contemporary events,* 1876

Chapter 12. Lawyers, Doctors and others

BEATSON, Robert, *A Chronological Register of both Houses of the British Parliament* . . . *1708 to* . . . *1807,* 3 vols, 1807

BOND, Maurice F., *The Records of Parliament: a guide for genealogists and local historians,* 1964

BULLOCH, John Malcolm, 'Theatrical Families', *Genealogists' Magazine,* VI, 339 (Dec. 1933)

BURGESS, Frederick, 'County Masons', *Genealogists' Magazine,* XI, 274 (Dec. 1952)

COLVIN, Howard Montague, *A Biographical Dictionary of English Architects 1660-1840,* 1954

FOSTER, Joseph, *The Register of Admissions to Gray's Inn, 1521-1889, together with the register of marriages in Gray's Inn Chapel 1695-1754,* 1889

GIUSEPPI, J.A., 'Families of Long Service at the Bank of England', *Genealogists' Magazine,* X, 399 and 439 (Sept. and Dec. 1949)

GROVE, *Sir* George (ed.), *Dictionary of Music and Musicians*, 6th ed. edited by Stanley Sadie, 20 vols, 1981

GUNNIS, Rupert, *Dictionary of British Sculptors 1660-1851,* [1953]

INNER TEMPLE, *Students admitted to the Inner Temple, 1547-1660* [1877]

JACOBS, Phyllis M. (compiler), *Registers of the Universities, Colleges and Schools of Great Britain,* 1965

JARVIS, Rupert C., 'The Records of the Customs and Excise Services', *Genealogists' Magazine* X, 219 (Sept. 1948)

JOHNSTON, William, *Roll of Commissioned Officers in the Medical Service of the British Army, who served on full pay within the period between the accession of George II and the formation of the Royal Army Medical Corps,* ed. by Lt-Col. Harry A.L. Howell, 1917

JOSLIN, David M., 'London Private Bankers, 1720-1785', *Economic History Review,* 2nd ser. VII (1954)

JUDD, Gerrit Parmele, *Members of Parliament, 1734-1832,* New Haven, U.S.A., 1955

LINCOLN'S INN, *The Records of the Honorable Society of Lincoln's Inn,* 2 vols [Vol 1 Admissions 1420-1799, Vol II. Admissions 1800-1893], 1896

MIDDLE TEMPLE, *Register of Admissions to the Honorable Society of the, from 15th Century to 1944, compiled under the direction of Sir Henry F. Macgeach by H.A.C. Sturgess, Librarian and Keeper of the Records,* 3 vol, 1949

NAMIER, *Sir* Lewis *and* BROOKE, John, *History of Parliament – The House of Commons, 1754-1790,* 3 vols, 1964 [Vols II and III consist of list of members for the period with biographical notes]

REDGRAVE, Samuel, *Dictionary of Artists of the English School,* new ed. rev. to the present date [by F.M. Redgrave], 1878

ROBSON, Robert, *The Attorney in Eighteenth-Century England,* 1959

SEDGWICK, Romney, *The House of Commons 1715-1754,* 2 vol, 1949

SLONIMSKY, Nicolas (ed), *Biographical Dictionary of Musicians,* 5th ed. New York, 1958

STURGESS, Herbert Arthur Charles, *Register of admissions to the . . . Middle Temple. From the 15th century to . . . 1944,* 3 vols, 1949

Chapter 13. Naval Ancestors

ALLEN, Joseph, *The New Navy Lists and General Record of the Services of Officers of the R.N. and R. Marines, 1846-55,* 1846-55 [a continuation of *The New Navy List compiled by an Old Commander (C. Houltain) 1839-45*]

CALLENDER, *Sir* Geoffrey Arthur Romane, *Bibliography of Naval History,* Parts 1 and 2. [Historical Assoc. Leaflets 58, 61, 1924, 1925: a brief selected list]

CAMPBELL, John, *Lives of British Admirals,* 4 vols, 1779

CHARNOCK, John, *Biographia Navalis,* 6 vols, 1794-98 [memoirs of officers of the Royal Navy from 1660 to 1797]

CLOWES, *Sir* William Laird, *The Royal Navy: a history from the earliest times to the present,* 7 vols, 1897-1903

COLLINGE, J.M., *Office Holders, vii. Navy Board Officers 1660-1832,* Inst. of Hist. Research, 1978

Commissioned Sea Officers of the Royal Navy, 3 vols [1954] [pub. by the Nat. Maritime Museum, Greenwich]

FOTHERGILL, Gerald, *Records of Naval Men*, 1910 [*Genealogists Pocket Library*, Vol 8]

HAMILTON-EDWARDS, Gerald Kenneth Savery, 'Naval Ancestry', *Amateur Historian*, I, 325 (Apr.-May, 1954)

JAMES, G.F., 'Collected Naval Biography', *Bulletin of Inst. of Historical Research*, XV, 162, 1937-8

LEWIS, Michael Arthur, *England's Sea-Officers*, 1939

LEWIS, Michael Arthur, *The Navy in Transition, 1814-1864, a social history*, 1965

LEWIS, Michael Arthur, *The Navy of Britain*, 1948

LEWIS, Michael Arthur, *A Social History of the Navy, 1793-1815*, 1960

MAINWARING, George Ernest, *A Bibliography of British Naval History*, 1930 [primarily a guide on MS material and to periodical articles, with author and subject headings]

Mariner's Mirror, 1911-date [the journal of the Society for Nautical Research]

MARSHALL, John, *Royal Naval Biography*, with supplements, 12 vols. [There is a TS index of this at the Society of Genealogists and at P.R.O.]

MERRIMAN, Reginald Dundas, 'Naval Records', *Genealogists' Magazine*, X. 95 (Dec. 1947)

Navy List, 1815-1870. [The official list, published quarterly from 1818, cont. in 2 pts 1870-1924, Active and Retired Officers (not published 1915).]

Navy Lists. The British Museum Printed General Catalogue gives printed lists of naval personnel etc. under 'England' (columns 2490-95)

O'BYRNE, William Richard, *A Naval Biographical Dictionary, comprising the life and services of every living officer in Her Majesty's Navy from the rank of Admiral of the Fleet to that of Lieutenant* [serving in 1845], 1849

O'BYRNE, William Richard, *Naval Biographical Dictionary*, new and enlarged ed., vol I and 4 pts of vol II 1861 [incomplete, to name 'H.G.S. Giles' only, but includes R. Marines, Pursers, Chaplains]

O'BYRNE, William Richard *and* O'BYRNE, Robert Henry, *The Sailor's Home Journal* [afterw. *The Naval Chronicle*] 1853-63

PERRIN, William Gordon, *Admiralty Library: Subject Catalogue of Printed Books, Part 1. Historical Section*, 1912 [Titles arranged under subject headings, but no general index]

RALFE, James, *The Naval Biography of Great Britain*, 4 vols, 1828 [a rare book]

STEEL, *List of the Royal Navy*, 1780-1816

Chapter 14. Merchant Services Record

LLOYD'S *Captains' Register, containing the names and services of certified masters of the British Mercantile Marine now afloat, compiled from the records of the Registrar-General of Seamen*, 1869 [does not include those who during the five years prior to publication have not been afloat but gives full name of masters (incl. those so qualified but serving as mates) place and date of birth, port at which examined, date of examination, and details of ships served in since receiving master's certificate]

MATHIAS, Peter *and* PEARSALL, A.W.H., jt. editors, *Shipping: a survey of historical records*, 1971 [undertaken by the Business Archives Council with the collaboration of the National Maritime Museum]

Chapter 15. Army Records

APPLEBY, C.B., 'The National Army Museum and Genealogy', *Genealogists' Magazine* XV, 14 (March 1965)

ARMY LISTS. See British Museum Printed Catalogue under 'England' columns 1485-91. The official printed lists have been published annually since 1754

DALTON, Charles, *English Army Lists and Commission Registers, 1661-1714,* 6 vols, 1892-1904

DALTON, Charles, *George I's Army 1714-1727,* 2 vols, 1910

DWELLY, E., *Muster Roll of British N.C.O.'s and Men at the Battle of Waterloo,* which only covers the Cavalry

FELLOWES, Edmund Horace, *The Military Knights of Windsor 1352-1944* [1944]

FORTESCUE, Sir John William, *A History of the British Army,* 13 vols and 6 atlases, 1899-1930

HAMILTON-EDWARDS, Gerald Kenneth Savery, *In Search of Army Ancestry,* 1977

HART, H.G., *Hart's Army List,* 1840-1916 [later New Annual Army List and cont. under varying titles]

Journal of the Society for Army Historical Research, 1921-date

Chapter 16. The East India Company

Asiatic Annual Register, or a view of the history of Hindustan, 1800-12.

Asiatic Journal and Monthly Register for British India, Vols 1-25, 1816-28, vols 26-28, 1828, cont. under various titles to 1845 [45 vols]

BULLOCK, Humphrey, 'Anglo-Indian Family History', *Amateur Historian,* I, 117 (Feb.-March 1953)

CRAWFORD, Dirom Grey, *A History of the Indian Medical Service, 1600-1930,* 2 vols, 1914

CRAWFORD, Dirom Grey, *Roll of the Indian Medical Service, 1615-1930, compiled by . . . D.G. Crawford,* 1930

DANVERS, F.C. (ed.), *List of Marine Records of the late East India Company, preserved in the Record Department of the India Office,* 1895. [Useful information, including lists of ships' journals, logs and various miscellaneous papers]

DODWELL, Edward *and* MILES, James Samuel, *East India Company's Bengal Civil Servants, 1780-1838,* 1839

DODWELL, Edward, *and* MILES, James Samuel, *East India Company's Bombay Civil Servants, 1798-1839,* 1839

DODWELL, Edward, *and* MILES, James Samuel, *East India Company's Madras Civil Servants, 1780-1839,* 1839

DODWELL, Edward, *and* MILES, James Samuel, *Medical Officers of the Indian Army, 1764-1838,* 1839

DODWELL, Edward, *and* MILES, James Samuel, *Officers of the Indian Army, 1760-Sept. 30, 1837,* 1838

DODWELL, Henry Herbert, *A Calendar of the Madras Despatches 1744-1765,* 2 vols, Madras, 1920-30.

DODWELL, Henry Herbert, *A Calendar of the Madras Records, 1740-1744,* Madras, 1917

East India Register and Directory [cont. under various titles] 1803-1895 [after which date the official *India Office List* and *Indian Army List* took its place]

FOSTER, Sir William, *Guide to the India Office Records, 1600-1858,* 1919

HARDY, Charles, *A Register of Ships employed in the Service of the . . . East India Company from 1760 to 1810 . . . rev. with considerable additions by H.C. Hardy,* 1811

HILL, Samuel Charles, *Bengal in 1756-1757: a selection of public and private papers dealing with the affairs of the British in Bengal during the reign of Siraj-Uddaula ed. with notes and an historical introduction by S.C.H.,* 3 vols, 1905 etc.

HILL, Samuel Charles, *Catalogue of the Home Miscellaneous Series of the India Office Records,* 1927

HILL, Samuel Charles, *List of Europeans and others in the English Factories in Bengal at the time of the Siege of Calcutta in the year 1756, with an appendix containing lists of European Sufferers,* Calcutta, 1902

HODSON, Vernon Charles Paget, 'India Office Records', *Genealogists' Magazine*, VI, 198 (March 1933)

HODSON, Vernon Charles Paget, *List of the Officers of the Bengal Army 1758-1834,* 4 pts, 1927-47

HODSON, Vernon Charles Paget, 'Some Families with a long East India Connection', *Genealogists' Magazine,* VI, 18, 63 103, 159, 247, 294, 355 (March 1932-Dec. 1933)

HYDE, Henry Barry, *The Parish of Bengal 1678 to 1788,* Calcutta, 1899

HYDE, Henry Barry, *Parochial Annals of Bengal: being a history of the Bengal Ecclesiastical Establishment of the Honourable East India Company in the 17th and 18th centuries, compiled from original sources,* Calcutta, priv. pr. 1901.

IVES, Edward, *A Voyage from England to India in the year 1754*, 1773 [mainly a description of the war]

LOVE, Henry Davison, *Vestiges of Old Madras 1640-1800,* 4 vols, 1913 [drawn from original records and well documented and indexed]

LOW, Charles Rathbone, *History of the Indian Navy 1613-1863,* 2 vols. 1877

PHILIPS, Cyril Henry, *The East India Company 1784-1834,* 1940 [Univ. of Manchester Historical Series No 77]

PRINSEP, Charles Campbell, *Record of Services of the Honourable East India Company's Civil Servants in the Madras Presidency, from 1741 to 1858 etc.,* 1885

SAINSBURY, Ethel Bruce (ed.), *A Calendar of the Court Minutes etc. of the East India Company. 1635-1639* [etc.] 1907-[in progress]

VIBART, Henry Meredith, *The Military History of the Madras Engineers and Pioneers from 1743 to the present time,* 2 vols, 1881-3

WILSON, William John, *History of the Madras Army,* 3 vols, Madras, 1882-3

Chapter 17. Jews, Huguenots and Other Immigrants

Jews
Anglo-Jewish Notabilities, their arms and testamentary dispositions, 1949. [Jewish Hist. Soc. of England publication]

ARNOLD, Arthur P., *A List of Jews and their Households in London, extracted from the census list of 1695*

BEVIS MARKS RECORDS, Part II. *Abstract of the Kutuboth or Marriage Contracts of the Congregation from the earliest times until 1837,* with index, 1949

FRANKLIN, Arthur Ellis, 'Jewish Forenames', *Genealogists' Magazine*, VII, 244 (March 1936)

HYAMSON, Albert Montefiore, 'The Jewish Obituaries in the Gentleman's Magazine [1731-1868]', *Miscellanies of the Jewish Historical Society of England,* Pt IV, 1942

HYAMSON, Albert Montefiore, *Plan of a Dictionary of Anglo-Jewish Biography . . . repr. from Anglo-Jewish Notabilities* [1949]

HYAMSON, Albert Montefiore, *The Sephardim of England: a History of the Spanish and Portuguese Jewish Community 1492-1951,* 1951

HORTON-SMITH, Lionel Graham Horton, 'Naturalisation and where to look', *Genealogists' Magazine,* X, 451 (Dec. 1949)

JACOBS, Joseph *and* WOLF, Lucien, *Bibliotheca Anglo-Judaica*, new ed. rev. and enlarged by Cecil Roth, 1937

JEWISH HISTORICAL SOCIETY OF ENGLAND, *Transactions*, 1895-date

LIPMAN, Vivian David, *Social History of the Jews in England 1850-1950,* 1954

ROTH, Cecil, *Archives of the United Synagogue,* 1930

ROTH, Cecil, *A History of the Jews in England,* 1941

ROTH, Cecil, *Magna Bibliotheca Anglo Judaica: a bibliographical guide to Anglo-Jewish history,* new ed., 1937

RYE, Walter, *The Persecutions of the Jews in England . . . a lecture . . . repr. from the 'Anglo-Jewish Exhibition Papers',* 1887

SAMUEL, Edgar R., 'Jewish Ancestors and where to find them'. *Genealogists' Magazine,* XI, 412 (Dec. 1953)

SAMUEL, Wilfred S., 'Sources of Anglo-Jewish Genealogy', *Genealogists' Magazine,* VI, 146 (Dec. 1932)

WOLF, Lucien, 'Old Anglo-Jewish Families', in *Essays in Jewish History,* Jewish Hist. Soc., 1934

Huguenots and Other Immigrants

AGNEW, David Carnegie A., *Protestant Exiles from France in the Reign of Louis XIV; or, the Huguenot Refugees and their Descendants in Great Britain and Ireland,* priv. pr., 1866

HORTON-SMITH, L.G.H., 'Naturalisation and Where to Look', *Genealogists' Magazine,* X, 451 (Dec. 1949)

LART, Charles Edmund, 'French Records', *Genealogists' Magazine,* VII, 1 (March 1935)

LART, Charles Edmund, 'French Noblesse', *Genealogists' Magazine,* VII, 229 (March 1936)

LART, Charles Edmund, *Huguenot Pedigrees,* 1924—

LART, Charles Edmund, *The Huguenot Regiments,* 1911 [fr. *Proceedings of the Huguenot Soc.,* IX, 3 (1885)]

LART, Charles Edmund, 'The Huguenot Society and its work', *Genealogists' Magazine,* III, 50 (Sept. 1927)

MINET, Miss S., 'Huguenot Records', *Genealogists' Magazine,* XII, 149 and 185 (March and June 1956)

REAMAN, George Elmore, *The Trail of the Huguenots in Europe, the United States, South Africa and Canada,* 1964

WEINER, Margery, *The French Exiles,* 1960

WULCKO, Laurance M., 'Naturalisation and Where to Look (II)', *Genealogists' Magazine,* X, 496 (March 1950)

Chapter 18. Scottish Records I: Civil and Parish Records

BLACK, George Fraser, *The Surnames of Scotland: their origin, meaning and history,* New York 1946

Book of the Old Edinburgh Club, 19 vols-[in progress] 1908-date

DONALDSON, Gordon, 'Scottish Registration', *The Scottish Genealogist,* July and October 1955

HAMILTON-EDWARDS, Gerald Kenneth Savery, *In Search of Scottish Ancestry,* repr. 1979, ch. II & III.

HOGAN, E.A. 'Scottish Registration', *The Scottish Genealogist,* April 1956

JOHNSTON, W. and A.K., *and others, Gazetteer of Scotland* (incl. a glossary of the most common Gaelic names), 2nd ed. 1958

STUART, Margaret, 'Genealogical Records in Scotland', *Genealogists' Magazine,* V, 277 (March 1931)

TURNBULL, William Barclay David Donald, *Scottish Parochial Registers: memoranda of the state of the parochial registers of Scotland,* 1849

WHYTE, Donald, *Introducing Scottish Genealogical Research,* 2nd ed, rev. and enl., Edinburgh, Scottish Genealogy Society, 1979

Chapter 19. Scottish Records 11: Sasines, Services, Testaments and other records

ADAM, Frank, *The Clans, Septs and Regiments of the Scottish Highlands,* 8th edn, revised by Sir Thomas Innes of Learney, 1970

ADAMS, Ian H., *Descriptive List of Plans in the Scottish Record Office,* vol. 1, 1967

ANDERSON, A., 'The Scottish Record Office', *Genealogists' Magazine,* XV, 64 (June 1965)

BAIN, Robert, *The Clans and Tartans of Scotland,* 4th ed. enlarged and re-ed. by Margaret O. Macdougall, 1959

BALFOUR-MELVILLE, Evan W.M. ed., *The Register of the Privy Council of Scotland,* 3rd ser., vol. 15, A.D. 1690, 1967

DALTON, Charles, *The Scots Army, 1661-1688, with memoirs of the commanders-in-chief,* 2 pts, 1909

Epitaphs and Inscriptions from Burial Grounds and Old Buildings in the North East of Scotland, with historical, biographical, genealogical etc., notes, 2 vols, 1875-9

EVANS, David Ellis, *Gaulish Personal Names: a study of some Continental Celtic formations,* 1967

Faculty of Advocates in Scotland, 1532-1943, 1944

FERGUSON, Joan Primrose S., *Scottish Family Histories held in Scottish Libraries,* 1960 [includes MSS and TS papers, pedigrees and genealogical charts]

FERGUSON, Joan Primrose S., *Scottish Newspapers held in Scottish Libraries,* 1956

FOSTER, Joseph, *Members of Parliament, Scotland, 1357-1882,* 2nd ed. rev. and corrected, 1882

GENERAL REGISTER HOUSE, EDINBURGH, *Detailed List of the Old Parish Registers of Scotland,* 1872

GIBSON, James, *Inscriptions on the Tombstones and Monuments in Memory of the Covenanters,* 1881

GILCHRIST, George [Monumental Inscriptions] [from surveys by Robert A. Shannon] *Applegarth and Sibbaldbie parishes,* 1971, *Kirkpatrick-Juxta parish,* 1972, *Trailflatt parish* (now incl. in Tinwald pa.), 1971, *Moffatt parish,* 1971, *Meigle parish,* 1972, *Bewcastle parish,* 1973 [from surveys by Alexander McCracken and Arthur Tolson], *Castleton parish* (new edn), 1972, *Langholm parish,* vol. 3, *Staplegordon parish,* 1971

GRAHAM, Henry Grey, *The Social Life of Scotland in the 18th Century,* 4th ed., 2 vols, 1937

GRANT, *Sir* Francis James, *The County Families of the Zetland Islands,* 1893

GRANT, *Sir* Francis James, *Index to Genealogies, Birth-briefs and Funeral Escutcheons in the Lyon Office, Edinburgh,* 1908

GRANT, *Sir* Francis James, 'Presbyterian Court Records 156-1935', in *Sources and Literature of Scots Law,* Stair Society Vol. 1 (1935)

HAMILTON-EDWARDS, Gerald Kenneth Savery, *In Search of Scottish Ancestry,* 1972, repr. with amendments, 1979

INNES of LEARNEY, *Sir* Thomas, 'Descent of the Chiefship and Chieftancy of Clans', *Genealogists' Magazine,* VIII 191, 255 (Dec. 1938 and March 1939)

INNES OF LEARNEY, *Sir* Thomas, *The Tartans of the Clans and Families of Scotland,* 8th edn, 1972

INNES OF LEARNEY, *Sir* Thomas, *Scots Heraldry* new edn rev. by Malcolm R. Innes, 1978

JOHNSON, J. Bolam, *Scottish Records,* 1908 [*Genealogists' Pocket Library* series, bound up with *Royal Descents*]

LART, Charles Edmund, *The Pedigrees and Papers of James Terry, Athlone Herald at the Court of King James II in France, 1690-1725,* 1938

List of Owners of Property in Edinburgh 1634-6, in *The Book of the Old Edinburgh Club,* 1924

LIVINGSTONE, Matthew, *A Guide to the Public Records of Scotland deposited in H.M. General Register House, Edinburgh,* 1905. [See also Supplements to this in the *Scottish Historical Review,* vols 26 and 27 (1946-7)]

LORD LYON, (Court of), *An Ordinary of Arms contained in the Public Register of All Arms and Bearings in Scotland, 1902-1973,* vol. 2 [of the work by Sir J.B. Paul] compiled in the Lyon Office [by David Reid of Robertland and Vivien Wilson] Edinburgh, 1977

M'CONNELL, Ernest Whigham Jardine (ed.), *Marriages at Gretna Hall, 1829-1855,* 1949

Handlist of Scottish and Welsh Records Publications, Scottish Section by Peter Gouldebrough and A.P. Kup; Welsh Section by Idwal Lewis, Br. Records Assoc. Publications Pamphlet No. 4, 1954

MACFARLANE, Walter, *Genealogical Collections concerning Families in Scotland,* ed. by J.T. Clarke, 2 vols, 1887 [Scottish History Society]

MACKENZIE, Agnes Muir, *Scotland in Modern Times, 1720-1939,* 1941

MACLEOD, Walter (ed.), *A List of Persons concerned in the Rebellion* [1745-6], 1890 [*Scot. Hist. Soc.,* Vol. VIII: gives 2,590 names, mainly from East-Central Scotland]

MITCHELL, John Fowler *and* MITCHELL, Sheila, *Monumental Inscriptions (pre-1855) in: Kinross-shire,* 1967; *Clackmannanshire,* 1968; *West Lothian,* 1969; *Dunbartonshire,* 1969; *Renfrewshire,* 1969; *East Fife,* 1971; *East Stirlingshire,* 1972; *West Fife,* 1972; *West Stirlingshire,* 1973; *South Perthshire,* 1974 (Scottish Genealogy Society)

MUNRO, Robert William, *Kinsmen and Clansmen,* 1971

New Statistical Account of Scotland by the Ministers of the Respective Parishes, 15 vols, 1845 [under 'Scotland, Appendix-Miscellaneous' in Br. Mus. printed Catalogue]

PATON, Henry (ed.), *The Lyon in Mourning; or, A collection of speeches, letters, journals, etc., relative to the affairs of Prince Charles Edward Stuart by the Rev. Robert Forbes . . . 1746-1775,* 3 vols, 1895-6

PATON, Henry M., *The Scottish Records, their history and value,* 1933 (Hist. Assoc. of Scotland pamphlets New Ser. No. 7)

PAUL, *Sir* James Balfour, *The Scots Peerage,* 9 vols, 1904-14. [Vol. 9 is an index]

RENNIE, James Alan, *The Scottish People; their clans, families and origins,* 1960

RIDDELL, 'MS Baronetage of Scotland', in Scottish National Library

ROGERS, Charles, *Monuments and Monumental Inscriptions in Scotland,* 2 vols, 1871-2

SANDISON, Alexander, 'Shetland Surnames', *Genealogists' Magazine,* XIII, 45 and 76 (June and Sept. 1959)

SANDISON, Alexander, *Tracing Ancestors in Shetland,* 2nd edn, 1978

SCOTT, Hew, *Fasti Ecclesiae Scoticanae, the succession of ministers in the parish churches of Scotland from . . . 1560,* New ed. rev. [ed. by W.S. Crockett and F.J. Grant] 7 vols, 1915-28

Scottish Family Histories: a list of books for consultation in the Edinburgh Reference Library 1958

SCOTTISH GENEALOGY SOCIETY, *Monumental Inscriptions (Pre-1855) in Peebleshire,* recorded by Sheila A. Scott, 1971

SCOTTISH GENEALOGY SOCIETY, *Pre-1855 Tombstone Inscriptions in Berwickshire* [recorded by David C. Cargill, Snr and others], 2 vols, 1971

SCOTTISH RECORD SOCIETY publications, 72 vols, 1898-date. [Lists of commissariot records, burgesses and guild-brethren, and apprentices for various burghs and towns]

Sectional List No 24 – *Record Publications,* H.M.S.O., 1965 [includes the indexes to Sasines and the Register of Deeds so far published]

SETON, *Sir* Bruce Gordon *and* ARNOT, Jean Gordon (editors), *The Prisoners of the '45,* 3 vols, 1928-9

SIMPSON, Grant G., *Scottish Handwriting, 1150-1650,* 1973

SINCLAIR, *Rt. Hon. Sir* John, *Bart,* The Statistical Account of Scotland; drawn up from the communications of the ministers of the different parishes, 21 vols, 1791-9

STEEL, Donald John, *Sources for Scottish Genealogy and Family History,* 1970. (Nat. Index of Parish Registers, vol. 12)

STUART, Margaret, *Scottish Family History,* 1930

TAYLER, Alistair *and* TAYLER, Henrietta, *Jacobites of Aberdeenshire and Banffshire in the Rising of 1715,* 1934

TAYLER, Alistair *and* TAYLER, Henrietta, *Jacobites of Aberdeenshire and Banffshire in the Forty Five,* 1928

THOMSON, John Maitland, *The Public Records of Scotland,* 1922

TURNBULL, William Barclay David Donald, *Catalogue of the MSS relating to Genealogy and Heraldry preserved in the Library of the Faculty of Advocates,* 1852 [only 10 copies printed]

WHYTE, Donald, ed., *A Dictionary of Scottish Emigrants to the U.S.A.,* Magna Carta Book Co., Baltimore, U.S.A., and Heraldry Today, London, 1972

Chapter 20. Irish Records

AINSWORTH, John Francis, 'Research in Ireland', *Genealogists' Magazine,* VIII, 249 (March 1939)

BURKE, M. *and others, Walker's Hibernian Magazine: Index to Deaths in Walker's Hibernian Magazine, vols 1-35; compiled by M. Burke and others for the Fellowship of the Library Association of Ireland* [to be published]

BURTCHAELL, George Dames and SADLEIR, Thomas Ulick (editors), *Alumni Dublinenses; a register of the students, graduates, professors and provosts of Trinity College, in the University of Dublin,* new ed. [1593-1860], 1935

CLARE, Wallace, *A Simple Guide to Irish Genealogy,* 3rd edn revised by Rosemary ffolliott, 1966

CLARKE, Richard Samuel Jessop, compiler, *Gravestone Inscriptions* Ulster-Scot Historical

Society, Belfast, 1966-74: *County Down:* [For details of Baronies covered see British Library Catalogue (printed) under his name]

Clerical Directory for Ireland; containing a list of the benefices, with their patrons; the names of the incumbents and curates etc., 1858

CONNELL, Kenneth Hugh, *The Population of Ireland 1750-1845,* 1950

CRONE, John Smythe, '*Bibliography of the Irish Family History*', *Irish Book Lover,* V, 91, 110, 151, 168, 204, 223 (1913-14); VI, 83, 116 (1914-15)

CRONE, John Smythe, *A Concise Dictionary of Irish Biography,* rev., and enlarged, 1937 [contains some 3,000 five-line biographies]

DARWIN, Kenneth, 'The Irish Records Situation', *Journal of the Society of Archivists,* II, No. 8 (Oct. 1963) [describes the record repositories in Ireland and their contents]

EAGER, Alan Robert, *A Guide to Irish Bibliographical material; being a bibliog. of Irish bibliographies and some sources of information,* 1964

FALLEY, Margaret Dickson, *Irish and Scotch-Irish Ancestral Research: a guide to the genealogical records, methods and sources in Ireland,* 2 vols, U.S.A., Evanston [1961-2]

FARRAR, Robert Henry, *Irish Marriages . . . an index to Walker's 'Hibernian Magazine', 1771 to 1812, with an appx fr. notes of Sir Arthur Vicars . . . of the births, marriages and deaths in 'The Anthologia Hibernica, 1793 and 1794,* 2 vols, 1897 [75 copies priv. pr.]

GARDNER, David E., HARLAND, D. *and* SMITH, F., *Genealogical Atlas of Ireland,* U.S.A., Salt Lake City, 1964

HALLIDAY, Bernard, *Ireland and Irish Families: catalogue of special collections of books on Ireland and collections of MSS, 1500-1850, relating to principal families of Ireland . . . mostly from the collection of the Rev. J. Graves,* 1904

LEADER, Michael, 'Irish Records', *Genealogists' Magazine,* XII, 512, 540 (Sept. and Dec. 1958)

LIMERICK, 'Farrar's Limerick Directory, 1769', *Irish Genealogists,* III, No. 9 (Oct. 1964) [a reprint of the first Limerick directory]

MACLYSAGHT, Edward, *Irish Families: their names, arms and origins,* 3rd edn, revised, Dublin, 1978

MACLYSAGHT, Edward, *More Irish Families,* 1960

MACLYSAGHT, Edward, *The Surnames of Ireland,* 1973 [a paperback of the 1969 edn]

MACLYSAGHT, Edward, *Survey of Documents in private keeping,* 1st ser. *Anal. Hib.* No. 15, 1944 2nd series by John F. Answorth and Edward MacLysaght, *ibid.* No. 20, 1958

O'BRIEN, A., *An Index of Deaths and Marriages from the Waterford Mirror 1800-1843.* [In preparation: for Fellowship of the Library Association of Ireland – to be published shortly]

O'BRIEN, George Augustus Thomas, *The Economic History of Ireland in the Eighteenth Century,* [1918]

O'HART, John, *The Irish and Anglo-Irish Landed Gentry,* 1969 [1st edn reprinted with intro. by Edward MacLysaght—facsimile reprints]

PENDER, Séamus, *A Guide to Irish Genealogical Collections,* 1935. [*Analecta Hibernica,* VII]

PHAIR, P.B., 'Guide to the Register of Deeds', *Analecta Hibernica,* XXIII, 257 (1966)

SADLER, Thomas Ulick, 'Ulster Officer Records', *Genealogists' Magazine,* VI, 434 (June 1934)

YOUNG, Arthur, *A Tour in Ireland, with general observations on the present state of that kingdom made in the years 1776, 1777 and 1778,* 2nd ed. 2 vols, 1780

Chapter 21. Welsh Records

DAVIES, Trefor Rendell (compiler), *A Book of Welsh Names,* 1952
Dictionary of Welsh Biography (400-1940), 1959
HALL, Hubert, 'Welsh Local Records: details and classified topographical list', *Transactions of Hon. Cymmrodorion Society,* pp. 16-24, 1914-15
Handlist of Scottish and Welsh Records Publications, . . . Welsh Section by Idwal Lewis, Br. Records Assoc. Publications Pamph. No. 4, 1954
JONES, E.D., *The Department of MSS and Records in the National Library of Wales,* 1947 [repr. from the *N. Lib. of Wales Journal*]
JONES, E.D., 'Material for the Genealogist in the National Library of Wales', *Genealogists' Magazine,* IV, 313 (June 1964)
JONES, Francis, 'An Approach to Welsh Genealogy', *Transactions of the Hon. Soc. of Cymmrodorion* (Session 1948)), 1949
Lewis's Topographical Dictionary of Wales, 1849
MEYRICK, Samuel Rush, *Heraldic Visitation of Wales and part of the Marches between the years 1586 and 1613,* 2 vols, 1846 (from the MS of Lewis Dwnn)
NICHOLAS, Thomas, *Annals and Antiquities of the counties and country families of Wales,* 2nd ed., rev. and enlarged, 2 vols, 1875
WILLIAMS, David, *A Short History of Modern Wales,* 1961
WILLIAMS, William Retlaw, *The Parliamentary History of the Principality of Wales . . . 1541-1895, comprising lists of representatives with biographical . . . notices of the members,* 1895

Chapter 22. The Dominions, the U.S.A. and Other Countries

Australian Dictionary of Biography, 1788-1850, 2 vols, Melbourne, 1966-7, *1851-1890 4 vol.* Melbourne, 1969-72; *1891-1939, 1 vol,* 1979
BALLEINE, George Reginald, *A Biographical Dictionary of Jersey* [1948]
BAKER, Edward Cecil, *A Guide to Records in the Leeward Islands,* 1965
BAKER, Edward Cecil, *A Guide to Records in the Windward Islands,* 1967
BIRD, Jack, 'Some Sources for French Genealogy and Heraldry', *Genealogists' Magazine,* XIII, 237 (Dec. 1960)
BIRD, Jack, 'Some Sources for German Genealogy and Heraldry', *Genealogists' Magazine,* XIII, 143 (March 1960)
BOLT, Alan, *The Sailing Ships of the New Zealand Shipping Company,* 1972
CAMAJANI, *Count* Guelfo Guelfi, 'Some Sources for Italian Genealogy', *Genealogists' Magazine,* XIV, 66 (Sept. 1962)
CHANDLER, M.J., *A Guide to Records in Barbados,* 1965
CUNNINGHAM, J.R.,'The Genealogical Work of the Latter-Day Saints', *Genealogists' Magazine,* XIV, 369 (Sept. 1964)
CURRER-BRIGGS, Noel, *English Adventurers and Colonial Settlers: Abstracts of legal proceedings in seventeenth-century English and Dutch courts relating to immigrant families: a source material guide,* 1971
CURRER-BRIGGS, Noel, *English Adventurers and Virginia Settlers: the co-ordinated use of seventeenth-century British and American Records by genealogists,* 3 vols (Genealogical Research series: source material guide), 1969

DAVIES, C.E.S., 'Tracing Ancestors and Constructing Family Trees . . . Pt. I. Enquiries to make in Australia', *The Ancestor,* Dec. 1962 [Quarterly Journal of the Genealogical Society of Victoria, Australia]

Dictionary of Canadian Biography, vol. 1, *1000 to 1700,* 1966; vol. 2, *1701 to 1740,* 1969; vol 10, *1871 to 1880,* 1972; vol. 9, *1861-1870,* 1976

FAHY, T.G., 'Genealogical Research in the Netherlands', *Genealogists' Magazine,* XIII, 366 (Dec. 1961)

FAHY, T.G., 'Some Sources for Dutch Genealogy', *Genealogists' Magazine,* XIV, 24 (March 1962)

FELTHAM, John *and* WRIGHT, E., *Memorial of God's Acre; being monumental inscriptions in the Isle of Man,* 1868 [from a MS mainly copied in 1797, representing some 2,000 inscriptions and ed. by W. Harrison]

Dictionary of New Zealand Biography, 2 vols, 1940

FOTHERGILL, Gerald, *American Emigrants: How to trace their English Ancestry,* 1908 [being Vol. I of *Some Special Studies in Genealogy]*

GRAY, Nancy *and* others, 'Compiling a Family History: A guide to procedure and use of Australian records', *Descent,* II, iii, 84 (1965)

GUILLET, Edwin Clarence, *The Great Migration: the Atlantic Crossing by Sailing Ships since 1770,* 2nd ed., 1963

JOSEPH, Anthony P., 'On Tracing Australian Jewish Genealogy', *Genealogists' Magazine, XIV, 425 (Dec. 1964)* [although particularly dealing with Jewish ancestry, much of the information is equally applicable to Australian genealogy in general]

KAMINKOW, Jack *and* KAMINKOW, Marion (editors), *A List of Emigrants from England to America, 1718-1759 . . . transcribed from records at the Guildhall, London,* 1964 [not incl., in Lancour's *Bibliography]*

LANCOUR, Adlore Harold, *A Bibliography of Ship Passenger Lists, 1538-1825,* 3rd ed. (of Passenger lists of ships coming to North America, 1607-1825) rev. and enlarged by R.J. Wolfe, with a list of passenger arrival records in the national archives, by F.E. Bridgers, New York, 1963

LANGTON, C., 'Records and Record Searching in Jersey', *Genealogists' Magazine,* V, 314 (June 1931)

LAWRENCE-ARCHER, James Henry, *Monumental Inscriptions of the British West Indies . . . with genealogical and historical annotations etc.,* 1875

LIVINSTON, Sir Nöel B., *Sketch Pedigrees of some of the Early Settlers in Jamaica . . : . with a list of the inhabitants in 1670 etc.,* 1909

MOORE, Arthur William, *Manx Names . . . with a preface by Professor Rhys,* 2nd ed., rev, 1903

NICHOLSON, Cregoe Donaldson Percy, 'Some Early Emigrants to America', *Genealogists' Magazine,* XII-XIII (March 1955 to Dec. 1960)

PAYNE, James Bertrand, *An Armorial of Jersey: an account, heraldic and antiquarian, of its chief native families with pedigrees, biographical notices etc.* [issued in parts and incomplete], 1859-65

PINE, Leslie Gilbert, *American Origins,* New York, 1960. [Gives information of sources in most European countries]

PUBLIC ARCHIVES OF CANADA, *Tracing your Ancestors in Canada,* 1966 [This booklet is reprinted in the *Genealogists' Magazine,* XV, 293 (Dec. 1966)]

PUGH, Ralph Bernard, *The Records of the Colonial and Dominions Offices,* 1964 [Public Record Office Handbook 3]

RABINO di BORGOMALE, H.L., 'Genealogical Research in France', *Genealogists' Magazine,* X, 1 (Sept. 1946)

SERLE, Percival, *Dictionary of Australian Biography,* 2 vols, Sydney, 1949

WALLACE, William Stewart, (ed.) *The Macmillan Biography of Canadian Biography,* 3rd ed. rev. and enlarged, 1963

WRIGHT, Phillip Richard Turta, *Monumental Inscriptions in Jamaica*, 1966

SOME ARTICLES IN THE GENEALOGISTS' MAGAZINE ON OVERSEAS GENEALOGICAL SOURCES

AUSTRALIA

JOSEPH, Anthony P., Anglo-Australia Genealogy, Mch & Jne 1981

BAHAMAS

WHITTLETON, Eric H., Family History in the Bahamas, Dec 1975

BARBADOS

STANFORD, C.J., Genealogical Sources in Barbados, Mch 1974

BELGIUM

HILLE, Philippe van, Genealogy in Belgium, Sept. 1968

BYZANTIUM

BIERBRIER, M.L., Modern Descendants of Byzantine Families, Sept. 1980

CANADA

Tracing your ancestors in Canada [repr. from booklet of the Public Archives of Canada, publ. Aug. 1966], Dec 1966

CHANNEL ISLES

BURNESS, Lawrence R., Genealogical Research in the Channel Isles, Mch 1978

FRANCE

AUDIN, Margaret, Tracing Ancestors in France, Dec 1981

GERMANY

BIRD, Jack, Some Sources for German Genealogy, Mch 1960

IRELAND

FFOLLIOT, Rosemary, Ireland's Records Regained, 1973

JAMAICA

WRIGHT, Philip, Material for Family History in Jamaica, Sept. 1966

NETHERLANDS

RESANDT, W. Wijnaendt van, Genealogy in the Netherlands, Jne 1974

POLAND

KLEC-PILEWSKI, Bernard, Compiler, Some Sources for Polish Genealogy, Dec 1969

SOUTH AFRICA

LOMBARD, R.T.J., Genealogical Research in South Africa, Dec 1978
BOTHA, C. Graham, Further Monumental Inscriptions, Cape of Good Hope, Mch 1951

UNITED STATES OF AMERICA

BOAM, T.L., Modern Sources for Genealogical Research in the United States, Mch 1977

Chapter 23. Various Other Sources

ARROWSMITH, R.L., *Charterhouse Register, June 1769-May 1872,* 1974
BERNAU, Charles Allan, *The Genealogy of the Submerged,* 1908 [Vol III of *Some Special Studies in Genealogy]*
'Bibliography of Lists of Apprenticeships', Genealogists' Magazine, VII, 18 and 74 (March and June, 1935)
BURGESS, Frederick, *English Churchyard Memorials,* 1963
COLBY, Reginald, 'The Bryant Index', *Genealogists' Magazine,* X, 488 (March 1950)
DRENNAN, Basil St George, *Keble College Centenary Register, 1870-1970,* 1970
EMDEN, A.B., *A Biographical Register of the University of Oxford to A.D. 1500,* 3 vols, 1957-9
GUILDHALL LIBRARY, *London Business House Histories: a handlist* [1964]
HABAKKUK, Hrothgar John, 'Marriage Settlements in the Eighteenth Century', *Transactions of the Royal Historical Society,* XXXII (1950)
JACOBS, Phyllis M., ed., *Registers of the Universities, Colleges and Schools of Great Britain and Ireland* (Inst. of Historical Research publication), 1964
KETCHLEY, C.P., 'Apprentices – Trade and Poor', *Amateur Historian,* II, 357 (June-July 1956)
LEESON, Francis, *A Guide to the Records of British State Tontines and Life Annuities of the 17th and 18th centuries* (Pinhorn Handbook No. 3) 1968
MATTHEWS, William, *British Autobiographies,* Univ. of California, U.S.A., 1955
MATTHEWS, William, *British Diaries: an annotated bibliography of British Diaries, written between 1442 and 1942,* 1950 [Diaries in MS are recorded, with author index]
TRINICK, Michael, 'A Country House Index', *Genealogists' Magazine,* XI, 89 (Sept. 1951) [*The Bryant Index,* see also under Colby, Reginald]
UNWIN, George, *The Guilds and Companies of London,* 2nd ed., 1962 [includes bibliog. of printed works on the different guilds of London additional to those in his 1908 edition]

Chapter 24. Places of Search: I. The Society of Genealogists

CAMP, Anthony John, 'Collections and Indexes of the Society of Genealogists', *Genealogists' Magazine,* XIII, 311 (June 1961)
Guide to the Library of the Society of Genealogists, [mimeographed] 1965
PERCY-SMITH, Hubert Kendall, 'The Headquarters of Genealogy in Britain', *Amateur Historian,* I, 70 (Dec.-Jan. 1953)
RAYMONT, J.L., *Notes on the recording of monumental inscriptions,* 3rd edn, Plymouth, Fed. of Fam. History Soc., 1981
WARD, W.R., *Administrations of the Window and Assessed Taxes (1696-1798),* 1963

Chapter 25. Places of Search: II The Public Record Office

FINES, J., 'Documents in the Public Record Office: III The Early Chancery Proceedings', *Amateur Historian* VI, 254 (Summer 1965)

GALBRAITH, Vivian Hunter, *An Introduction to the Use of the Public Records,* repr. with corrections, 1952

GALBRAITH, Vivian Hunter, *Studies in the Public Records,* 1948

Guide to the Contents of the Public Record Office, rev. and extended (to 1960) from the Guide by the late M.S. Giuseppi, F.S.A., 2 vols, 1963: Vol. 1 Legal Records; Vol. 2 State Papers and Departmental Records; Vol. 3, Documents Transferred 1960-1966, 1968 [the official guide, pub. by H.M.S.O.]

HECTOR, L.C., 'Genealogy in the Public Records, *Genealogists' Magazine,* VIII, 57 (June 1938)

JOHNSON, Charles, *The Public Record Office,* 1932 [S.P.C.K. Helps]

LATHAM, R.L., 'Interpreting the Public Records' [various articles], *Amateur Historian,* I, 5 47, 77, 112, 155 (Aug. 1952-May 1953)

NEWTON, K.C., 'Reading Medieval Local Records', *Amateur Historian,* III, 81 (Winter 1956-7)

PUBLIC RECORD OFFICE, *Information for Readers,* 1963 [a 4 pp. useful pamphlet]

Record Publications (Sectional List No 24) 1965. [See under bibliog. Chapter 9, *Government Publications*]

VIRGINIA STATE LIBRARY, *The British Public Record Office: history, description, record groups, finding aids and materials for American history with special reference to Virginia,* Richmond, Virginia, U.S.A., 1960 [a useful account in 178 pp from the U.S.A. point of view]

Chapter 26. Places of Search III. The British Museum and other Libraries

DOPSON, Laurence, 'The John Rylands Library, Manchester', *Amateur Historian,* II, 202 (August.-Sept. 1955)

GILSON, Julius Parnell, *A Student's Guide to the MSS of the British Museum* [S.P.C.K. *Helps for Students of History* No. 31], 1920

HAMILTON-EDWARDS, Gerald Kenneth Savery, 'The Burnet Morris Collection at Exeter', *Genealogists' Magazine* XIV, 180 (June 1963)

HEPWORTH, Philip, *Archives and Manuscripts in Libraries, 1961,* 1962

HISTORICAL MANUSCRIPTS COMMISSION, *Record Repositories in Great Britain: a list prepared by a joint committee of the Hist. MSS Com. and the British Records Assoc.,* 1964

IRWIN, Raymond *and* STAVELEY, Ronald, (editors), *The Libraries of London,* 2nd, rev. ed., 1964

JONES, Philip Edmund, *and* SMITH, Raymond, *A Guide to the Records in the Corporation of London Records Office and the Guildhall Library Muniment Room etc.,* 1951

JONES, Philip Ernest H., 'Genealogy and the City of London Records', *Genealogists' Magazine,* XI, 134, 167 (Dec. 1951, March 1952)

REDSTONE, Lilian Jane *and* STEER, Francis William (editors), *Local Records: their nature and care,* 1953

RYE, Reginald Arthur, *The Libraries of London: a guide for students etc.* 3rd ed. 1928

SMITH, Francis Raymond S., 'The Guildhall Library in War and Peace', *Genealogists' Magazine,* X, 175 (June 1948)

WAGNER, *Sir* Anthony Richard, *The Records and Collections of the College of Arms,* 1952
WALLACE, A., 'Genealogical MSS in the Newcastle-upon-Tyne Reference Library', *Genealogists' Magazine,* XIV, 194 (Sept. 1963)

Chapter 27. Genealogy and Heraldry

BOUTELL, Charles, *English Heraldry,* rev. by C.W. Scott-Giles and J.P. Brooke-Little, 1965
BOUTELL, Charles, *Boutell's Heraldry,* revised by J.P. Brooke-Little, 1970
BROOKE-LITTLE, John Philip, *An Heraldic Alphabet,* 1973
BURKE, *Sir* John Bernard, *The General Armory of England, Scotland, Ireland and Wales,* 1884, repr. 1962
CHESSHYRE, David Hubert Boothby, *The Identification of Coats of Arms on British Silver,* 1978
CHILD, Heather, *Heraldic Design,* 1965
Coats of Arms, Rolls, Great Britain, Rolls of Arms Henry III, 1967 [Contents; Matthew Paris shields—Glover's roll—Walford's roll—Sir Anthony Wagner's additions and corrections to 'A Catalogue of English Rolls of Arms']
DENHOLM-YOUNG, Noël, *History and Heraldry, 1254 to 1310: a study of the historical value of the Rolls of Arms,* 1965
FAIRBAIRN, James, *Fairbairn's Crests of the Families of Great Britain and Ireland ... revised by Laurence Butters,* 1968 [originally publ. in 2 vols, Edinburgh, 1860]
FOSTER, Joseph, *Grantees of Arms named in Docquets and Patents between the years 1687 and 1898, preserved in various MSS ...* ed. by W.H. Rylands, 2 vols, 1916 [Harleian Society, Vols 67 and 68]
FOSTER, Joseph, *Grantees of Arms named in Docquets and Patents to the end of the 17th century, in the MSS. preserved in the British Museum ... and elsewhere, alphabetically arranged etc.,* ed by W.H. Rylands, 1915 [Harleian Socity, Vol. 66]
FOSTER, Joseph, *Some Feudal Coats of Arms from Heraldic Rolls, 1298-1418,* 1902
FOSTER, Joseph, *Two Tudor Books of Arms: being Harleian MSS. 2169 and 6163,* 1904 [De Walden Library]
FOX-DAVIES, Arthur Charles, *A Complete Guide to Heraldry,* rev. ed. repr. 1961 [still the best general work on English heraldry]
FOX-DAVIES, Arthur Charles, compiler and ed., *Armorial Families* [7th edn repr.], 1970
FOX-DAVIES, Arthur Charles, *A Complete Guide to Heraldry* revised and annotated by J.P. Brooke-Little, 1969
FRANKLYN, Julian, *Shield and Crest,* 3rd edn, 1967
FRANKLYN, Julian *and* TANNER, John, *An Encyclopaedic Dictionary of Heraldry,* 1970
GATFIELD, George, *Guide to Printed Books and Manuscripts relating to English and Foreign Heraldry and Genealogy,* 1892
GAYRE *of Gayre and Nigg,* Robert, *Heraldic Standards and Other Ensigns,* 1959
GODFREY, Walter Hindes, assisted by *Sir* Anthony Wagner, *The College of Arms ... being the 16th and final monograph of the London Survey Committee,* 1963 [contains biographies of the heralds and their coats of arms]
HALL, Winifred, *Canting and Allusive Arms of England and Wales,* 1966
HUMPHERY-SMITH, Cecil R., ed., *General Armory Two,* 1974
INNES of Learney, *Sir* Thomas, *Scots Heraldry,* 2nd ed., rev. and enlarged 1956
JOUGLA DE MORENAS, Henri, *Grand Armorial de France, 6 vols + 1 Suppl., Paris, 1934-52* [*Les Editions Héraldiques,* later *Société de Grand Armorial de France*]

LOW, Charles, *A Roll of Australian Arms*, illustrated by Alan K. Chatto, Kent Town, S. Australia, 1971

LYNDSAY, Sir David, *Facsimile of an Ancient Heraldic Manuscript emblazoned by Sir David Lyndsay, Lyon King of Arms, 1542,* 1878

MATHIEU, Rémi, *Le Système Héraldique Français*, 5th ed., Paris, 1946

MONCREIFFE *of that Ilk, Sir* Rupert Iain Kay, *bart. and* POTTINGER, Don, *Simple Heraldry, cheerfully illustrated,* 1953 [amusingly written and illustrated and full of sound accurate information on the subject]

MOULE, Thomas, *Bibliotheca Heraldica Magnae Britanniae: An Analytical Catalogue of Books on Genealogy, Heraldry, etc.,* 1882

NATIONAL ART LIBRARY, *Victoria and Albert Museum Classed Catalogue of Printed Books; Heraldry,* 1901

PAPWORTH, John Woody *and* MORANT, Alfred William Whitehead, *Ordinary of British Armorials, reproduced from the original edition of 1874:* intro. by G.D. Squibb [and] A.R. Wagner, 1961

PARKER, James, *A Glossary of Terms used in Heraldry* (new edn), 1970

PAUL, Sir James Balfour, *Heraldry in Relation to Scottish History and Art,* 1899

PHILLIPS, Sir Edward *and* MORANT, James, *Catalogue of the Library of the Heraldry Society,* 1963

PINE, Leslie Gilbert, 'Family History from Heraldry', *Amateur Historian,* I, 238. (Oct.-Nov. 1953)

REYNOLDS, John, *A Display of Heraldry of the Particular Coat Armours now in use . . . in the six counties of North Wales,* 1739 [24 pp. containing about 60 coats of arms: a facsim. of this ed. has been published]

RIETSTAP, Johannes Baptist, *Armorial Général*, 2nd ed. rev. and augmented, Gouda, 1884-7 [see also below under Rolland, Victor]

ROLLAND, Victor *and* ROLLAND, Henri, *J.B. Rietstap: General Illustrated Armorial,* 3rd ed. [Plates illustrating the text of *l'Armorial Général* de J.B. Rietstap] 6 vols [1954]

ROLLAND, Victor *and* ROLLAND, Henri, *Supplément à l'Armorial Général* de J.B. Rietstap [vols. 1-5 by V. Rolland; vol. 6 by Henri Rolland], 6 vols, Paris, 1904. *Table du Supplément, etc.,* Lyon, 1951

ROGERS, Hugh Cuthbert Basset, *The Pageant of Heraldry: an explanation of its principles and its uses today . . . with an introduction by Col. H.A.B. Lawson, Rothesay Herald and Lyon Clerk,* 1955

SCOTT-GILES, Charles Wilfred, *The Romance of Heraldry,* 1951

SETON, George, *The Law and Practice of Heraldry in Scotland,* 1863

SMITH, Christopher J., 'Funeral Hatchments', *Amateur Historian,* II, 138 (Apr.-May 1955)

STEVENSON, John Robert Horne, *Heraldry in Scotland, incl. a Recension of 'The Law and Practice of Heraldry in Scotland' by the late George Seton,* 2 vols, 1914

STODART, Robert Riddle, *Scottish Arms: being a collection of Armorial Bearings, 1370-1678,* 2 vols, 1881

SUMMERS, Peter G., 'A Survey of Hatchments', *Genealogists' Magazine,* XII, 443 (March 1958)

SWAN, Conrad, *Heraldry—Ulster and North American Connections: being the text of the inaugural Sir William Scott memorial lecture delivered by Conrad Swan on 2nd December 1968 at Belfast* (Ulster-Scot. Hist. Foundation), 1972

WAGNER, *Sir* Anthony Richard, *Heraldry in England,* 1949
WAGNER, *Sir* Anthony, *Heralds of England: a history of the office and College of Arms,* 1967
WAGNER, *Sir* Anthony Richard, *Historic Heraldry of Britain,* 1939

Chapter 28. Genealogy and Biography

The main sources for biography are mentioned in this bibliography in Chapter 28 itself and in Chapters 9 and 10. It should also be noted that the British National Bibliography since it began publication annually in 1951 in its section on biography (920) gives all biographies published in each year. See also the author's article in the *Genealogists' Magazine XV, 68 (June 1965)* on 'Genealogy and Biography'.

Chapter 29. Manorial, Chancery and other legal records

BERESFORD, Maurice Warwick, *The Lay Subsidy Rolls: Pt. i. 1290-1334; Pt ii. After 1334: The Poll Taxes of 1377, 1379 and 1381,* 1963
Bibliography of British History, 3 vols, 1933-51. 1. Tudor period, 1485-1603; 2. Stuart Period, 1603-1714; 3. Eighteenth Century, 1714-1789
BOWLER, *Dom* Cyril Hugh, *Recusant Roll No. 2 (1593-1594): An Abstract in English,* 1965. [*Recusant Rolls of the Exchequer, temp, Elizabeth I*]
CARR, A.D., 'Short Guides to Records No. 12: Deeds of Title', *History,* Oct. 1965 [incl. inform. on Bargain and Sale, Lease and Release and Fines]
CHIBNALL, Albert Charles *and* WOODMAN, A. Vere (editors) *Buckinghamshire Village,* 1965 ['Study of the feudal and economic development of a village from Norman times to the 19th century . . . from little known documents in the Public Record Office with local and private records']
CHIBNALL, Albert Charles *and* WOODMAN, A. Vere (editors) *Subsidy Roll for the County of Buckinghamshire, anno, 1524* 1950 [Bucks. Record Soc., Vol. 8]
CHIBNALL, Marjorie (ed.), *Select Documents of the English Lands of the Abbey of Bec,* 1951 [Camden Soc, 3rd Ser., Vol 73]
CLAYTON, Muriel, *Catalogue of Rubbings of Brasses and Incised Slabs, Victorian and Albert Museum,* 1929
CORNWALL, Julian, 'A Tudor Domesday: the Musters of 1522', *Journal of Society of Archivists,* III, No. 1 (April 1965)
ELLIS, *Sir* Henry, *Introduction to Domesday Book,* 2 vols [includes index of tenants in capite, of under-tenants and of persons of the time of Edward the Confessor, with biographical and genealogical notes on landowners]
EMMISON, Frederick George, *Archives and Local History,* 1966, new edn 1974
FARRER, William, *Honors and Knights' Fees,* 3 vols, 1923 [attempts to trace descent of tenants of these, 11th to 14th centuries]
FURNIVALL, Frederick J., *The Fifty Earliest English Wills in the Court of Probate, London,* A.D. *1387-1439 . . . copied and edited from the original registers in Somerset House by F.J.F.,* 1882, repr. 1964. [Early English Text Soc.]
GARRETT, Robert Edmund Francis, *Chancery and other Legal Proceedings* (Repr. by *Pinhorns* from the *Genealogists' Magazine,* vol. 15 Nos. 3 and 4), 1965
GOODER, Eileen A., *Latin for Local History: an introduction,* 1961 [intended for use with B.H. Kennedy's *The Shorter Latin Primer*]

GROSS, Charles, *Sources and Literature of English History from the Earliest Times to about 1485,* 2nd ed., 1914

HALL, Hubert (ed.), *A Repertory of British Archives Pt I: England,* 1920 [R. Historical Soc.]

HASSALL, William Owen, *Wheatley Records,* 1956

HECTOR, Leonard Charles, *The Handwriting of English Documents,* 2nd ed., 1966

HONE, Nathaniel J., *The Manor and Manorial Records,* 3rd ed. 1925 [includes a bibliog.]

HOSKINS, William George, *Local History in England,* 1959 [one of the most useful books, with a valuable bibliog. Does not include Wales or London, which the author explains require separate books]

IREDALE, D., *Enjoying Archives,* 1973 [good on information on county record offices]

LATHAM, Lucy Clare, *The Manor,* 1931 [Historical Assoc. Leaflet No. 83]

LATHAM, R.E., 'Coping with Medieval Latin', *Amateur Historian* I, 331 (Apr.-May 1954)

MCGUINESS, Mary, 'Inquisitions Post Mortem', *Amateur Historian,* VI, No. 7 (Spring 1965)

MARTIN, Charles Trice, *The Record Interpreter: a collection of abbreviations, Latin words and names used in English Historical Manuscripts and Records,* 2nd ed., 1910

MONUMENTAL BRASS SOCIETY, *Portfolios,* 1894-1914, and 1935 onwards: *Transactions,* 1887-1914, 1935—

POWICKE, *Sir* Frederick Maurice *and* FRYDE, Edman Boleslav, *Handbook of British Chronology,* 2nd ed., 1961 [useful for regnal years etc.]

PURVIS, John Stanley, *The Archives of the York Diocesan Registry,* 1952

RYE, Walter, *Records and Record Searching: a guide to the Genealogists and Topographer,* 2nd ed., 1897

RYE, Walter, *Norfolk Records: being an index to four series of Norfolk Inquisitions: The Tower series; the Chancery or Rolls series; the Exchequer series, the Wards and Liveries series,* 1892. [Norfolk and Norwich Arch. Soc.]

RYE, Walter, *Scandinavian Names in Norfolk,* 2nd ed., 1920

RYCRAFT, Ann, *English Mediaeval Handwriting,* 1971 [12 facsimiles and transcripts]

SHEENAN, Michael M., 'A List of Thirteenth-Century English Wills', *Genealogists' Magazine,* IX, 259 (March 1961)

SHERWOOD, Leslie, 'The Court Baron', *Amateur Historian,* II, 374 (June-July 1956)

STEPHENSON, Mill, *List of Monumental Brasses in the British Isles, with appendix by Ralph Griffin,* 1964

TOMLINS, *Sir* Thomas Edlyne, *The Law Dictionary . . . defining and interpreting the terms etc.,* 3rd ed., 2 vols, 1820

TORR, V.J., 'Brasses and the Monumental Brass Society', *Amateur Historian,* I, 159 (Apr.-May 1953)

UNETT, John, *Making a pedigree,* 2nd edn, 1971. [Good on manorial records, Chancery proceedings and Mediaeval Sources.]

WEST, John, *Village Records,* 1963, new edn Phillimore, 1982 [devotes considerable space to mediaeval records]

WILLIAMS, J. Anthony, 'Short Guides to Records No. 11 Recusant Rolls', *History,* June, 1965

WILLIAMS, William Morgan, *The Sociology of an English Village: Gosford, Cumberland,* 1956 ['of general value for methods and materials involved in the study of the recent history of a community', W.G. Hoskins]

Chapter 30. The Development of Family History

CAMP, Anthony John, *Everyone has roots: an introduction to genealogy,* 1978

COLWELL, Stella, *The Family History Book: a guide to tracing your ancestors,* Oxford, 1980

CURRER-BRIGGS, Noel, ed. *A Handbook of British Family History: a guide to methods and sources, ed. by N. C-B. & others,* Family History Services, 1979

MATTHEWS, Constance Mary, *Your Family History*, 2nd edn., 1982

STEEL, Donald John, *Discovering your Family History* published in conjunction with the BBC T/V series "Family History", 1979

STEEL, Donald John *and* TAYLOR, Lawrence, *Family History in Schools*, 1973

STOREY, Richard I. *and* MADDEN, Lionel, *Primary Sources for Victorian Studies,* Phillimore, 1977

WRIGLEY, Edward Anthony, ed., *An Introduction to English Historical Demography: from the 16th to the 19th century, etc.,* D.E.C. Eversley, P. Laslett and E.A. Wrigley, *etc.,* 1966 [Cambridge Group for the History of Population and Social Structure, Publication No. 1]

INDEX